Jonathan Edwards at 300

Essays on the Tercentenary of His Birth

Edited by
Harry S. Stout
Kenneth P. Minkema
Caleb J. D. Maskell

UNIVERSITY PRESS OF AMERICA,® INC.
Lanham • Boulder • New York • Toronto • Oxford

Copyright © 2005 by
University Press of America,® Inc.
4501 Forbes Boulevard
Suite 200
Lanham, Maryland 20706
UPA Acquisitions Department (301) 459-3366

PO Box 317
Oxford
OX2 9RU, UK

All rights reserved
Printed in the United States of America
British Library Cataloging in Publication Information Available

Library of Congress Control Number: 2005927099
ISBN 0-7618-3227-0 (paperback : alk. ppr.)

∞™ The paper used in this publication meets the minimum
requirements of American National Standard for Information
Sciences—Permanence of Paper for Printed Library Materials,
ANSI Z39.48—1992

Contents

Introduction   v

Theology of History

"Does History Matter to God? Jonathan Edwards's Dynamic
Re-conception of God's Relation to the World,"   1
Sang H. Lee

"Edwards as American Theologian: Grand Narratives and
Pastoral Narratives,"   14
Amy Plantinga Pauw

Scripture

"Longing for More and More of It"? The Strange Career Of
Jonathan Edwards's Exegetical Exertions,"   25
Douglas A. Sweeney

"The Sacred and the Profane Connected: Edwards, the Bible, and
Intellectual Culture,"   38
Robert E. Brown

"Jonathan Edwards and the Cultures of Biblical Violence,"   54
Stephen J. Stein

Culture

"Franklin, Jefferson and Edwards on Religion and the Religions,"   65
Gerald R. McDermott

"Lost and Found: Recovering Edwards for American Literature," 86
  Philip F. Gura

"Jonathan Edwards's Freedom of the Will Abroad," 98
  Mark A. Noll

Society

"Jonathan Edwards And The Politics Of Sex In
  Eighteenth-Century Northampton," 111
  Ava Chamberlain

"Forgiveness and the Party of Humanity in
  Jonathan Edwards's World," 123
  Mark Valeri

Race

"Lessons from Stockbridge: Jonathan Edwards and the
  Stockbridge Indians," 131
  Rachel Wheeler

"African American Engagements with Edwards in the Era of the
  Slave Trade," 141
  John Saillant

Biography

"Jonathan Edwards in the Twenty-First Century," 152
  George M. Marsden

Index 165

Introduction

The year 2003 marked the tercentenary of the birth of Jonathan Edwards, the man perpetually hailed as "America's most original religious thinker." In his lifetime, which spanned the first half of the eighteenth century, Edwards was a college tutor and president, pastor, revivalist, Indian missionary, philosopher, scientist, and theologian. His impact, both on colonial religious life and on the Anglo-American world of his day, was internationally acknowledged, and his legacy for the century and a half and more after his death in 1758 has been profound. Even to this day, Edwards's life is studied and his writings consulted on a global basis more than any other American theologian.

It therefore came as no surprise that Edwards's three-hundredth birthday elicited a rich variety of observations and commemorations. Conferences were held, among other places, at Lancaster and Pittsburgh, Pennsylvania; Princeton, New Jersey; Wethersfield and New Haven, Connecticut; Minneapolis, Minnesota; and of course Northampton and Stockbridge, Massachusetts, where Edwards spent most of his career. What is interesting to note is that most of these gatherings were religious in nature, sponsored by or held at churches and addressing explicitly spiritual and theological concerns. Besides these events, special lectures, conference sessions, and a deluge of religious and scholarly articles and books marked the milestone.[1] Edwards appeared on the cover of *The New York Review of Books* (with his cultural alter ego, Benjamin Franklin, whose tercentenary comes in 2006). And, last but not least, a new biography by Prof. George Marsden published during the Edwards tercentenary has won numerous awards.[2]

Several scholarly conferences were sponsored by the Yale Edition of *The Works of Jonathan Edwards*, which also celebrated its fiftieth anniversary in 2003. The Yale Edition was founded in 1953 by Perry Miller of Harvard

University, the renowned Puritan scholar and biographer of Edwards. To add even more luster to the celebrations, the Yale Edition realized Miller's founding goal, namely, to complete a twenty-six volume series of Edwards's selected writings, published by Yale University Press. One goal Miller could not have imagined was that, even as the letterpress series was coming to a close, the Edition was preparing to launch a comprehensive online archive of Edwards's writings, which promises to revolutionize study and immensely broaden reading of him.[3] So, a celebration—a capstone conference—was doubly in order, marking goals completed and goals newly envisioned.

The most significant scholarly conference sponsored by the Edwards *Works* took place at the Library of Congress in Washington, D.C., a fitting place to acknowledge Edwards's place in the pantheon of America's greatest figures. On October 3–4, 2003, about two hundred academics, religious practitioners, students, and interested members of the general public met to hear papers by major scholars specializing in Edwards, theology, and American religious and cultural life. The presenters were selected to represent much of the best and most recent work being done on Edwards. Their papers, suitably revised and expanded, are presented in this volume. Their arrangement here—Theology of History, Scripture, Culture, Society, Race, and Biography—follows nearly the same order in which they were originally delivered.

The meeting in our nation's capital came amidst an ongoing resurgence of interest—a renaissance, if you will—in Edwards scholarship voluminously summarized in two bibliographies of secondary literature tracing commentary and interpretation on Edwards from his death in 1758 to 1993.[4] These reference guides list an astounding total of over 3,000 books, articles, dissertations, theses, and other publications on Edwards, making him one of the most studied figures in American history and *the* most studied figure in the colonial period. As the bibliographies in part recorded, the two decades preceding the Edwards tercentenary saw a dramatic and steady rise in the amount of work being done on Edwards and the number of reprints of his writings, whether single or collected sermons, major treatises, and other assortments.

From the topics represented in this volume, it is clear that Edwards scholarship has changed dramatically since the observance of the bicentennial of Edwards's birth in 1903. Then, admirers gathered at Stockbridge, Andover Seminary, East Windsor, and other locations across New England. Interests were, to a great extent, antiquarian, genealogical, and provincial, with descendants giving orations or composing hymns and odes. Material relics—a swatch of Sarah Pierpont Edwards's wedding dress, fragments from the elm trees that once stood in front of the Edwards manse in Northampton—were assembled and solemnly viewed. Other commentators dwelt on Edwards's philosophical originality and legacy, but with little sense of contemporary relevance. The philosophical world of turn-of-the-century America, not to mention popular culture, had largely bypassed Edwards and his followers. The first three decades of the twentieth century were the period of the Progressive Era, the Jazz Age, and the Scopes "Monkey" Trial, when Puritan-bashing was the vogue and figures like Edwards were lampooned for their repressive and backward-looking creeds. One writer in 1918 stated that Edwards "believed in the worst God, preached the worst sermons, and had the worst religion of any human being who ever lived on this continent," while another a decade later blamed Edwards for the violent gangsterism of the Prohibition Era— from Edwards to John Dillinger.[5] What's more, virtually no one took exception to these estimations.

But during the 1920s, isolated scholars labored to begin a reappraisal of the Puritans and Edwards that would render Edwards "relevant" to mid-twentieth century America. Harvard professors Kenneth Murdock and Samuel Eliot Morison began this quiet revolution, which was taken up by their students, especially Perry Miller. Uncontestably, Miller did more than any one scholar to determine the shape and direction of American intellectual and literary history during the middle decades of the twentieth century. This, despite the fact that he wasn't a proponent or defender of Edwards's religious outlook but a secular historian who brought more attention to Edwards by ignoring spirituality and sin and concentrating on the philosophical and literary legacies.

Over the half century from the 1940s to the 1990s, the number of works on Edwards increased more than sevenfold. Why all this interest? Besides Miller's own charismatic influence, we can point to several reasons. First, new methods and perspectives encouraged scholars to re-visit Edwards and Edwardsean topics. Second, the availability of new texts by Edwards prompted new interpretations of traditional themes or explorations of new ones. Finally, the rise of conservative Christianity and "born again" politics in the last quarter of the twentieth century has led people of faith from many different backgrounds and allegiances to the person a recent biography has dubbed "America's Evangelical."[6]

Throughout the 1960s and 1970s, American history-writing veered away from intellectual history to a preoccupation with the New Social history, family studies, ethnography, cliometrics, and the long train of hyphenated histories. But interest in Edwards endured through this sea change as established and younger scholars alike applied these new approaches to his life and thought. The 1980s also saw a spate of dissertations and monographs on a range of Edwardsean subjects by a generation of younger scholars who have been pumping out books and articles on an ever-increasing range of topics and disciplines, from ethnicity and race to gender and sexual mores to the life cycle and speechways.[7]

While influences *on* Edwards are an important topic among historians, Edwards's legacies have become even more an area of exploration. Traditionally, the "New Divinity"—the name given to the school of Edwards's followers—has been portrayed as a pale imitation of its founder. But since the 1980s with the work of scholars such as Mark Noll, William Breitenbach, and Joseph Conforti,[8] an interest in reassessing the nature and evolution of the "New Divinity" through the nineteenth century has led to a burgeoning literature that ranges from popular culture to missiology to women's studies.[9]

During the middle decades of the last century, significant neo-orthodox theologians, notably H. Richard Niebuhr in *The Kingdom of God in America* and Joseph Haroutunian in his study of the "ossification" of the New Divinity, returned to Edwards.[10] Yet the quantity of theological considerations of Edwards remained small. Not until the 1970s did studies of Edwards's theology begin a dramatic rise in numbers and themes that has continued to the present. In fact, in the 1990s there was nearly double the output in this field from the previous decade. Studies in history amounted to over one quarter of the literature on Edwards during the decade, while theological ones came in at one third. Analyses of dispositional ontology and rational biblical theology, comparative and semi-systematic studies, and examinations of doctrinal loci —the Trinity, justification, atonement, and hell—figured significantly.[11] And studies of Edwards on the nature of the church—ecclesiology, sacraments, and psalmody—were also evident as never before.[12]

By the late 1980s and through the 1990s, Edwards was "appropriated" for constructive theology and church growth on an unprecedented scale. Robert Jenson's *America's Theologian* (1988) was suggestively subtitled *A Recommendation of Jonathan Edwards*. This category of "recommendation" set the tone for claiming Edwards less for secular appreciation than as a "resource" for current evangelical discourse or for "the future of Reformed theology." A 1996 conference in Philadelphia, sponsored by Princeton Theological Seminary, Westminster Theological Seminary, and *The Works of Jonathan Edwards*, led to a book of essays entitled *Edwards in Our Time*.[13] Dissertations, theses, articles, and handbooks oriented pastors and church leaders to Edwards as a model for preaching, as an expert on the signs of grace and revival, or a guide for delineating gender roles in the church, family issues, and Christian education.[14] Relatedly, polemical use of Edwards returned in a way not seen since the nineteenth century, as leaders of charismatic churches and revival movements used Edwards to legitimate their claims, while critics used Edwards to discredit them.[15]

During the 1990s, theological commentary on Edwards was the highest that it had been in more than a century. Up to that point, major theological pieces on Edwards had been confined largely to "mainline" religious publications. Now, however, interpretive essays are regularly found in an assortment of evangelical journals. In fact, *over half* of the theological considerations of Edwards during the '90s appeared in evangelical publications. For example, in compiling a survey of journal articles on Edwards published during the 1990s, Kenneth Minkema shows, of 105 articles tallied, the following breakdown among types of journals: Evangelical: 64 (61.0%); Mainline: 7 (6.7%); Non-religious: 34 (32.3%).[16] Likewise, religious presses of all sizes have been churning out new editions of Edwards's writings as well as monographs geared towards popular audiences. Reformed, evangelicals, and charismatics—the "new evangelicals" from across a broad spectrum—have embraced Edwards like never before.

All indications are that this trend will continue, as younger scholars and religious leaders take up work in the Edwards vineyard. For instance, at least thirty-two dissertations on Edwards have been submitted from 2001–2003 alone. Of these, fourteen were done at state or secular private universities, while eighteen were completed at seminaries, schools of theology, or religiously affiliated institutions. Within this latter group, it is interesting to note that the two institutions supporting the most graduate work on Edwards (three dissertations each) within these three years were a Presbyterian seminary (Westminster Theological) and a Jesuit university (Marquette). Recently, too, we have been treated to a vigorous string of publications on Edwards's formulation of the doctrine of justification and on the nature of his "occasionalism."[17]

The papers presented in this volume reflect the widely divergent interests, motives, and methods in studying Edwards, from those addressing controversial issues in Edwards such as racism and violence to those who find in Edwards a remarkable voice for today. The first two papers, gathered under the rubric of "Theology of History," address Edwards's conception of God as involved in time.[18] Prof. Sang Hyun Lee of Princeton Theological Seminary argues that "history matters" to God, that "the world matters and is important to God," because of God's relation to the world as creator and communicator. Edwards's dispositional ontology allowed him to see God and created being as one. Creation is an "emanation" of God, through which God "enlarges" and repeats God's self. In Edwards's conception, history is infinite and heaven is progressive and dynamic. Prof. Amy Plantinga Pauw of Louisville Presbyterian Theological Seminary looks at *A History of the Work of Redemption* as Edwards in his role as "theologian of the grand narrative." The Psalmist sings that the heavens "declare the glory of God," but for Edwards so too do nature and human experience. Edwards sought in his grand narrative to unite all of these realms of existence in one story, told from "God's point of view." Complementing the grand narrative, however, was the "pastoral narrative," the perspective of religious leaders rooted in "ordinary life in the church." Edwards was intimately acquainted with this sort of narrative too. But, as Plantinga Pauw points out, the grand and the pastoral narratives "had an uneasy co-existence in Edwards's thought."

If human experience and nature are ways through which God reveals God's self, an even more important means of revelation for Edwards was Scripture. Outside of a small circle of religious scholars,[19] very little attention has been paid to Edwards's view of Scripture and his achievements as an exegete. Here, addressing the theme of "Scripture," three papers begin the process of bringing this aspect of Edwards into the mainstream of scholarship. Trinity Evangelical Divinity School's Prof. Douglas Sweeney points to the lack of study of Edwards's biblicism, which was actually the work he took most seriously. Edwards had a high view of the Bible as divinely inspired and argued that supernatural revelation of God's will through the Bible was necessary—and more important than reason alone—if humans were to understand it. Like Sweeney, Prof. Robert E. Brown of Lehigh University baldly admits the lack of adherents to Edwards's hermeneutic but nonetheless argues that it is vital to understanding not only Edwards's place in American culture but American culture itself. What are at stake are ways of articulating "the relationship between sacred text and profane knowledge"—a challenge no less demanding today than in Edwards's time. Edwards was intent on showing that sacred text stood up to the emerging emphasis on empirically verifiable facts as the basis for political authority and moral credibility. Brown examines Edwards's efforts to address the controversial issue of the authenticity of the Pentateuch as a way of seeing his methodological solution. Foremost among Edwards's editors in making his scriptural commentary available is University of Indiana Religious Studies professor Stephen J. Stein, who has edited "Notes on the Apocalypse," "Notes on Scripture," and the voluminous and ironically named "Blank Bible." If Edwards never inspired a school of biblical interpretation, Stein would argue, there was a reason. Stein warns of some of the "negative" things we will find in Edwards's commentary, especially relating to scriptural accounts of "biblical violence." Salient among these disturbing aspects of Edwards's thought as discovered through his exposition are anti-Semitism and a virulent anti-Catholicism. When encountering these interpretations, we see how Edwards was a person of his culture who, for all his acumen, could not rise above the prejudices of his time and place.

For Edwards, reason continued to be confined within the limits of revelation but still had a major role. Considering Edwards under the broad topic of "Culture," Prof. Gerald McDermott of Roanoke College presents three eminent Americans—Benjamin Franklin, Thomas Jefferson, and Edwards—and their views on "religion and the religions." The deistic Franklin and Jefferson subordinated things religious to reason, but in his time Edwards spent much effort and ink to show what reason could *not* do. Ultimately, in their effort to make religion "non-mysterious," Franklin and Jefferson reduced it to morality. For Edwards, however, morality was not an end in itself. As it turned out, America did not subscribe wholly to the religious dictates of either Franklin, Jefferson, or Edwards. One unappreciated area of Edwards's influence, interjects University of North Carolina English professor Philip Gura, is his place as an American literary figure. Edwards's emphasis on aesthetics and the prominence of his works, including *Religious Affections*, *The Life of David Brainerd*, and *Personal Narrative*, distinguish him in the canon of American authors. Particularly important was Edwards's part in the formation of nineteenth-century sentimentalism. Although his influence was significant enough to spawn an "Edwardsean culture" in antebellum America, he and his followers were also widely reviled. If Edwards as a prophet was not loved in his own country, he certainly had admirers in Great Britain, as Wheaton College's Mark Noll demonstrates by looking at Scottish and English reactions to Edwards's famous treatise on the *Freedom of the Will*. From Edwards's lifetime through the early nineteenth century, four philosophers and theologians—Lord Kames, Baptist minister Andrew Fuller, political theorist William Godwin, and Presbyterian minister Thomas Chalmers. Each had different approaches and differences with Edwards on the will, but all found the work transformative to their thinking.

"Society" here represents a broad range of inquiry into Edwards along a number of fronts associated with social and cultural history, anthropology, family and life cycle studies, and gender and women's studies. One episode from Edwards's pastorate at Northampton crystallizes several issues and unites several disciplines. For Ava Chamberlain, Professor of Religious Studies at Wright State University, the paternity suit of 1748 involving Elisha Hawley and Martha Root provides a case study in the construction of femininity and masculinity and evolving legal standards. Specifically, the way that the courts treated men and women accused of fornication demonstrated a double standard that greatly favored males. Another dimension of religious and political life in Northampton was ongoing factionalism and "party spirit." From the beginning of his pastorate, Edwards inveighed against the contention but, aside from brief interludes of harmony during revivals, was unsuccessful. Mark Valeri of Union Theological Seminary in Virginia combines an historical approach to this pastoral problem with recent explorations among theologians into "lived religion," or practices and rituals constituting religious communities. Valeri focuses on Edwards's teaching on forgiveness to highlight his efforts to legitimize the revivals of the 1730s and '40s.

A recent category for Edwards Studies is represented here by two papers on "Race." With interest in native American cultures and Euro-Indian and

Euro-African contact at unprecedented heights, Edwards's involvement with Indian missions and African slavery has come under renewed scrutiny. Edwards owned slaves and defended the institution of slavery, though he did come to realize that the transatlantic slave trade had to end.[20] Also, Edwards's tenure as a missionary at Stockbridge, ministering to Mahicans and Mohawks, raises questions about the content of his preaching and his views of Indians and the role of missions.[21] Prof. Rachel Wheeler of Indiana University-Purdue University in Indianapolis has systematically read through all of Edwards's Stockbridge sermons and found an interesting connection between his missionary experience and the argument of *Original Sin* that helps to advance our understanding of Indian Christians and how Europeans interacted with them. For Edwards, the doctrine of total depravity had egalitarian implications for Indian and European alike. As Prof. John Saillant of Western Michigan University shows from his work on "African Calvinists," black abolitionists also found in Edwards's teachings ammunition for their crusade against slavery. Edwards's views on virtue, providence, and will, among others, found resonance among black writers of the early republic and antebellum periods, as did Edwardsean and New Divinity typological interpretations.

Our concluding paper, delivered originally as the conference keynote by Edwards biographer George Marsden of Notre Dame University, proposes an Edwards for the twenty-first century. From his magisterial study of Edwards, Marsden the historian steps out of his traditional role and into an apologetic one, addressing American society as a whole, Christian as well as non-Christian. Marsden particularly points to Edwards as a model for selecting from the legacies of the Enlightenment and "enlightened modernity" in a discriminating, critical manner rather than accepting or rejecting them wholesale. Edwards himself was an avid reader of the "new learning" of his time, eclectically co-opting and adapting new scientific and philosophical discoveries to his inherited worldview. For people who share Edwards's particular religious faith, Marsden holds up Edwards as a corrective for the "superficiality" of evangelicalism. Edwards's expansive concept of beauty, for example, combines concern for practicality as well as theological and spiritual depth. But for all, Marsden points out, Edwards provides a healthy corrective to knee-jerk optimism and faith in the "progress" of humankind's nature and destiny.

These papers, then, present a snapshot of scholarship on Edwards at the three hundredth anniversary of his birth. If there is no common theme, interpretation, or approach in these pieces, they only reflect the great diversity in Edwards Studies—historical and theological, secular and religious. But the contributions of these authors also provide direction for inquiry on Edwards in the near future. In doing so, they augur a lively, thriving industry in the study of Edwards for subsequent generations of scholars.

Many people assisted in organizing the Library of Congress conference. We would especially like to thank Librarian of Congress James H. Billington, Manuscript Curator James Hutson, and Facilities Director Kim Moden. Our appreciation, too, to the presenters who originally took part in the event and revised their papers despite busy schedules. We would be remiss if we did not recognize and thank all of the enthusiastic and thoughtful attendees of the conference, including what was probably the largest gathering of past and present members of the Edwards *Works*. In seeking out a publisher for the papers, we did not have to look far. David Chao of University Press of America expressed an early interest and has been most gracious and encouraging every step of the way.

MANUSCRIPT CITATIONS

Unless otherwise noted, all manuscript references in this volume are to the Edwards Papers in the Beinecke Rare Book and Manuscript Library, Yale University.

FREQUENTLY CITED VOLUMES

The Works of Jonathan Edwards (New Haven: Yale University Press, 1957–2005), referred to as "*WJE*" followed by the volume and page numbers:

Vol. 1, *Freedom of the Will*, ed. Paul Ramsey
Vol. 2, *Religious Affections*, ed. John E. Smith
Vol. 3, *Original Sin*, ed. Clyde A. Holbrook
Vol. 4, *The Great Awakening*, ed. C. C. Goen
Vol. 5, *Apocalyptic Writings*, ed. Stephen J. Stein
Vol. 6, *Scientific and Philosophical Writings*, ed. Wallace E. Anderson
Vol. 7, *The Life Of David Brainerd*, ed. Norman Pettit
Vol. 8, *Ethical Writings*, ed. Paul Ramsey
Vol. 9, *A History Of The Work Of Redemption*, ed. John F. Wilson
Vol. 10, *Sermons and Discourses, 1720–1723*, ed. Wilson H. Kimnach
Vol. 11, *Typological Writings*, eds. Wallace E. Anderson & Mason I. Lowance, with David Watters
Vol. 12, *Ecclesiastical Writings*, ed. David D. Hall
Vol. 13, *The "Miscellanies," a-500*, ed. Thomas A. Schafer
Vol. 14, *Sermons and Discourses, 1723–1729*, ed. Kenneth P. Minkema
Vol. 15, *Notes on Scripture*, ed. Stephen J. Stein

Vol. 16, *Letters and Personal Writings*, ed. George S. Claghorn
Vol. 17, *Sermons and Discourses, 1730–1733*, ed. Mark Valeri
Vol. 18, *The "Miscellanies," 501–832*, ed. Ava Chamberlain
Vol. 19, *Sermons and Discourses, 1734–1738*, ed. M. X. Lesser
Vol. 20, *The "Miscellanies," 833–1152*, ed. Amy Plantinga Pauw
Vol. 21, *Writings on the Trinity, Grace And Faith*, ed. Sang Hyun Lee
Vol. 22, *Sermons and Discourses, 1739–1742*, eds. Harry S. Stout & Nathan O. Hatch, with Kyle P. Farley
Vol. 23, *The "Miscellanies," 1153–1360*, ed. Douglas A. Sweeney
Vol. 24 (Parts 1 & 2), *The "Blank Bible,"* ed. Stephen J. Stein
Vol. 25, *Sermons and Discourses, 1743–1758*, ed. Wilson H. Kimnach
Vol. 26, *Catalogue of Books*, ed. Peter J. Thuesen

NOTES

1. A sampling of tercentennial monographs, collected essays, edited collections, and reference works on Edwards includes Robert E. Brown, *Jonathan Edwards and the Bible* (Bloomington, Ind.: University, of Indiana Press, 2002); *The Salvation of Souls: Nine Previously Unpublished Sermons on the Call of Ministry and the Gospel by Jonathan Edwards*, ed. Richard Bailey and Gregory Wills (Wheaton, Ill.: Crossway, 2003); *Jonathan Edwards: Philosophical Theologian*, ed. Paul Helm and Oliver Crisp (London: Ashgate, 2003); *The Princeton Companion to Jonathan Edwards*, ed. Sang Hyun Lee (Princeton: Princeton University Press, 2005); *The Printed Writings of Jonathan Edwards*, comp. M.X. Lesser (Princeton: Princeton Theological Seminary, 2004); George M. Marsden, *Jonathan Edwards: A Life* (New Haven, Yale University, Press, 2003); *The Blessing of God: Previously Unpublished Sermons of Jonathan Edwards*, ed. Michael McMullen (Nashville, Tenn.: Broadman & Holman, 2003); Stephen Nichols, *An Absolute Sort of Certainty: The Holy Spirit and the Apologetics of Jonathan Edwards* (Phillipsburg, N.J.: Presbyterian & Reformed Publishing, 2003); Mark Noll, *America's God: From Jonathan Edwards to Abraham Lincoln* (New York: Oxford University, Press, 2002); Amy Plantinga Pauw, *The Supreme Harmony of All: The Trinitarian Theology of Jonathan Edwards* (Grand Rapids, Mich.: Eerdmans, 2003); Douglas A. Sweeney, *Nathaniel William Taylor, New Haven Theology, and the Legacy of Jonathan Edwards* (New York: Oxford University Press, 2003); Avihu Zakai, *Jonathan Edwards's Philosophy of History: The Reenchantment of the World in the Age of Enlightenment* (Princeton, Princeton University, Press, 2003).

2. Garry Wills, "Mismatched Americans," *New York Times Book Review*, July 6, 2003; Marsden, *Life of Jonathan Edwards*.

3. The site of the Jonathan Edwards Center and Online Archive at Yale can be found at http://edwards.yale.edu.

4. M. X. Lesser, *Jonathan Edwards: A Reference Guide* (Boston: G. K. Hall, 1981) and *Jonathan Edwards: An Annotated Bibliography, 1979–1993* (Westport, Conn.: Greenwood Press, 1994).

5. Marilla M. Ricker, *Jonathan Edwards: The Divine Who Filled the Air with Damnation and Proved the Total Depravity of God* (New York: American Freethought Tract Society, 1918); Struthers Burt, "Jonathan Edwards and the Gunman," *The North American Review* 227 (June 1929): 712–18.

6. Philip Gura, *Jonathan Edwards: America's Evangelical* (New York: Hill & Wang, 2005).

7. Mary Ava Chamberlain, "Jonathan Edwards Against the Antinomians and Arminians," Ph.D. dissertation, Columbia University,, 1990; Allen C. Guelzo, "The Unanswered Question: The Legacy of Jonathan Edwards's *Freedom of the Will* in Early American Religious Philosophy," Ph.D. dissertation, University of Pennsylvania, 1986, published as *Edwards on the Will: A Century of American Theological Debate* (Middletown, Conn.: Wesleyan University Press, 1989); John R. Fitzmier, "The Godly Federalism of Timothy Dwight, 1752–1817: Society, Doctrine, and Religion in the Life of New England's 'Moral Legislator,'" Ph.D. dissertation, Princeton University, 1986, published as *New England's Moral Legislator: Timothy Dwight, 1752–1817* (Bloomington, Ind.: Indiana University, Press, 1998); Mark R. Valeri, "Joseph Bellamy: Conversion, Social Ethics, and Politics in the Thought of an Eighteenth-Century Calvinist," Ph.D. dissertation, Princeton University, 1985, published as *Law and Providence in Joseph Bellamy's New England: The Origins of the New Divinity in Revolutionary America* (New York: Oxford University Press, 1994).

8. Mark A. Noll, "Moses Mather (Old Calvinist) and the Evolution of Edwardseanism," *Church History* 49 (Sept. 1979): 273–85; Noll, "Jonathan Edwards and Nineteenth-Century Philosophy," in *Jonathan Edwards and the American Experience*, ed. Nathan O. Hatch and Harry S. Stout (New York: Oxford University Press, 1987), 260–87; Mark A. Noll, "The Contested Legacy of Jonathan Edwards in Antebellum Calvinism: Theological Conflict and the Evolution of Thought in America," *Canadian Review of American Studies* 19 (Summer 1988): 149–64; William Breitenbach, "Unregenerate Doings: Selflessness and Selfishness in New Divinity Theology," *American Quarterly* 34 (Winter 1982): 479–502; William Breitenbach, "The Consistent Calvinism of the New Divinity Movement," *William and Mary Quarterly* 41 (Apr. 1984): 241–64; William Breitenbach, "Piety *and* Moralism: Edwards and the New Divinity," in *Jonathan Edwards and the American Experience*, 177–204; Joseph A. Conforti, "Samuel Hopkins and the New Divinity: Theology, Ethics, and Social Reform in Eighteenth-Century New England," *William and Mary Quarterly* 34 (Oct. 1977): 572–89; Conforti, *Samuel Hopkins and the New Divinity Movement: Calvinism, the Congregational Ministry, and Reform in New England between the Great Awakenings* (Grand Rapids, Mich.: Eerdmans, 1981).

9. Conforti, "Mary Lyon, the Founding of Mount Holyoke College, and the Cultural Revival of Jonathan Edwards," *Religion and American Culture* 3 (Winter 1993): 69–89; Conforti, "The Invention of the Great Awakening," *Early American Literature* 26 (Fall 1991): 99–118; Conforti, *Jonathan Edwards, Religious Tradition, and American Culture* (Chapel Hill, N. C.: University, of North Carolina Press, 1995); Bruce Kuklick, *Churchmen and Philosophers: From Jonathan Edwards to John Dewey* (New Haven: Yale University Press, 1985); Genevieve E. McCoy, "Sanctifying the Self and Saving the Savage: The Failure of the ABCFM Oregon Mission and

the Conflicted Language of Calvinism," Ph.D. dissertation, University of Washington, 1991; David W. Kling, *A Field of Divine Wonders: The New Divinity and Village Revivals in Northwestern Connecticut, 1792–1822* (University Park, Pa.: Penn State University Press, 1993); Amanda Porterfield, *Mary Lyon and the Mount Holyoke Missionaries* (New York: Oxford University Press, 1997; Douglas A. Sweeney, *Nathaniel William Taylor, New Haven Theology, and the Legacy of Jonathan Edwards.*

10. H. Richard Niebuhr, *The Kingdom of God in America* (New York: Harper & Brothers, 1937); Joseph G. Haroutunian, *Piety Versus Moralism: The Passing of the New England Theology* (New York: Henry Holt & Co., 1932).

11. Stephen R. Holmes, "The Justice of Hell and the Display of God's Glory in the Thought of Jonathan Edwards," *Pro Ecclesia* 9 (Fall 2000): 389–403; John E. Colwell, "The Glory of God's Justice and the Glory of God's Grace: Contemporary Reflections on the Doctrine of Hell in the Teaching of Jonathan Edwards," *Evangelical Quarterly* 67 (Oct. 1995); Bruce W. Davidson, "Reasonable Damnation: How Jonathan Edwards Argued for the Rationality of Hell," *Journal of the Evangelical Theological Society* 38 (Mar. 1995): 47–56; Bruce M. Stephens, "An Appeal to the Universe: The Doctrine of the Atonement in American Protestant Thought from Jonathan Edwards to Edwards Amasa Park," *Encounter* 60 (Winter 1999): 55–72; Stephen Nichols, *An Absolute Sort of Certainty.*

12. David Rightmire, "The Sacramental Theology of Jonathan Edwards in the Context of Controversy," *Fides et Historia* 21 (Jan. 1989): 50–60; Richard A. S. Hall, *The Neglected Northampton Text of Jonathan Edwards: Edwards on Society and Politics* (Lewiston, N.Y.: Edwin Mellen, 1990); Rowena R. Jones, "Edwards, Dickinson, and the Sacramentality of Nature," *Studies in Puritan American Spirituality* 1 (Dec. 1990): 225–53; David D. Hall, "Editor's Introduction," in *WJE* 12; William J. Danaher, Jr., "By Sensible Signs Represented: Jonathan Edwards's Sermons on the Lord's Supper," *Pro Ecclesia* 7 (Summer 1998): 261–87.

13. Robert Jenson, *America's Theologian: A Recommendation of Jonathan Edwards* (New York: Oxford University. Press, 1988); Amy Plantinga Pauw, "The Future of Reformed Theology: Some Lessons From Jonathan Edwards," in *Toward the Future of Reformed Theology: Tasks, Topics, Traditions*, ed. David Willis-Watkins and Michael Welker (Grand Rapids, Mich.: Eerdmans 1999), 456–69; *Edwards in Our Time: Jonathan Edwards and the Shaping of American Religion*, ed. Sang H. Lee and Allen C. Guelzo (Grand Rapids, Mich.: Eerdmans, 1999).

14. Gary Benfold et al, *God at Work? Signs of True Revival* (London: Grace Publishing Trust, 1995); Doreen Moore, "Jonathan Edwards: Ministry and the Life of the Family," *Reformation & Revival* 4 (Summer 1995): 99–120; Beth A. McDermott, "Jonathan Edwards and the Redefinition of American Masculinity: From the Power of Fathers to the Power of Men," M.A. Thesis, University of New Hampshire, 1998; B. Edwards, *Men, Women, and Authority: Serving Together in the Church* (Bromley, Kent: Day One Pub., 1996); T. M. Moore, "A Brief Introduction to an Edwardsean View of Christian Instruction," *Presbyterion* 25 (Spring 1999): 21–31.

15. Bruce Hindmarsh, "The 'Toronto Blessing' and the Protestant Evangelical Awakening of the Eighteenth Century Compared," *Crux* (Dec. 1995), 3–13; James A. Beverly, *Revival Wars: A Critique of* Counterfeit Revival (Pickering, Canada: Evan-

gelical Research Ministries, 1997); John D. Hannah, "Jonathan Edwards, the Toronto Blessing, and the Spiritual Gifts: Are the Extraordinary Ones Actually the Ordinary Ones?" *Trinity Journal* 17 (Fall 1996): 167–89.

16. Kenneth P. Minkema, "Jonathan Edwards in the Twentieth Century," *Journal of the Evangelical Theological Society* 47 (Dec. 2004): 659–87, esp. p. 677.

17. On justification, see, for example, the string of articles in the *Westminster Theological Journal* of 2004 by George Hunsinger, John Bombaro, and Jeffrey Waddington; and on occasionalism and dispositional ontology, see the essays by Paul Helm, Oliver Crisp, and Stephen Holmes in *Jonathan Edwards: Philosophical Theologian*, ed. Helm and Crisp.

18. On the theme of history in Edwards, see Brown, *Jonathan Edwards and the Bible*; Zakai, *Jonathan Edwards's Philosophy of History*; and Harry S. Stout, "Jonathan Edwards's Tri-World Vision," in *The Legacy of Jonathan Edwards: American Religion and the Evangelical Tradition*, ed. D. G. Hart, Sean Michael Lucas, and Stephen J. Nichols (Grand Rapids, Mich.: Baker, 2003), 27–46.

19. Chief among them John H. Gerstner, as epitomized in his *Rational Biblical Theology of Jonathan Edwards* (3 vols., Powhatan, Va.: Berea Publications, 1991–93).

20. Kenneth P. Minkema and Harry S. Stout, "The Edwardsean Tradition and the Antislavery Debate, 1741–1865," *Journal of American History* 92 (June 2005): 1–28.

21. See, for example, Gerald R. McDermott, "Jonathan Edwards on American Indians: The Devil Sucks Their Blood," *New England Quarterly* LXXII (Dec. 1999): 539–57.

Does History Matter to God? Jonathan Edwards's Dynamic Re-conception of God's Relation to the World

Sang Hyun Lee

Princeton Theological Seminary

One of the most remarkable aspects of Edwards's thought is his understanding of the relation between God and the world, according to which God is not only perfect within himself but capable of being increased or self-enlarged through the world. For Edwards, the essential nature of God's being is an eternal disposition as well as an actuality at once fully actual and also continuously tending to further actualizations and thus to further self-enlargement. This dynamic view of the divine being leads, in Edwards's thought, to a view of the creation of the world as God's repetition, outside of himself in time and space, of his prior actuality. The created world, then, is the framework in and through which God adds to God's own being. What God does in time and history through some human beings and nature, in other words, is a part of God's own life. Edwards brought an element of becoming into God's being without compromising God's prior actuality, and thereby made it in principle possible for the creatures in the realm of becoming to participate in the life of God himself. In short, what God does in the world matters to God. In this sense, the world matters and is important to God.

DISPOSITIONAL ONTOLOGY AND THE REALITY OF THE WORLD

Edwards's view of the omnipresence of God's direct causal involvement in the world is often given such emphasis in interpretations of Edwards's thought that the nature of the reality of the created world is not sufficiently noticed. We must, therefore, begin with a brief discussion of Edwards's dispositional re-conception of the nature of reality. Edwards saw reality not in terms of substances and forms, as had been done for so many centuries, but rather as a network of law-like habits and dispositions. What made this fundamental metaphysical reformulation possible for Edwards was his realist, as opposed to nominalist, idea of habits and dispositions. For him, a habit or disposition has a mode of reality apart from their manifestations in actual actions and events. A habit as an abiding principle is also law-like for Edwards in that it actively and prescriptively governs the occurrence and character of actual events. "All habits," writes Edwards, are "a law that God has fixed, that such actions upon such occasions should be exerted." When there is a habit or disposition, it functions like a prescriptive law that certain events will, and not only may, occur whenever certain circumstances prevail. Habits and dispositions, in short, are ontologically real and causally active law-like powers.[1]

Redefining Aristotelian metaphysics, Edwards declared in a remarkable sentence in "Subjects to Be Handled in the Treatise on the Mind," that "it is the laws that constitute all permanent being in created things, both corporeal and spiritual." In "Of Atoms," Edwards stated that "all body is nothing but what immediately results from the exercise of divine power in such a particular manner."[2] An actual entity, in other words, is God's immediate activity occurring in "a particular manner," and this "particular manner" refers to habit-like law that God has previously established. Without God's immediate activity, nothing can exist. But the divinely established and now-abiding laws also "govern" the way God acts in time and space.[3] To put the matter differently, a habit is the law that is triggered into exertion only when certain conditions are met. The primary condition is God's immediate activity of causing existence; without this divine action, no habit or law could be exercised and bring about actual existence or actual event.[4] In his early notes to "Natural Philosophy," Edwards wrote that "the universe is created out of nothing every moment." This statement has led many scholars to characterize Edwards's view of God's relation to the world as one of "occasionalism," the view that the universe is newly created moment-by-moment.[5] Edwards's remark in his early notes for "Natural Philosophy" is overshadowed by his lifelong belief that God establishes the laws according to which he would cause "resistance," and once established these laws are sustained by God's continuously immediate action of resistance.

Edward was not a simple occasionalist. The habit-like laws constitute the relative and yet abiding reality and structure of the world as distinguished from God, and are observed by God in his actions in the world. Habits and laws are active and causal powers. Since human beings and physical entities, according to Edwards, are essentially dispositions and habits, human beings have a reality distinguishable from God and are in principle capable of actively participating in what God does in the world. So Edwards can write:

"God has made intelligent creatures capable of being concerned in these effects, and being the willing active subjects, or means; and so they are capable of actively promoting God's glory." Non-sentient physical entities participate in God's life in time and space through the converted sentient beings' perception of them as the images of God's beauty.[6]

GOD AS DISPOSITION AND ACTUALITY: THE TRINITY

For Edwards, the ground of God's creation of the world and continuing activity in the world is rooted in the nature of God's own internal being. And Edwards articulates God's own being in terms of the doctrine of the Trinity. Edwards makes a new beginning in the development of the doctrine of God in Western theology by re-conceiving God's being as essentially a disposition rather than a substance. "It is [God's] essence to incline to communicate himself." This disposition to "communicate himself" is what we must conceive of as being originally in God as a perfection of his nature. Edwards then resolves this communicative disposition into God's "disposition effectually to exert himself."[7] In other words, God's disposition to operate as God is the essence of the divine being. God is dispositional. And since God, for Edwards, is also true beauty, and knowing and loving being, God is the eternal disposition to know and love true beauty.

Edwards follows the Western theological tradition by affirming that God is fully actual. He points out that God "is an eternal adequate and infinite exercise of perfect goodness that is completely equal to such an inclination in perfection."[8] This eternal and infinite exercise of the divine disposition to know and love true beauty is articulated through Edwards's doctrine of the immanent Trinity.

Edwards articulates the doctrine of the Trinity using both the logic of dispositional ontology and also John Locke's psychology of the self—namely, the self, the self's reflexive idea of the self, and the self's love of the reflexive idea. The three distinctions in God, says Edwards, are "God, the idea of God, and delight in God." The first subsistence of the divine being, or the Father, is God in his first true actuality. As Edwards states, "The Father is the deity subsisting in the prime, in-originated and most absolute manner, or the deity in its direct existence." In other words, the Father is the first, true, and full exercise of the divine dispositional essence to know and love true beauty and, therefore, the first actuality of God as truly knowing and loving true beauty. The Father is the first "instance" of God in full actuality or "direct existence." But the divine disposition remains a disposition even after its full exercise. In the Father, actuality coincides with disposition.[9]

Consequently, God as the Father is a disposition to communicate himself, just as he is an eternally perfect actuality. God as the Father is disposed to further exercise, and this exercise brings about a repetition of what God already is. This repetition occurs because God is primordially actual. So the Son, "God's Idea of himself," is the intellectual exercise of the Father as actuality-disposition, or the Father's reflexive knowing of himself. In this way, the second person of the Trinity is "generated." The eternal generation of the Son is not the actualization of God as God, because the Father already is God in full actuality. The Son's generation as the Father's exercise of his dispositional essence can only be the intellectual repetition or communication of what the Father already is. Thus, in the Son "the deity is truly and properly repeated by God's thus having an idea of himself . . . [and] by this means the Godhead is really generated and repeated." Like the Father, the Son is the eternal disposition communicating himself. But he also has full actuality in the intellectual repetition of the Father. "The Son is the adequate communication of the Father's goodness, and the express image of him. But yet the Son also has an inclination to communicate himself."[10] The Son is different from the Father in that the Father is "un-originated" as the first exercise of the divine disposition, while the Son is "generated" by the Father, or is the repetition of the Father. The Son in his full deity is, like the Father, both actuality and disposition to communicate further.

The Father's and the Son's dispositional essences are now exercised affectionally, as "the Father and the Son infinitely lov[e] and [delight] in each other."[11] In this way, the Father's and the Son's prior actuality is affectionally repeated, and the third person is "proceeded" from the Father and the Son. And like the Father and the Son, the Holy Spirit is the full actuality of God's affectional repetition of his prior actuality and the disposition to love further.

In short, God in his intra-trinitarian life is at once fully actual qua God and also essentially disposed to communicate himself. Within the Trinity, God as the eternal disposition to know and love true beauty is exercised and also repeated in a way that is "an eternal, adequate and infinite exercise" of the divine dispositional essence.[12] Unlike contemporary process theology, God for Edwards is fully self-actualized as God as well as eternally disposed to further self-communication. In this dynamic re-conception of the immanent Trinity, Edwards lays the foundation for a doctrine of God's creation and activity in the world through which God's actual being is further increased and enlarged and thus is genuinely affected.

GOD'S END IN CREATION

Edwards uses his concept of the divine being as essentially dispositional along with the *ad intra/ad extra* distinction to explain God's creation of the world. God is fully *ad intra*, but also remains essentially a disposition to communicate himself. Now this divine disposition "delights in all kinds of its exercises"—that is, exercises *ad extra*, or outside of himself, as well as *ad intra*, or inside himself. So the "same disposition" that inclines him to delight in his glory now seeks to be exercised *ad extra*. Now a disposition is the law that a certain event will occur when a certain occasion arises. The divine disposition entails that God will delight when a delightful occasion, such as God's idea of himself in God *ad intra*, arises. But outside of God there is nothing that can function as the occasion for the exercise of the divine disposition. This is the point where we recognize that the divine disposition according to Edwards is in some ways radically different from the finite, created dispositions. The divine disposition is a sovereign and absolutely self-sufficient disposition that can bring into being the occasions themselves for the exercise of that disposition. God's disposition is a disposition that "will make occasion for the communication." So the creatures "are made that God may have in them occasions to fulfill his pleasure in manifesting and communicating himself."[13]

How can a perfectly actualized God aim at any goal? Edwards says that God can only seek the highest good, which is nothing else than God himself as true beauty. But since God himself *ad intra* is already fully actualized, there is nothing for God to actualize or achieve in order for God to be God. The only possible answer is that in creating the world God aims at himself, "existing *ad extra*." "His own glory was the ultimate, himself his end—that is himself communicated." The aim is not God's prior actuality as God, which is eternally accomplished *ad intra*. What God aims at is God's prior actuality existing *ad extra*, or "increase, repetition or multiplication" *ad extra* of the divine actuality *ad intra*—that is, in time and space.[14] Intelligent beings are created so that through their acts of knowing and loving true beauty, God's internal Trinitarian knowing and loving may be repeated in time and space. The physical universe, of which humanity is a sentient part, is also created to repeat God's glory as the "images or shadows" of divine things, though their actualization as the physical repetition of God's infinite glory happens only through the converted human beings' acts of knowing and loving the physical universe as images of God's beauty.

The end of repeating God's own glory in time and space, according to Edwards, is subordinate to the end of making creatures happy. By this subordination Edwards does not wish in any way to belittle the dignity of the creatures. According to Edwards, "an ultimate end is that which the agent seeks in what he does for its own sake," or something "which he values upon its own account." In this sense, God's end of glorifying himself and giving creatures being and happiness are both ultimate ends. God delights in the creation for its own sake and upon its own account, and thus it is of value to him. But

Edwards says there are different *kinds* of ultimate ends. A "chief or highest end" is an end that is most valued and therefore most sought after by the agent in what he does. Now "to be an end more valued than another end is not exactly the same thing as to be an end valued ultimately, or for its own sake." Thus, "two different ends may be both ultimate ends, and yet not be chief ends. They may be both valued for their own sake . . . and yet one valued more highly and sought after more than another." Edwards also puts the issue another way. Between two ultimate ends, one is "an original, independent ultimate end and the other consequential and dependent." Edwards concludes that God's repetition of himself *ad extra* is the chief, highest and original ultimate end in creating the world, while making creatures happy is also an ultimate end that is implied by, and comprehended in, the other. Edwards's perspective is thoroughly theocentric. Yet he wants to preserve the dignity and ultimate significance of the happiness of the creature. The end of the creature is to be understood strictly within the larger framework of God's chief end of glorifying himself, although it does possess a dependent and yet ultimate meaning as a reality distinguishable from God.

Now the process of God's self-repetition in time, according to Edwards, takes an infinite amount of time because God's internal actuality and its internal repetition are infinitely perfect. The repetition of the infinite fullness of God *ad intra* will take an "eternal duration, with all the infinity of its progress and infinite increase of nearness and union to God." Indeed, "the time will never come when it can be said it has already arrived at this infinite height."[15] The world will everlastingly continue to repeat in a spatio-temporal way the infinite glory of God. But the world will never become God. The God-world distinction is never abolished.

It is important to note here that Edwards in his discussion of God's creation of the world freely mixes emanationist and teleological languages. God's creation of the world, Edwards says, is a "flowing forth," a "diffusion" of God's internal fullness, as well as an act in which God "aims at" a goal and "seeks" to achieve an end. Edwards's emanationist language can give the impression of a Neo-platonic influence. Whatever Neo-platonic elements there may be in Edwards's thought, his view of creation certainly is not Neo-platonic emationism. Edwards is neither using a Neo-platonic concept of creation as a nonpurposive "over-flowing," nor is Edwards using language carelessly. He speaks as he does because he sees the creation as both a purposive act and also as an ontological self-enlargement. The exercise of the divine disposition in God's creative act is an ontological increase of God's fullness because the exercise of a disposition brings a real possibility to actuality, thereby increasing the degree of actuality. In this sense, God's creation of the world is an ontologically productive extension of his own prior actuality—hence Edwards's emanationist language. But at the same time, the exercise of the divine disposition is a teleological movement, because what the disposition is disposed to is the aim brought about by the disposition's exercise. Actuality is aimed at by the disposition's exercise. On this point, Edwards's re-conception of the divine creativity must be distinguished clearly from that of Plotinus, for whom the category of necessary emanation excludes any room for teleology. For Edwards, God's emanation of himself is a purposive activity. The marriage in Edwards of emanationist and teleological languages is made possible by the logic of his dispositional re-conception of the divine being.

THE MEANING OF TEMPORALITY FOR GOD'S OWN LIFE

If the same disposition exercised fully in God *ad intra*—"the original property of [God's] nature"—is exercised in God's creation of the world, then the world brings about "more" of God's actuality, though God does not need such an increase to be God. In asserting this consequence of his dynamic re-conception of the divine being, Edwards is anxious to reaffirm the historic Christian doctrine of the perfection of God. Especially in regard to God's aseity or self-sufficiency (the belief that God is and does what he is, and does so completely, without depending upon any other being), Edwards is resolute in refusing to make any compromises. Whenever Edwards denies that God cannot be added to, he has in mind an addition to God that comes from the creature's own power. Edwards states that "nothing that is from the creature adds to or alters God's happiness, as though it were changeable either by increase or diminution." The latter half of this statement does give the impression that Edwards might be denying the possibility of any increase of God's being in principle. But at the end of the paragraph in which the quote above appears, Edwards makes his point clear by asserting that God's joy "can't be added to or diminished by the power or will of any creature; nor is in the least dependent on anything mutable or contingent."[16]

So the sovereign self-sufficiency and independence of God is uncompromisingly affirmed. But when it comes to classical theism's doctrine of God's immutability in the Aristotelian sense, the tradition cannot contain or restrain Edwards's dynamic re-conception of the deity any longer. As long as the divine self-sufficiency is not questioned, Edwards forcefully asserts that God indeed can be "added to" and that God takes "proper delight" in what God does in time and history. Edwards observes:

> God's joy is dependent on nothing besides his own act, which he exerts with an absolute and independent power. And yet, in some sense it can be truly said that

God has the more delight and pleasure for the holiness and happiness of his creatures: because God would be less happy, if he was less good, or if he had not that perfection of nature which consists in a propensity of nature to diffuse of his own fullness.[17]

Given that God did not create the world grudgingly but out of his nature to delight in self-communication, and given that God's creation was an intentional and purposive act, Edwards just cannot see why God cannot be seen as taking proper delight in the fulfillment of his will and thus having his being and happiness increased. Edwards goes on in *The End of Creation*:

> If the last end which [God] seeks in the creation of the world, be truly a thing grateful to him (as certainly it is if it be truly his end and truly the object of his will), then it is what he takes a real delight and pleasure in . . . It may therefore be proper here to observe that let what will be God's last end, that he must have a real and proper pleasure in whatever be the proper object of his will, he is gratified in.

Edwards explains further:

> But we have reason to suppose that God's works in creating and governing the world are properly the fruits of his will, as of his understanding. And if there be any such thing at all as what we mean by *acts of will* in God, then he is not indifferent whether his will be fulfilled or not. And if he is not indifferent, then he is truly gratified and pleased in the fulfillment of his will: or which is the same thing, he has a pleasure in it. And if he has a real pleasure in attaining his end, the attainment of it belongs to his happiness.[18]

Furthermore, if God's real pleasure in the attainment of his will in creating the world "belongs to his happiness," then God is really "happier" and is thereby "enlarged" and "increased" by his self-communication *ad extra*. So God's self-sufficiency, in Edwards's way of thinking, does not prevent God's actuality from being "added to." Edwards in fact repudiates explicitly the view that God's self-sufficiency and immutability would prevent God from taking real delight in what he does through creation:

> Many have wrong notions of God's happiness, as resulting from his absolute self-sufficiency, independence, and immutability. Though it be true that God's glory and happiness are in and of himself, are infinite and can't be added to, unchangeable for the whole and every part of it, he is perfectly independent of the creature; yet it don't hence follow, nor is it true, that God has no real and proper delight, pleasure or happiness, in any of his acts or communications relative to the creature.[19]

The Aristotelian picture of God as the unmoved mover who is incapable of being affected in any way is clearly left behind by Edwards through his dynamic conception of God's creation of the world as a purposive act. God creates the world because he is who he is in his original nature.

There is a paragraph in *The End For Which God Created the World* in which Edwards makes a comment on the eternal nature of God's knowledge, which at first gives the impression of not fitting well with his position on God's self-enlargement through his activity in time. Edwards's concern here is that God's taking a real and proper delight in what happens in time is not inconsistent with the traditional concept of God as eternal. The passage reads:

> Nor does anything that has been advanced in the least suppose or infer that it does, or is it in the least inconsistent with the eternity, and most absolute immutability of God's pleasure and happiness. For though these communications of God, these exercises, operations, effects and expressions of his glorious perfections, which God rejoices in, are in time; yet his joy in them is without beginning or change. They were always equally present in the divine mind. He beheld them with equal clearness, certainty and fullness in every respect, as he doth now. They were always equally present, as with him there is no variableness or succession. He ever beheld and enjoyed them perfectly in his own independent and immutable power and will. And his view of, and joy in them is eternally, absolutely perfect, unchangeable and independent.[20]

Eternity, or sense of timelessness, has to be asserted in the case of the Father's act of knowing and loving himself. In other words, there was no time when God did not know and love himself. There was no time when the Son had not been begotten by the Father, and the Holy Spirit had not proceeded from the Father and the Son. God's knowledge and love of himself are truly timeless and without succession.

But in the above paragraph from *The End of Creation*, Edwards is talking about God's knowledge of the world in time, which involves succession and duration. The question arises: Is Edwards asserting here that the infinite God's knowledge of the events in time involves no duration or succession whatsoever? If so, then temporal events would not be known by God as temporal (that is, involving duration and succession) and thus would not be ultimately meaningful to God. But Edwards, as we have seen, insists that God takes a real and proper delight in certain events as they occur in time. We find further help in interpreting the above-quoted paragraph when we read Edwards's discussion of what God had in view as the ultimate end, particularly in regard to the creation of creatures. Edwards writes, "In this view, those elect creatures which must be looked upon as the end of all the rest of the creation, considered with respect to the whole of *their eternal duration*, and as such made God's end, must be viewed as being, as it were, one with God." In regard to the same point, Edwards adds, "As the creatures' good was viewed in this manner when God made the world for it, viz. with respect to the whole of *the eternal duration* of it, and the *eternally progressive* union and communion with himself."[21]

Such statements as these suggest that in God's view of the events in time, according to Edwards, duration and progressive succession are somehow included in what God knows. Thus, the interpretation that suggests itself is that, for Edwards, God timelessly knows the events in time in their succession and progress. This would make sense in analogy with the human experience of knowing now, without succession and in a simultaneous instant, two events that occurred in succession in the past.[22] For Edwards, then, God timelessly knows time in succession (i.e. temporality as temporality). Time, as such, matters to God when God acts in time to enlarge God's own actuality.

THE IMPORTANCE OF TEMPORALITY IN EDWARDS'S THOUGHT

For Edwards, although God does not need temporality for his internal actuality and perfection, God needs or uses the world in space and time to exercise his dispositional essence outside of his own internal being. What God does in time and space makes time and space important to God. In other words, it is not that the created world as such can increase the divine being; it is rather what God himself does in and through the world in time and space that affects the divine being by adding to his own being. In this specific sense, nevertheless, the world in space and time really matters to God's own life. The point we are highlighting here, however, is that it is *time as such*, and *space as such*, that is indispensable in God's own activity of enlarging himself *ad extra*, although not all space and time, and not space and time as separated from God's self-expanding, communicating activity, is indispensable to God.

Edwards and Plotinus both spoke of the world as overflowing from the fullness of God. But for Plotinus, the overflowing is neither teleologically nor ontologically incremental to God's own life in any sense. In such a perspective, the temporal world is not of any meaning or importance to God himself, who remains eternally and absolutely unaffected by anything. We can safely say that Edwards clearly left behind the old classical theism's Aristotelian concept of God as the unmoved mover who is absolutely impassible and unaffected by what happens in the world in space and time. Further, whatever Neo-platonic influences there may be in Edwards's thought, his dynamic new thinking on the God-world relation is certainly not one of them.

This new thinking of Edwards on the God-world relation could not but have had a profound impact upon his theology as a whole. The impact appears in Edwards's heightened attention to the place of time and space in God's scheme of things. In this essay we have space only to mention some of those areas in Edwards's thought where temporality and spatiality are taken with a particular seriousness. For example, in Edwards's theological epistemology, the act of knowing and loving the transcendent beauty of God is not conceived of in any way as an act of leaving behind the temporal and spatial world. The "sensible knowledge" that the Holy Spirit makes possible is not some new information that is separate from the words of the Scripture but rather a new apprehension of what already is in Scripture. The finite, creaturely ideas and the concrete ideas of the physical universe are all necessary "stuff" in and through which the transcendent is experienced and known. For God to repeat God's intra-triune knowing and loving in the world, they have to be repeated in time and space. Yet, Edwards is not a "mystic," if the term refers to one who contends that true knowledge of the ultimate reality involves a departure from the sensible and the mundane.

Edwards's emphasis upon Christian practice as the most important "sign" of the veracity of a person's conversion is well known. His understanding of regeneration as the indwelling of the Holy Spirit, or a new disposition in the regenerate, implies a stress upon the actual practice of the regenerate. Given appropriate occasions, a disposition will necessarily be exercised in the form of a certain type of action. Christian practice necessarily follows regeneration. But the deeper reason, I suggest, for Edwards's strong emphasis upon Christian practice has to be found in God's creation—namely, repeating God's intra-trinitarian acts in time and space. The actual holy deeds of a converted person in this temporal and spatial world are what are required for God's own end in creation. God delights, Edwards observes, "in the devotions, grace and good works of the saints."[23] There cannot be a more profound grounding for Christian ethics.

Finally, we should mention Edwards's eschatology to indicate the heightened importance of temporality and spatiality in his thought. According to him, the end of the world will be the day when God's work of redeeming the elect will be completed. On that day the world as we know it will come to an end, but history will not be finished. What has to be repeated in time and space is the infinite fullness of God's being, which will take an infinite duration of time. So "there never will come the moment, when it can be said, that now this infinitely valuable good has been actually bestowed." On the "last day," Christ the bridegroom and the church as bride will be reunited and will marry before the Father. But this "wedding day" will be a wedding that will never end . . . the joys of the wedding day will continue to all eternity."

History will continue in the "new heaven and new earth"; the increase and repetition of God's glory in time and history will go on "throughout the never-ending ages of eternity."[24]

In the new heaven and the new earth, the saints will behold God's beauty with their bodily eyes, mainly as manifested in the person of the Redeemer. The saints will "see" the beauty of God, "most of all mediate ways, in the man Jesus Christ." Further, the beauty of God in the physical universe will be more intense in heaven than upon earth, appearing "chiefly on the bodies of the man Christ Jesus and the saints."[25] For Edwards, unlike in medieval theology, the beatific vision is mediated by the incarnate Jesus Christ. The temporality and humanity of Jesus Christ continue in heaven, since God's work of repeating his glory in time and space continues there.

The late Paul Ramsey astutely observed that, in Edwards's vision, Christ's mediatorial role as the incarnate Son of God continues in heaven. Ramsey calls this "the eternality of the incarnation" in Edwards's eschatology. Ramsey concludes: "In the entire history of Christian theology, there is no more dynamic understanding of the relation of God to his creatures than that of Jonathan Edwards."[26] I would only add that Edwards's "dynamic understanding" of God's relation to the world went even further than Ramsey might have thought: namely, that God in that relation is enlarged and increased, thereby making what happens in time and history, by God's grace, a participation in God's own life.

NOTES

1. "Miscellanies," no. 241, in *WJE* 13:358. For a fuller discussion of Edwards's concept of habit or disposition and of his dispositional ontology, see my *The Philosophical Theology of Jonathan Edwards* (Princeton: Princeton University Press, 2000), 34–114.

2. *WJE* 6, 391, 215.

3. "Miscellanies," no. 1263, in *WJE* 23:201–12.

4. In "Of Atoms," Edwards asserted that the "resistance" (or existence) of an entity (and thus by implication, an event or action) is the result of the immediate activity of God abiding by the previously established laws of nature (*WJE* 6:214–15).

5. *WJE* 6:241. See, for example, Norman Fiering, *Jonathan Edwards's Moral Thought and Its British Context* (Chapel Hill: University of North Carolina Press, 1981), 279–80, 307–308.

6. "Miscellanies," no. 1218, in *WJE* 23:150–53; Lee, *Philosophical Theology of Jonathan Edwards*, 89–94.

7. "Miscellanies," no. 107, in *WJE* 13:277–78; *The End For Which God Created the World*, in *WJE* 8:433–34; "Miscellanies," no. 1218, in *WJE* 23:150–53.

8. "Miscellanies," no. 104, in *WJE* 13:272.
9. "Miscellanies," no. 94, in *WJE* 13:262; "Discourse on the Trinity," in *WJE* 21:131; Lee, *Philosophical Theology of Jonathan Edwards*, 188.
10. "Discourse on the Trinity," in *WJE* 21:114–20, 114; "Miscellanies," no. 104, in *WJE* 13:272.
11. "Miscellanies," no. 94, in *WJE* 13:256–63
12. "Miscellanies," no. 104, in *WJE* 13:272.
13. "Miscellanies," no. 553, in *WJE* 18:97; *End For Which God Created the World*, in *WJE* 8:452; "Miscellanies," no. 445, in *WJE* 13:494; "Miscellanies," no. 448, in *WJE* 13:496.
14. *The End For Which God Created the World*, in *WJE* 8:527; "Miscellanies," no. 247, in *WJE* 13:361; *The End For Which God Created the World*, in *WJE* 8:433.
15. *The End For Which God Created the World*, in *WJE* 8:534.
16. *The End For Which God Created the World*, in *WJE* 9:435, 448.
17. *The End For Which God Created the World*, in *WJE* 8:447.
18. *The End For Which God Created the World*, in *WJE* 8:449.
19. *The End For Which God Created the World*, in *WJE* 8:445–46.
20. *The End For Which God Created the World*, in *WJE* 8:448.
21. *The End For Which God Created the World*, in *WJE* 8:443, 459.
22. I am indebted to Robert W. Jenson for his suggestion of the interpretation offered here.
23. "Miscellanies," no. 107b, in *WJE* 13:278.
24. *The End For Which God Created the World*, in *WJE* 8:536; *WJE* 9:508, 508–509.
25. "Miscellanies," nos. 137 and 182, in *WJE* 13:295–96, 328.
26. Paul Ramsey, "Heaven Is a Progressive State," in *WJE* 8:720, 716.

Edwards as American Theologian: Grand Narratives and Pastoral Narratives

Amy Plantinga Pauw

Louisville Presbyterian Theological Seminary

Jonathan Edwards was a theologian of the grand narrative. His grand narrative, interspersed throughout his writings, and above all in his *History of the Work of Redemption*, tells of God's immanence in human history. It is a triumphant narrative, told from the deity's point of view.[1] The God of this narrative is working out his sovereign purpose in the world, and nothing will stand in the way of its realization. In a fast-day sermon preached during Britain's ongoing conflict with Spain, Edwards declared that God

> orders and governs all the public commotions that are in the world. None of the ferments and quarrels and uproars that are in nations, or between one nation and another, come to pass without his ordering. Those changes that God has ordained of old in his eternal counsels shall come to pass, and no others; and they shall come to pass no otherwise than just as he has determined. Their manner, nature and extent, and all their circumstances and their whole issue, is ordered by him.[2]

For Edwards, God is in the details. History is a story of God's continuing and intimate presence and agency in human affairs, and the glorious result will be the complete conquest of evil and the victory of God's saints.

In his grand narrative, Edwards had utter confidence not merely in God's governing of human affairs, but also in the human ability to discern the patterns and aims of this divine ordering. All the ferments, quarrels, and uproars of Edwards's day served God's magnificent work of human redemption, which was "the great end and drift of all God's works and dispensations from the beginning."[3] In a world marked by sin and decay, God's redemptive intentions for humanity require a struggle against all that stands in the way of intimate union with God. So for Edwards the drama of the earthly work of redemption is a gradual, conflict–ridden process, though its ultimate conclusion is never in doubt.

History was not the only arena of God's providential ordering. God, according to Edwards, is a communicative being. "The heavens declare the glory of God," said the Psalmist. But for Edwards, so do the worlds of nature and of ordinary human affairs. The entire creation preaches aloud about God's great work of redemption. As Edwards put it, "I expect by very ridicule and contempt to be called a man of a very fruitful brain and copious fancy, but they are welcome to it. I am not ashamed to own that I believe that the whole universe, heaven and earth, air and seas, and the divine constitution and history of the holy Scriptures, be full of images of divine things, as full as a language is of words."[4] At the center of this universe of images of divine things are human creatures. The eternal communication of wisdom and love *within* the Trinity finds fitting external expression in God's communication of wisdom and love to human creatures. This saving divine communication is "the great and universal end of God's creating the world."[5] Human creatures are brought into existence to know and love God, and to rejoice in God's glorious excellency. They are the primary beneficiaries of God's communication, and of the great work of redemption itself.

God, then, governs both creation and human history towards the goal of the great work of redemption. As part of his grand narrative in the *History of the Work of Redemption*, Edwards also described the *means* of God's redemptive work. As he reflected from his colonial perch in Northampton, Massachusetts, on how the work of redemption advanced, Edwards became convinced that it was "by remarkable pourings out of the Spirit of God" at "special seasons of mercy," or revivals.[6] God's work of redemption in human history does not flow smoothly or predictably. The Spirit moves by fits and starts, flaring up in unlikely places at surprising times.

This insight about revivals being the means of advancing God's work of redemption came to Edwards, not incidentally, in the wake of a surprising revival in his own congregation. Nor did his grand narrative omit a starring role for "eminent ministers" like himself: "the deliverance of the Christian church will be preceded by God's raising up a number of eminent ministers that shall more plainly and fervently and effectually preach the gospel than it had been before, and reprove his own church, and show her her errors, and also shall convince gainsayers, and shall thoroughly detect the errors of the false church."[7] The method of God's immanent workings was splendidly clear. In Edward's account of the progress of the work of redemption, his role as revivalist in the colonial hinterlands took on supreme significance as part of sacred, providential history. As Edwards's recent biographer, George Marsden, has noted, Edwards "characteristically saw himself as involved in grand historical moments."[8]

We see here one of the dangers of a grand narrative. The attempt to give an account of things from God's point of view so often bestows leading roles in the drama on the little parts of Christ's realm that the author knows best. In *Some Thoughts on the Revival*, his fullest account of the ongoing revivals in New England, Edwards reached for biblical typology to portray the significance of the "new world," particularly New England, in God's overarching purposes. The new world is like Joseph, who "fed and saved the world when [it was] ready to perish with famine, and was a fruitful bough by a well, whose branches ran over the wall, and was blessed with all manner of blessings and precious things, of heaven and earth, through the good-will of him that dwelt in the bush." In the same way, America would feed and save the old world spiritually, having been given "the honor of communicating religion in its most glorious state" to the rest of humanity.[9]

It has to be said right away that Edwards was far more restrained than many of the subsequent American narrators of this land's divine promise. According to Edwards, God's selection of obscure places like colonial New England and ancient Israel reflected more the divine sense of humor than special human virtue. Edwards called the work of God in Northampton "surprising" not least because of the Spirit's choice of subjects and venue. Edwards was always eager to remind his parochial parishioners of "God's grace carried on in other places."[10] These "other places" of God's great work of redemption encompassed not only distant regions of earth, but also the worlds of heaven and hell. America had at best a cameo appearance in Edwards's far-flung divine drama.

Religion, not geography, determined the leading roles in Edwards's drama of redemption. In keeping with the tendency of grand narratives to differentiate sharply between the forces of good and evil, the *History of the Work of Redemption* neatly divides the world into the true church, that is the Protestant church, and the enemies of the church. For now, God's immanent presence is glimpsed in worldwide outbreaks of revival, military defeats of Catholic countries, and other signs of encouragement to the beleaguered saints. But the earthly sufferings of the righteous will finally be avenged by God's fierce and pitiless wrath against all evildoers. The ultimate manifestation of the immanent divine presence will be in "the terrible judgments and fearful destruction . . . executed on God's enemies,"[11] among them blasphemers, deists, and obstinate heretics, including what Edwards regarded as the twin kingdoms of Satan, Roman Catholicism and Islam. There is no getting around the fact that violence and exclusion of others have often been part of Christian grand narratives. The claim that Christianity provides a uniquely peaceful, all-encompassing alternative to other metanarratives does not withstand historical scrutiny.[12]

Alongside grand narratives, both nationalist and religious, another sort of narrative of God's immanence has existed since colonial times—what we may term the pastoral narrative. Jonathan Edwards was also a theologian of the pastoral narrative, which can be traced throughout his letters, notebooks, and sermons.[13] The pastoral narrative is also a narrative of the immanence of God in human history, but it stays much closer to ordinary life in the church, including its difficult, intractable bits. Rather than surveying the work of redemption from God's luxury box,[14] pastors find themselves on most days at the level of its ruts and bumps in the lives of particular persons and communities. They do not observe human ferments and quarrels and uproars from on high—they find themselves in the middle of them.

As a pastor, Edwards witnessed "the disordering rhythms of everyday life," the gaping "intermittances" in the spiritual lives of many of the faithful, the endless communal and individual negotiations around religious convictions and practices.[15] While the ultimate end of God's work of redemption might be certain, the earthly life of faith is a tangle of ambiguities, inconsistencies and contingencies. Edwards as pastor found that "distinguishing marks of the Spirit's work" are awfully hard to discern on the micro level, because the human capacity for spiritual self-deception is huge, and divine grace has many counterfeits. Even what Edwards judged to be the genuine work of the Spirit was unsettling, resisting the institutional control of "eminent ministers" like himself, and sowing agitation, innovation, and dissension. And if revivals were indeed the appointed means of establishing Christ's reign, the spiritual gains they brought seemed disturbingly transitory. Edwards lamented how the surprising outpourings of the Spirit in a community could be closely followed by a deluge of party spirit, moral confusion and spiritual arrogance. From the perspective of the pastoral narrative, the redeeming work of God eludes human comprehension and control. "The methods of grace," Edwards opined, "are obscure, as those of nature."[16] Pastoral vision is blurry, and pastoral power is always brokered and partial. In the pastoral narrative, God's immanent presence, while undeniable, rarely lends itself to stories of triumph and glory.

Chastened by disappointment in his parishioners and perhaps by his own continuing struggles against pride, Edwards as pastor looked back ruefully on his confident grand narrative of the 1730s revivals in Northampton: "Was there too much of an appearance of a public pride, if I may so call it? Were we not lifted up with the honor that God had put upon us as a people, beyond most other people? . . . Did it not make us something self-sufficient in our way of talking to others, as though we thought we were the *people*, and we were confident that we ourselves were guides to the blind, and a light of them that are in darkness, and instructors of the foolish, and teachers of babes?"[17]

The pastoral narrative invites this kind of humility; it acknowledges that the Spirit's earthly work of regeneration is a protracted and complex business, of which God alone is judge.

The pastoral narrative typically elicits a different ecclesiology than the grand narrative. The distinction between the righteous and the unrighteous is much less clear. The visible church is less an elite gathering of the saints than a means of grace for the spiritually needy. In his *Notes on Scripture*, Edwards declared that "in the Christian church are gathered together persons of all nations, kindreds, tongues, and peoples, persons of all degrees, all kinds of tempers and manners." Just as the door of Noah's ark "was open to receive all sorts of creatures—tigers, wolves, bears, lions, leopards, serpents, vipers, dragons—such as men would not by any means admit into the doors of their houses," so likewise "Christ stands ready to receive all, even the vilest and worst."[18] In the pastoral narrative, the ongoing struggle against the forces of evil takes place within Christian hearts and Christian communities, in the midst of chronic human disorder and imperfection. God's work of redemption is so agonizingly difficult and slow because it aims at nothing less than opening heaven and converting earth, bringing "the vilest and worst" into joyful, eternal fellowship with the triune Godhead. God triumphs over evil not by annihilating evildoers, but by winning sinners over to the good.

The pastoral narrative requires that the church's authentic ministry be more than simply a recital of God's saving deeds, a matter of standing above the fray of daily experience and witnessing to the history of God's glorious work of redemption. The pastoral narrative finds "images of divine things" in the rhythms of "human birth, suffering, and dying—bodily and communal processes in which the mystery of human life is lodged."[19] It situates the great work of redemption in the midst of God's relations to the nourishing, ongoing, and reliable order of creation. The church does not only recite or display God's salvation—it mediates it through patient attention to the ordinary tasks of pastoral ministry: feeding the hungry, teaching children, encouraging the spiritually weak, visiting the sick, comforting the bereaved.

Intertwined as they were in his writing and preaching, the grand narrative and the pastoral narrative had an uneasy co-existence in Edwards's thought. We see especially in Edwards's early ministry in Northampton among English settlers and in his missionary work among the Stockbridge Indians at the end of his life a deep attention to this unassuming work of pastoral ministry. Week after week, from Edwards's time until our own, it is this kind of work that has quietly funded the spiritual and moral capital of American churches. Yet it is understandable that a person who characteristically saw himself as involved in grand historical moments would tire of the prosaic tasks of pastoral ministry—especially in the context of the pragmatic, family-oriented religiosity of Northampton, Massachusetts. His earnest spiritual resolutions to the contrary, the cardinal virtues of pastoral ministry—patience, humility and generosity of spirit— did not come easily for Edwards. When in his treatise on *Religious Affections* he criticized the person who acts as if he were "by just right the head of all the Christians in the town, and is assuming, self-willed, and impatient of the least contradiction or opposition," he could have been describing himself.[20]

As David D. Hall has noted, Edwards the pastor "craved in his parishioners the same intensity of commitment he felt within himself."[21] The lack of this spiritual intensity in Northampton and the congregation's increasing resentment of Edwards's coercive pastoral attempts to revive it became a source of frustration and bitterness for him. In matters of religious devotion, Edwards had little tolerance for "neutrality, or lukewarmness, or a middle sort of persons with a moral sincerity."[22] But the church, then as now, has always been full of such persons. Edwards's spiritual expectations for his Northampton parishioners were clearly unrealistic. In a sermon probably preached to them more than once, Edwards portrayed a group of Christians all caught up "in a just and righteous, meek, peaceable, quiet, loving conversation one among another, far from all revenge and ill will, all living in love, studying to promote one another's good, abounding in deeds of righteousness and mercy, apt to forbear with one another, apt to forgive one another, ready to deny themselves one for another, living together like a society of brethren in all Christian and holy behavior one towards another."[23] This description resembles Edwards's vision of the divine society of the Trinity, the "supreme harmony of all," much more than any earthly congregation, let alone Northampton.

Ken Minkema has described Edwards as a "fair-weather friend to his congregation."[24] During times of revival, Edwards was quick to see the town as "full of the presence of God, full of love and joy as never before." But when this love and joy languished, Edwards's unforgiving and unrelenting criticism of his Northampton parishioners only increased their bitterness and divisions. His vision of communal love within the Trinity set an impossible standard for his congregation. When the people failed to attain it, Edwards's trinitarianism could inscribe a narrow moralism, which ironically undermined his theology of a self-dispossessing, communicative God of wisdom and love. As Edwards's national and international stature as an expert on "religious affections" grew, so did the mutual resentment and disaffection between him and his congregation.

By defining the advance of God's work of redemption in terms of special seasons of revival and awakening, Edwards was tempted to view ordinary life in the church, in Sidney Mead's words, as "a struggle across dull plateaus between peaks of spiritual refreshing."[25] As the 1740s wore on, Edwards became increasingly isolated from the ferments and quarrels and uproars close at hand in his congregation. Instead of patient dealings with his all-too-earthly parishioners, he devoted himself more and more to grand narratives of God's immanent presence far away and long ago—the trinitarian views of ancient Chinese, revivals of the true church in sixteenth-century Europe.[26] In *A History of the Work of Redemption*, written already in 1739, Edwards crafted a Constantinian grand narrative about the ultimate victory of Protestant Christianity, a narrative unmarred by the spiritual failings and flaws of actual Protestants.

Most twenty-first century readers of Jonathan Edwards have little taste for this kind of theology of glory. And it is academic fashion these days to be reflexively suspicious of grand narratives. So it is tempting at this point to conclude that the pastoral narrative should always trump the grand narrative. Taking Edwards as a cautionary example, perhaps pastors, like postmodernists, should view grand narratives with incredulity and try to get along without them.

But Edwards's pastoral practice argues for a more complex conclusion. A pastoral narrative without some vision of God's grand purposes for the whole of creation can leave Christian communities walled in by the mundane parochialisms of their particular locations. Serene Jones has described the larger doctrinal framework of Christian faith as an imaginative landscape, a conceptual territory within which Christians stand to get their conceptual bearings on the world and the reality of God therein.[27] In a similar way, narratives of God's great work of redemption provide an enormous landscape within which to orient and negotiate the complexities of daily lives of faith. These narratives remind us, in Edwards's words, "of God's grace carried on in other places," and unsettle Christians' comfortable assumptions about how God's grace is being carried on in their own place. Pastoral narratives need this larger landscape.

One of the great "landscape painters" of American Protestantism was H. Richard Niebuhr. In his stunning essay, "The Anachronism of Jonathan Edwards," he sketched the prominent lines of the Edwardsean landscape: "What Edwards knew, what he believed in his heart and with his mind, was that [hu]man[ity] was made to stand in the presence of eternal, unending absolute glory, to participate in the celebration of cosmic deliverance from everything putrid, destructive, defiling, to rejoice in the service of the stupendous artist who flung universes of stars on his canvas, sculptured the forms of angelic powers, etched with loving care miniature worlds within worlds."[28] While grand narratives are dangerous when removed from the messiness of ordinary Christian life, so too pastoral narratives are dangerous when abstracted from the larger landscape of God's immanent presence in the world. Without any grand narrative, pastoral ministry tends to turn in on itself, overwhelmed by myriad details, borne along by unchallenged prejudices and customs.

We see at various points in Edwards's ministry the capacity of the grand narrative to relativize, even delegitimate tribalist pretensions. As Rachel Wheeler points out in her essay in this volume, Edwards employed the grand narrative's insistence on the universality of human sin in his treatise on *Original Sin*, written in Stockbridge, to criticize the moral pretensions of the English settlers. Echoing the prophet Amos, he denounced the "deluge of infidelity, profaneness, luxury, debauchery and wickedness of every kind" that flooded "the Protestant countries at this day, and . . . our nation in particular." Compared to the European settlers, Edwards averred, the Native Americans are "mere babes and fools as to proficiency in wickedness."[29] The grand narrative functioned to deflate English claims to be superior to Natives in culture and virtue. Similarly, as Mark Valeri's essay shows in the case of his cousin Eunice Williams, Edwards appealed to a Christian grand narrative to commend a form of forgiveness that reached far beyond the Puritan tribe. Hating one's French and Indian enemies was the "reasonable" and "natural" human response, but the grand narrative created a new landscape in which "we ought not to hate them for we don't know but that God has a design of mercy towards them. We ought not to hate them, for we don't know but that God has from all eternity put his love upon them and that Christ shed his precious blood for them and bestowed his own Image upon them."[30] To those who had domesticated forgiveness into a parochial duty, designed to maintain social harmony at the local level, Edwards countered with an understanding of forgiveness that challenged New England's deepest social and political divisions.

Theologians have often ignored Edwards's pastoral labors in their estimates of his contributions to theological discourse. This is unfortunate, because Edwards was a better theologian when he let the rough textures of pastoral life show through in his theological reflections. His grand vision of God's great work of redemption was most powerful when tempered by his keen pastoral recognition of the messiness, the paradoxes, and the ambiguities of the life of faith. Likewise, his pastoral instincts and response were soundest when embedded within the larger landscape of God's great work of redemption. In Edwards's intertwining of the grand narrative and the pastoral narrative we find his most enduring theology.

Edwards was an American theologian. He remains an important figure for American Protestants in particular, not least because they have often indulged their taste for grandiose narratives about their nation's role in God's eternal purpose without the benefit of the relativizing force of Edwards's pastoral realism. The comments of Senator Albert Beveridge of Indiana, for example, are a textbook example of American imperialism at the turn of the twentieth-century: "God . . . has marked the American people to finally lead in the redemption of the world. This is the divine mission of America. . . . We are the trustees of the world's progress, guardians of its righteous peace."[31] In Beveridge's narrative, God's immanent presence and American fortunes are inextricably intertwined. We have to look no further than the daily newspapers for signs that this "Captain America complex" is alive and well in our time. As the Canadian historian George Rawlyk has argued, "no nation in modern history . . . has been as preoccupied as has been the United States with the conviction that it indeed has a *unique* mission in the world and a *special* hegemonic contribution to make."[32] The danger, in Edwards's time as in ours, is for grand narratives to lead to a "fatal short circuit" between national wrath and divine wrath, American glory and divine glory.[33]

Grand narratives about America are not going away anytime soon. Nor should they. Part of what we expect from our political and religious leaders is a wide-angled vision, a sense of perspective that comes from articulating the larger connections we have to other places, times, and peoples. Those who believe in God rightly desire to see their particular desires and struggles against a wider horizon of God's immanent presence in human history. Religious faith is not just a set of private beliefs to help individuals get through the day, but a comprehensive ground for reflection on how the world and human life hang together.[34] This involves people's lives both as citizens and as members of a global community.

On the other hand, attention to a civic version of what I've called the pastoral narrative can chasten our grand narratives, quashing tendencies toward self-righteous nationalism and religious sectarianism. In great American orators like Edwards, Abraham Lincoln and Martin Luther King, Jr., we see how frank recognition of national and religious failings imbues their grand narratives with a mixture of humility, irony, and hope, so that they still demand a hearing—40 years, 150 years, even 300 years later.

NOTES

1. For an account of Edwards's "grand narrative" of redemption history, see Avihu Zakai, *Jonathan Edwards's Philosophy of History: The Reenchantment of the World in the Age of Enlightenment* (Princeton: Princeton University Press, 2003). I am grateful to Joe Coalter and Ken Minkema for their comments on this paper.
2. "God's Care in Times of Public Commotions," in *WJE* 22:348.
3. "Miscellanies," no. 702, in *WJE* 18:284.
4. "Types Notebook," in *WJE*. 11:152.

5. "Miscellanies," no. 332, in *WJE* 13:410.
6. *WJE* 9:143.
7. "Miscellanies," no. 810, in *WJE*. 18:518.
8. Marsden, *Jonathan Edwards: A Life*, 387.
9. *Some Thoughts Concerning the Revival*, in *WJE* 4:354–55.
10. See Edwards's sermon by this title in *WJE*. 22:103–110.
11. *WJE* 9:475.
12. I would nevertheless argue that the church has abundant theological resources for repenting of its violence and exclusions.
13. I would argue that Edwards's letters are an underutilized resource for exploring his theology. See *WJE* 16.
14. I borrow this phrase from Merold Westphal, "Blind Spots: Christianity and Postmodern Philosophy," *Christian Century* 120, no. 12 (June 14, 2003): 33.
15. These phrases are drawn from David D. Hall, who has so acutely portrayed the texture of "lived religion" in colonial New England. See Hall, "Narrating Puritanism," in *New Directions in American Religious History*, ed. Harry S. Stout and D. G. Hart (New York: Oxford University Press, 1977), 51–83.
16. "Miscellanies," no. 899, in *WJE* 20:156, quoting Stephen Charnock.
17. "Bringing the Ark to Zion a Second Time," in *WJE* 22:255.
18. "Notes on Scripture," no. 297," in *WJE* 15:271.
19. Walter Brueggemann, "The Loss and Recovery of Creation in Old Testament Theology," *Theology Today* 53 (July 1996), 179.
20. *WJE* 2:411.
21. David D. Hall, "Editor's Introduction," in *WJE* 12:46.
22. *An Humble Inquiry*, in WJE 12:220.
23. "Mercy and Not Sacrifice," in *WJE*: 22:133.
24. Minkema, "The Edwardses: A Ministerial Family in Eighteenth-Century New England," Ph.D. Dissertation, University of Connecticut, 1988, p. 238.
25. Sidney E. Mead, *The Lively Experiment: The Shaping of Christianity in America*, (New York: Harper & Row Publishers, 1963), 125.
26. *WJE* 9:421–424; "Miscellanies," no. 1236, in *WJE* 23:171.
27. Jones, "Graced Practices: Excellence and Freedom in the Christian Life," in *Practicing Theology: Beliefs and Practices in Christian Life*, ed. Miroslav Volf and Dorothy Bass (Grand Rapids, Mich.: Eerdmans, 2002), 74.
28. H. Richard Niebuhr, "The Anachronism of Jonathan Edwards," in *Theology, History, and Culture*, ed. William Stacy Johnson (New Haven: Yale University Press, 1996), 128.
29. *WJE* 3:183, 198. See Rachel Wheeler's paper, below.
30. MS sermon on Matt. 5:44 (c. 1731–32), with the doctrine: "Men ought to love their enemies." See Mark Valeri's paper, below.
31. Robert Jewett, *The Captain America Complex: The Dilemma of Zealous Nationalism* (Philadelphia: Westminster Press, 1973), 9. See also Russell B. Nye, *This Almost Chosen People: Essays in the History of American Ideas* (Lansing, Mich.: Michigan State University Press, 1966).

32. George Rawlyk, "Politics, Religion, and the Canadian Experience: A Preliminary Probe," in *Religion and American Politics: From the Colonial Period to the 1980s*, ed. Mark A. Noll (New York: Oxford University Press, 1990), 254.

33. Robert Jewett, *The Captain America Complex*, 111.

34. I've borrowed some of this language from Rowan Williams, in his lecture entitled "Christian Theology and Other Faiths," delivered June 11, 2003, at Birmingham University, England.

"Longing for More and More of It"? The Strange Career Of Jonathan Edwards's Exegetical Exertions[1]

Douglas A. Sweeney

Trinity Evangelical Divinity School

"The Bible is full of wonderful things," preached Jonathan Edwards to his parishioners. It has stood the test of time as the world's "most comprehensive book." It is "divine." It is "unerring." Indeed, the light that it sheds on our world "is ten thousand times better than [the] light of the sun." The Bible's contents, Edwards contended, are "the most excellent things in the world." In fact, they tower "as much above those things" we study "in other sciences, as heaven is above . . . earth." Moreover, the knowledge gained from the Bible "is infinitely more useful and important" than the knowledge gained in "all other sciences." Edwards depicted the Bible accordingly as "a precious treasure," one "far exceeding all human writings." He encouraged his congregations to "search for" biblical treasure, "and that with the same diligence . . . with which men . . . dig in mines" for "gold." He assured them that the Bible "contains enough" within its covers so "to employ us to the end." Even at death, he averred, we "shall leave enough" of the Scriptures "uninvestigated to employ . . . the ablest divines to the end of the world," or better, "to employ the . . . saints and angels to all eternity." Edwards devoted the bulk of his time each day to searching the Bible's treasures, preparing to preach, write and counsel as a biblical theologian. He found what he called a "greater delight" in exegetical exertion "than in anything else" he did. And he confessed on many occasions that those who have ever "tasted the sweetness" of God's Scriptural divinity will live out their days in "longing for more and more of it."[2]

As this montage of quotations makes clear, Jonathan Edwards was a biblicist—one whose world revolved around the words of Scripture. And as this sample of statements implies, modern scholars have yet to come close to understanding the ways in which Edwards's life was animated by what he deemed God's Word. Three hundred years after Edwards's birth, and half a century into what some have called the Edwards renaissance, few have bothered to study Edwards's extensive exegetical writings.[3] While preoccupied with his roles in America's "public" life and letters, and failing to see the public significance of his biblical exegesis, we have neglected the scholarly work that he took most seriously. The lion's share of Edwards's time during every week of his adult life was spent wrestling with the words of holy writ. But though we know a great deal now about his ethics, metaphysics, epistemology and aesthetics—not to mention his pastoral ministry and his role in New England's revivals—few know much at all about Edwards's exegetical labors. Names such as Matthew Poole, for example, or Arthur Bedford, or Humphrey Prideaux, scarcely ring a bell today among Edwards scholars. But these were his interlocutors–much more than Locke, Berkeley and Newton.[4] They may not have played as great a role in shaping his intellectual agenda. But they played a much greater role in helping him prosecute that agenda. Edwards spent decades, quite literally, poring over their biblical writings, doing his most important work with them at hand.[5]

Edwards scholars have often treated this fact as an embarrassing family secret, one that would damage our reputations if widely known. And truth be told, this concern has not been completely misdirected, for many have little use at all for the Edwards of history. According to Bruce Kuklick, Edwards proved far more attractive and serviceable to secular intellectuals when portrayed by Perry Miller as "one of us–close to being an atheist for Niebuhr." But now that Edwards has been unmasked as a Bible-believing supernaturalist —ironically, by Miller's own Yale Edition of Edwards's *Works*—his thought "is not likely to compel the attention of intellectuals ever again. Indeed," argues Kuklick, "it is more likely to repel their attention."[6] To most disinterested observers Kuklick's claim will appear hyperbolic. Large numbers of intellectuals remain intrigued by Edwards's thought, as attested by the success of Perry Miller's Yale Edition, not to mention the number of people who honored the Edwards tercentennial. Nonetheless, Kuklick's statement represents a common (mis)perception that the real, historical Edwards may not be fit for polite company. And insofar as mainstream scholarship is a reliable indicator, most students could hardly care any less about Edwards's biblical orientation.

So what are Edwards scholars to do in the midst of this awkward situation? Must we hide his biblicism in order to save his place in the canon? Should we ignore this part of his life so that he appears a "retrievable" thinker? After juxtaposing Edwards's own perspective on the Bible against the neglect of his exegesis in most of the history of modern scholarship, I will begin to offer an answer to these questions. I will contend that we must find a way to address Edwards's biblicism head on–and not simply in a quixotic quest for the real

Edwards of history. The biblical Edwards, I will suggest, can also help us come to terms with other neglected forms of modern supernaturalism.

I.

Like most Christians before him, Edwards referred to the Bible regularly as the very "Word of God." But he also liked to call it "the word of Christ" or, as he phrased it once in a sermon he gave as a teenager in Manhattan, "the epistle of Christ that he has written to us." The Bible functioned, then, for Edwards as what he termed a "word of life; as the light of life; a sweet, . . . life-giving word." He called it "a perfect rule," a reliable "guide to true happiness." For as he insisted, it is "a book of divine instructions." Edwards maintained an exceptionally high view of the Bible's inspiration. He taught that God had "indited" (i.e. proclaimed, pronounced, or even composed) the Scriptures through the Bible's human authors, thus imbuing the biblical narratives with "a strange and unaccountable kind of enchantment." Not surprisingly, then, he believed the Bible to be "an infallible guide, a sure rule which if we follow we cannot err." And he exhorted his listeners frequently that "if God hath been so engaged in teaching" the world about himself, "certainly we should not be negligent in learning; nor should we make growing in [biblical] knowledge a by-business, but a great part of the business of our lives."[7]

Indeed, for Edwards, the appropriate posture for those who would understand the divine was "to sit at Jesus' feet and hear his word." They must "go to him whose Word it is and beg of him to teach," for "he has reserved to himself this work of enlightening the mind with spiritual knowledge, and there is no other can do it; there is none teaches like God." Like Mary of Bethany in the gospels, the sister of Lazarus and Martha—who took "a pound of ointment of spikenard, very costly, and anointed the feet of Jesus, and wiped his feet with her hair" (John 12:3)—we should know better than to busy ourselves with "[trouble] about many things." Rather, as Jesus said to Martha, only "one thing is needful: and Mary hath chosen that good part" (Luke 10:41–42), for she had clung to Christ and hung on His every word. Likewise, Edwards believed that "the word of God is the great means of our eternal good. . . . 'tis the most necessary means, and without which our souls must famish." It is like "MILK," he suggested, flowing "from the breasts of the church." It is like "rain" for which God's people have a "a great and earnest thirsting."[8]

Edwards spoke often of the need to study "what reason *and* Scripture declare." He affirmed the traditional Calvinist dictum that those who would understand the world and its relationship to God need both the "book of nature" *and* the "book of Scripture." But he emphasized consistently the priority of the Bible. As he wrote in his *Distinguishing Marks of a Work of the Spirit of God* (1741), "all that is visible to the eye is unintelligible and vain, without the Word of God to instruct and guide the mind." And as he had preached in a crucial sermon on this theme a few years earlier,

> We make a distinction between the things that we know by reason, and things we know by revelation. But alas we scarce know what we say: we know not what we should have known . . . had it not been for revelation . . . . Many of the principles of morality and religion that we have always been brought up in the knowledge of, appear so rational that we are ready to think we could have found 'em out by our own natural reason . . . . [But] all the learning, yea, all the common civility that there is in the world, seems to be either directly or indirectly from revelation, whether men are sensible of it or no. . . . Everything that is good and useful in this fallen world, is from supernatural help.

This would become a major theme in Edwards's response to the deists late in his life. In opposition to their call for a modern religion of nature and reason, Edwards insisted on the necessity of supernatural revelation–even for the maintenance of a healthy civic virtue. But this was also a major theme in Edwards's early preaching and writing. For as he drafted in his "Miscellanies" in 1728, "were it not for divine revelation, I am persuaded that there is no one doctrine of that which we call natural religion [but] would, notwithstanding all philosophy and learning, forever be involved in darkness, doubts, endless disputes and dreadful confusion." And as he preached to his congregation near the end of the 1730s, human reason can tell us a lot about the works of God in nature, but "there is nothing else that informs us what [the] scheme and design of God in his works is but only the holy Scriptures."[9]

Supernatural revelation and the spiritual light it provides were, for Edwards, essential for clarifying the nature of reality. It was not that the world could not be known at all without the Bible, or that the Bible served as a textbook in natural history, science or reason. Rather, for Edwards, God's Word and Spirit illuminate our worldly wisdom, enabling us to perceive its relationship to the supernatural order, and rendering our knowledge more clear, beautiful and real than ever before. In a remarkable notebook entry dating from 1729, Edwards depicted this point so vividly that it is worth quoting here at length:

> A mind not spiritually enlightened [by means of the Bible and God's Spirit] beholds spiritual things faintly, like fainting, fading shadows that make no lively impression on his mind, like a man that beholds the trees and things abroad in the night: the ideas ben't strong and lively, and [are] very faint; and therefore he has but a little notion of the beauty of the face of the earth. But when the light comes to shine upon them, then the ideas appear with strength and distinctness;

and he has that sense of the beauty of the trees and fields given him in a moment, which he would not have obtained by going about amongst them in the dark in a long time. A man that sets himself to reason without divine light is like a man that goes into the dark into a garden full of the most beautiful plants, and most artfully ordered, and compares things together by going from one thing to another, to feel of them and to measure the distances; but he that sees by divine light is like a man that views the garden when the sun shines upon it. There is as it were a light cast upon the ideas of spiritual things in the mind of the believer, which makes them appear clear and real, which before were but faint, obscure representations.

Edwards wrote scores of pages about this "divine and supernatural light," as well as its role in the production of what he termed "spiritual understanding." He taught that revelation elucidates the harmony of the cosmos; that it grants a teleological glimpse of the world's relationship to God; that spiritual knowledge of its contents constitutes a greater blessing "than any other privilege that ever God bestowed on . . . men." He went so far, in fact, as to say that those who "hear the Word . . . and keep it . . . bring forth Christ" himself in their hearts; that Christ is truly "formed in them"; that spiritual knowledge of the Bible intensifies our vital union with the living Word of God, the one through whom the world was created and for whom it is preserved; and that this union is "more blessed" than "to have Christ . . . in the arms, or at the breast, as the virgin Mary had." Spiritual knowledge even grants what Edwards referred to in one sermon as "an earnest" or "the dawnings" of the beatific vision. In sum, it enables the people of God to participate in the life of God. For the spiritual principle in the souls of those who enjoy this special blessing "is not only from the Spirit, but it also partakes of the nature of that Spirit." No wonder, then, these words from Edwards's spiritual autobiography: "I [have] had . . . the greatest delight in the holy Scriptures, of any book whatsoever. Oftentimes in reading it, every word seemed to touch my heart. I felt an harmony between something in my heart, and those sweet and powerful words. I seemed often to see so much light, exhibited by every sentence, and such a refreshing ravishing food communicated, that I could not get along in reading. Used oftentimes to dwell long on one sentence, to see the wonders contained in it; and yet almost every sentence seemed to be full of wonders."[10]

II.

How peculiar it is that scholars have largely neglected the biblical Edwards. Among the thousands of publications devoted to Edwards since his death, only a few, a tiny fraction, deal primarily with this theme. In fact, a survey of M. X. Lesser's massive Edwards bibliographies confirms this point with precision. In neither of Lesser's volumes on the history of Edwards scholarship (1729–1993) is there an entry in the index headed "Bible," "revelation," "Scripture" or even "Word of God." His first volume (covering 1729–1978) has six entries under "Edwards, Jonathan, Biblicism." His second volume (1979–1993) has one headed "Scripture and Society," and another titled "Word and Spirit in the Theology of Jonathan Edwards." Lesser lists several, scattered entries on related topics as well, such as general hermeneutics and typology. To be sure, his reference guides are not a foolproof scholarly indicator, for Edwards's biblicism is mentioned in works devoted to other themes. Nevertheless, and overall, they do reflect the relative scarcity of scholarship on Edwards's use of the Bible.[11]

Surely this neglect has something to do with the fact that the pioneers of the twentieth-century Edwards renaissance tended to denigrate his biblicism in tragic, not to say histrionic, terms. Ola Winslow, for example, while ignoring his exegesis, denounced Edwards's biblical theology as an "outworn, dogmatic system" that desperately "needed to be demolished." Perry Miller admired the system but thought it had little to do with the Bible. Highlighting Edwards's major achievements in the realm of Enlightenment science, Miller lamented that Edwards also spent so much time rehearsing the Bible. Indeed, Miller opined, "part of the tragedy of Edwards is that he expended so much energy upon an [exegetical] effort that has subsequently fallen into contempt." Alfred Owen Aldridge rendered Edwards a fundamentalist for his view of the Bible's authority. In contradiction to Miller, though sharing Miller's disappointment in Edwards's frequent appeal to Scripture, Aldridge wrote that "in vindicating revelation, nearly all of Edwards's inferences tended to depreciate reason." And Peter Gay spoke for many when in 1966 he labeled Edwards "the greatest tragic hero . . . that American Calvinism produced." According to Gay, Edwards's biblicism was nothing short of "medieval," and "the results" of his work "were, as they had to be, pathetic." Edwards "philosophized in a cage that his fathers had built and that he unwittingly reinforced." He should have known that "revelation . . . can be nothing more than an extension of reason," that "nearly all religious doctrine is either redundant or superstitious." Nevertheless, "Edwards went right on accepting the testimony of Scriptures as literally true."[12]

The cumulative effect of such assertions has been similar to that described by John Coolidge long ago with respect to the field of Puritan studies: "the one necessary presupposition for any attempt to defend [Puritanism], or even to make it interesting" was "that the Puritans really derived their convictions from some other source than the Bible. . . . In order to argue that Puritanism had a mind, it has seemed necessary to assume that Puritan writers regularly deluded themselves by a curious ritual, casting a dust of scriptural references over pages where, nevertheless, an ingenious modern investigator can discover traces of thought."[13] Much as such scholarly gymnastics distorted our view of Puritanism, so the frequent denigrations of and excuses for Edwards's biblicism have kept us from understanding his chief occupation.

Not everyone has shared this dismal view of Edwards's biblicism. Several conservative clergymen have championed Edwards's exegesis as a model for other pastors and seminarians.[14] Several other, more critical scholars—informed by the publication of exegetical material in *The Works of Jonathan Edwards*—have begun to recognize that, in the words of Harry S. Stout, Edwards's world "was entirely suffused with the Word of God."[15] But only a few critical scholars have offered extensive interpretations of Edwards's work on the biblical texts—most notably Stephen Stein, Robert Brown and a few of the editors of Edwards's sermon corpus for *The Works of Jonathan Edwards*. In addition to several articles on Edwards and the Bible, Stein has provided most of the textual work on Edwards's biblical manuscripts. Brown has written a book on Edwards's response to higher criticism—belying Gay's claim that the biblical Edwards was benighted.[16] Others have written as well on Edwards's engagement with biblical themes,[17] some in substantial contributions on Edwards's typology, eschatology, and philosophy of history as these relate to American literature and culture.[18] But no one has written much on Edwards's exegesis *per se*—on how he handled biblical doctrine in the texts of Scripture themselves, and on how his interpretations came to matter.

III.

No doubt Edwards would have attributed our neglect of his exegesis to "[man's] proneness to an exceeding stupidity and sottishness in those things wherein his duty and main interest are chiefly concerned."[19] But perhaps another explanation might be offered here as well.

The Edwards renaissance was inspired during and after World War II by scholars who sensed our nation's need for what H. Richard Niebuhr and several others have called an "American Augustine," a theological founding father who understood original sin, respected the limits of human potential, and who promoted moral rectitude, social realism and spiritual progress.[20] But as they nominated Edwards for this exalted cultural role, these scholars appeared but dimly aware of what it would mean to retrieve Edwards as a spiritual founding father in the wake of disestablishment. Augustine and Edwards lived and worked according to Constantinian principles, one at the dawn and one at the twilight of the age of Christendom. Their theological pronouncements carried the weight of legal authority and mainstream cultural privilege.

Thus their calls for cultural submission to Bible and church were not unreasonable.

But all that has changed now. The age of Christendom has ended and the likes of Augustine and Edwards speak as dissenters from mainstream culture. Ironically, Edwards himself contributed to the dissolution of Christendom with his call for "true" religion and critique of Christian formalism.[21] But he also feared what he foresaw as its corrosive cultural effects, worrying that "many" Enlightenment thinkers had become so "puffed up" by means of "great temporal knowledge" that they "can hardly bear to submit their reason to divine revelation."[22] During the age of Revolution this cultural fear materialized. The Christian churches and their Scriptures were disestablished as national authorities. America's leading founding fathers felt little compulsion to submit their reason to divine revelation. And ever since, the biblical Edwards has actually militated against the spirit of mainstream American culture. He has contradicted the American spirit of liberation from external authority, our spirit of independence, self-culture and self-sufficiency.[23] Consequently, our "Augustine" has had to be shorn of his biblicism in order to serve as a significant public symbol.

But perhaps this was never an appropriate role for Edwards to play after disestablishment. Mainstream American public culture has little use for a *real* Augustine. And our interest in perpetuating a national Edwards of faith has obscured our estimation of the Edwards of history — distracting attention from other roles that he has played in the modern world. Despite the claims of Peter Gay, Edwards was not a medieval throwback. His work gave rise to several influential modern movements, from New England's own Edwardseanism to international evangelicalism. Even the modern supernaturalism inherent in Edwards's biblicism continues to thrive around the world today.[24]

One of the understudied legacies of Edwards's life and work pertains to what might be termed the *disestablished public significance* of his approach to the Christian Bible. Though no longer privileged as a legally sanctioned form of religious belief, Edwards's biblical theology has exerted more spiritual force during the past 200 years than it ever did on America's eighteenth century. It continues to attract tens of thousands of adherents, and to interest many others who stand at a distance from his views. Indeed, if the rapid global spread of Edwards's evangelical movement were not enough to demonstrate the power of his biblical faith today, then surely the events of 9/11 and its global aftermath have awakened us to the fact that much of the world persists in maintaining a scriptural faith. Billions of people around the globe submit themselves to sacred texts, thus resisting the American spirit of self-construction — at least part of the time. Perhaps the real, biblical Edwards can help us to see how this can be. Perhaps it is time to pay due attention to Edwards's vast exegetical writings.

NOTES

1. My sincere thanks to Robert Brown, Joseph Conforti, David Kling, Scott Manetsch, Mickey Mattox, Gerald McDermott, Ken Minkema, Kevin Vanhoozer, John Wilson and John-Mark Yeats for expert help on drafts of this paper. All printed works cited below are by Jonathan Edwards, unless otherwise noted.

2. Sermon on Matt. 24:35 (n.d.), Box 7, f. 502, L. 2r.; *WJE* 9:290–91; *WJE* 1:438; "To the Mohawks at the Treaty," in *The Sermons of Jonathan Edwards: A Reader*, ed. Wilson H. Kimnach, Kenneth P. Minkema and Douglas A. Sweeney (New Haven: Yale University Press, 1999), 109; "Heeding the Word, and Losing It," in *WJE* 19:46, 44; "The Importance and Advantage of a Thorough Knowledge of Divine Truth," in *The Sermons of JE*, 33–36, 40, 43; and Sermon on I Peter 2:2–3 (n.d., Aug. 1755), Box 11, f. 855, L. 5, r., L. 2v.

3. For a brief survey of JE's exegetical writings, see Douglas A. Sweeney, "Jonathan Edwards," in *Historical Handbook of Major Biblical Interpreters*, ed. Donald K. McKim (Downers Grove, Ill.: Intervarsity, 1998), 309–12.

4. The works of Poole, Bedford and Prideaux that JE engaged the most extensively were: Matthew Poole, *Annotations Upon the Holy Bible*, 2 vols. (London, 1683–85–JE's father Timothy owned a copy of this work); Matthew Poole, *Synopsis Criticorum aliorumque Sacrae Scripturae Interpretum*, 5 vols. (London, 1669–76); Arthur Bedford, *The Scripture Chronology Demonstrated by Astronomical Calculations, and also by the Year of Jubilee, and the Sabbatical Year among the Jews: or, An Account of Time, from the Creation of the World, to the Destruction of Jerusalem; as it may be proved from the Writings of the Old and New Testament* (London, 1730); and Humphrey Prideaux, *The Old and New Testament Connected in the History of the Jews and Neighbouring Nations, from the Declension of the Kingdoms of Israel and Judah to the Time of Christ*, 4 vols. (London, 1716–1718–JE's copies of the ninth edition of this work are listed in his "Account Book" at the Beinecke and may be seen at the Forbes Library, Northampton, Mass.). Poole, Bedford and Prideaux, moreover, were but three of many exegetical influences on JE. For the most comprehensive summary of these exegetical influences, see Stephen J. Stein, "Editor's Introduction," in *WJE* 15:4–12, 22–24.

5. In this regard, JE made good on his early resolution "to study the Scriptures so steadily, constantly and frequently, as that I may find, and plainly perceive myself to grow in the knowledge of the same." As his student, ministerial colleague and first biographer, Samuel Hopkins, testified after JE's death, "he studied the BIBLE more than all other books, and more than most other divines do. . . . He took his religious principles from the Bible, and not from any human system or body of divinity." And as confirmed by JE's great-grandson, Sereno E. Dwight, in a moment of unguarded family pride, "his knowledge of the Bible . . . is probably unrivalled." What is more, "no other divine has as yet appeared, who has studied the Scriptures more thoroughly. . . . He took his religious principles from the Bible, and not from treatises, or systems of theology, or any work of man." *WJE* 16:755; Samuel Hopkins, *The Life and Character of the Late Reverend Mr. Jonathan Edwards* . . . (Boston, 1765), 40–41; and Sereno E. Dwight, "Memoirs of Jonathan Edwards, A.M.," in *The Works of Jonathan*

Edwards, 2 vols. (Carlisle, Penn.: Banner of Truth, 1974; 1834), 1:clxxxvii-clxxxix. Dwight's "Memoirs" were published originally in the less accessible Sereno E. Dwight, ed., *The Works of President Edwards . . . in Ten Volumes* (New York, 1829–1830).

6. Bruce Kuklick, "Review Essay: An Edwards for the Millennium," *Religion and American Culture: A Journal of Interpretation* 11 (2001): 116–17. On JE's "modern supernaturalism," see, *WJE* 23:20–23.

7. "Personal Narrative," in *WJE* 16:801; "Life Through Christ Alone," in *WJE* 10:526; "The Way of Holiness," in *WJE* 10:477; "Divine Love Alone Lasts Eternally," in *WJE* 8:363; Sermon on Ps. 119:162 (Nov. 1749), Box 3, f. 189, L. 1r.; "The Importance and Advantage of a Thorough Knowledge of Divine Truth," in *WJE* 22:38, 35; "Profitable Hearers of the Word," in *WJE* 14:265–66; Sermon on I Cor. 2:11–13 (May 7, 1740), Box 10, f. 719, L. 3v.; Sermon on Matt. 13:23 (n.d., June 1756), Box 6, f. 473, L. 22r.; *WJE* 2:438; "Stupid as Stones," in *WJE* 17:180; Sermon on Luke 10:38–42 (n.d., July 1754), Box 7, f. 560, L. 6v.; and "Miscellanies, no. 6, in *WJE* 13:202.

8. Sermon on Luke 10:38–42, L. 3r.; "Profitable Hearers of the Word," 266; "Heeding the Word, and Losing It," 47; "Images of Divine Things," no. 113, in *WJE* 11:93; and Sermon on Heb. 6:7 (Jan.-Feb. 1747), Box 11, f. 820, L. 17r.

9. *Concerning the End for Which God Created the World*, in *WJE* 8419–20 (emphasis mine); *The Distinguishing Marks of a Work of the Spirit of God*, in *WJE* 4:240; "Light in a Dark World, a Dark Heart," in *WJE* 19:720; *WJE* 13:421 (cf. *WJE* 13:422–26, 537, *WJE* 18:140, and *WJE* 20:52–53); and *WJE* 9:520. On JE's understanding of the relationship between reason and revelation as it was developed near the end of his life, see "Editor's Introduction," in *WJE* 23:19–29. On his response to the deists, see esp. Gerald R. McDermott, *Jonathan Edwards Confronts the Gods: Christian Theology, Enlightenment Religion, and Non-Christian Faiths* (New York: Oxford University Press, 2000).

10. *WJE* 13:469–70; Sermon on Luke 11:27–28 (n.d., Aug. 1751), Box 14, f. 1065, L. 1v., L. 6v.-7r.; "The Pure in Heart Blessed," in *WJE* 17:65–66; "Treatise on Grace," in *WJE* 21:178–80; and "Personal Narrative," in *WJE* 16:797. For JE's doctrine of spiritual understanding, see esp. *WJE* 2:205–206, 225, 266–91, 296–97, 301; *WJE* 10:286–87, 297–98, 462–63; *WJE* 18:156–57, 245–48, 452–66; and numerous sermons of JE, esp. "A Divine and Supernatural Light," in *WJE* 17:408–26; "A Spiritual Understanding of Divine Things Denied to the Unregenerate," in *WJE* 14:70–96; "False Light and True," in *WJE* 19:122–42; "Light in a Dark World, a Dark Heart," in *WJE* 19:704–33; "Profitable Hearers of the Word," in *WJE* 10:243–77; and "The Importance and Advantage of a Thorough Knowledge of Divine Truth," in *WJE* 22:80–102. For JE's notion of the mysterious power of the Bible, see also the suggestive comments in his "Miscellaneous Observations on the Holy Scriptures" (the "Blank Bible"), Box 17, f. 1216. In his notes therein on Ps. 29:3 (ms. pp. 414–15), he writes that "Lightning and thunder is a very lively image of the word of God upon many accounts. 'Tis exceeding quick, and exceeding piercing, and powerful to break in pieces, and scorch, and dissolve, and is full of majesty." And in his notes on Heb. 4:12 (ms. pp. 865–67), he makes reference to God's giving of the Law to Moses on

Mt. Sinai (Ex. 19ff.) "With thunders and lightnings and a voice so piercing awful and tremendous that the people could not endure it," and then compares the Hebrews text, which teaches in similar fashion that "the word in its powerful efficacy . . . does as it were cut the soul asunder."

11. See M. X. Lesser, *Jonathan Edwards: A Reference Guide* (Boston: G. K. Hall, 1981); and M. X. Lesser, *Jonathan Edwards: An Annotated Bibliography, 1979–1993* (Westport, Conn.: Greenwood Press, 1994).

12. Ola Elizabeth Winslow, *Jonathan Edwards, 1703–1758* (New York: MacMillan, 1940), 325–30; Perry Miller, "Introduction," in *Images or Shadows of Divine Things by Jonathan Edwards* (New Haven, 1948), ed. Miller, 25 and *passim* (cf. Perry Miller, *Jonathan Edwards*, The American Men of Letters Series [New York: Sloan, 1949]); Alfred Owen Aldridge, *Jonathan Edwards*, The Great American Thinkers Series (New York: Washington Square Press, 1966), 120–21, 150–62 (quotation taken from p. 158); and Peter Gay, *A Loss of Mastery: Puritan Historians in Colonial America* (Berkeley: University of California Press, 1966), 105, 113, 116.

13. John S. Coolidge, *The Pauline Renaissance in England: Puritanism and the Bible* (Oxford: Clarendon Press, 1970), 1–2.

14. See esp. Ralph G. Turnbull, *Jonathan Edwards The Preacher* (Grand Rapids: Baker, 1958), 68–78; Ralph G. Turnbull, "Jonathan Edwards–Bible Interpreter," *Interpretation: A Journal of Bible and Theology* 6 (1952): 422–35; Samuel T. Logan, Jr., "The Hermeneutics of Jonathan Edwards," *Westminster Theological Journal* 43 (1980): 79–96; John H. Gerstner, "Jonathan Edwards and the Bible," *Tenth: An Evangelical Quarterly* 9 (1979): 2–71; and John H. Gerstner, *The Rational Biblical Theology of Jonathan Edwards*, vol. 1 (Powhatan, Va.: Berea Pub., 1991).

15. Harry S. Stout, "Word and Order in Colonial New England," in *The Bible in America: Essays in Cultural History*, ed. Nathan O. Hatch and Mark A. Noll (New York: Oxford University Press, 1982), 34. See also Paul Ramsey, "Editor's Introduction," in *WJE* 8:8–9; Harry S. Stout, *The New England Soul: Preaching and Religious Culture in Colonial New England* (New York: Oxford University Press, 1986); Wilson H. Kimnach, "General Introduction to the Sermons: Jonathan Edwards's Art of Prophesying," in *WJE* 10:207; John E. Smith, *Jonathan Edwards: Puritan, Preacher, Philosopher* (Notre Dame: University of Notre Dame Press, 1992), 138–47; Kenneth P. Minkema, "Editor's Introduction," in *WJE* 14:15–16; and George M. Marsden, *Jonathan Edwards: A Life* (New Haven: Yale University Press, 2003), 472–89.

16. Stephen J. Stein, "Jonathan Edwards and the Rainbow: Biblical Exegesis and Poetic Imagination," *New England Quarterly* 47 (1974): 440–56; Stephen J. Stein, "Cotton Mather and Jonathan Edwards on the Number of the Beast: Eighteenth-Century Speculation about the Antichrist," *Proceedings of the American Antiquarian Society* 84 (1974), 293–315; Stephen J. Stein, "The Quest for the Spiritual Sense: The Biblical Hermeneutics of Jonathan Edwards," *Harvard Theological Review* 70 (1977): 99–113; Stephen J. Stein, "Editor's Introduction," in JE, *Apocalyptic Writings*, ed. Stephen J. Stein, *The Works of JE*, vol. 5 (New Haven, 1977), 1–93; Stephen J. Stein, "The Spirit and the Word: Jonathan Edwards and Scriptural Exegesis," in *Jonathan Edwards and the American Experience*, ed. Nathan O. Hatch and Harry S. Stout (New York: Oxford University Press, 1988), 118–30; Stein, "Editor's Introduction," in *WJE* 15:1–46; and Robert E.

Brown, *Jonathan Edwards and the Bible* (Bloomington: Indiana Univ. Press, 2002). See also Brown, "Edwards and Scripture," in *The Princeton Companion to Jonathan Edwards*, ed. Sang Hyun Lee (Princeton: Princeton University Press, 2005).

17. See esp. Karl Dietrich Pfisterer, *The Prism of Scripture: Studies on History and Historicity in the Work of Jonathan Edwards*, Anglo-American Forum (Frankfurt: Peter Lang, 1975); Conrad Cherry, "Symbols of Spiritual Truth: Jonathan Edwards as Biblical Interpreter," *Interpretation: A Journal of Bible and Theology* 39 (1985): 263–71; two books by Conrad Cherry that pay due attention to the Bible: *The Theology of Jonathan Edwards: A Reappraisal* (Bloomington: Indiana University Press, 1990; 1966), and *Nature and Religious Imagination: From Edwards to Bushnell* (Philadelphia: Fortress Press, 1980); Ava Chamberlain, "Brides of Christ and Signs of Grace: Edwards's Sermon Series on the Parable of the Wise and Foolish Virgins," and Kenneth P. Minkema, "The Other Unfinished 'Great Work': Jonathan Edwards, Messianic Prophecy, and 'The Harmony of the Old and New Testament,'" both in *Jonathan Edwards's Writings: Text, Context, Interpretation*, ed. Stephen J. Stein (Bloomington: Indiana University Press, 1996), 3–18, 52–65; and Shalom Goldman, *God's Sacred Tongue: Hebrew & the American Imagination* (Chapel Hill: University of North Carolina Press, 2004), 74–88.

18. On these themes, see esp. C. C. Goen, "Jonathan Edwards: A New Departure in Eschatology," *Church History* 28 (1959), 25–40; Mason I. Lowance, Jr., *The Language of Canaan: Metaphor and Symbol in New England from the Puritans to the Transcendentalists* (Cambridge, Mass.: Harvard University Press, 1980); John F. Wilson, "History, Redemption, and the Millennium," in *Jonathan Edwards and the American Experience*, 131–41; John F. Wilson, "Editor's Introduction," in *WJE* 9:1–109; Wallace E. Anderson, "Editor's Introduction to 'Images of Divine Things' and 'Types,'" and Mason I. Lowance, Jr. with David H. Watters, "Editor's Introduction to 'Types of the Messiah,'" both in *WJE* 11:3–33, 157–82; and Avihu Zakai, *Jonathan Edwards's Philosophy of History: The Re-Enchantment of the World in the Age of Enlightenment* (Princeton: Princeton University Press, 2003).

19. *WJE* 3:147.

20. On the notion of an American Augustine, see esp. H. Richard Niebuhr, *The Kingdom of God in America* (New York: Harper, 1959; 1937), xvi; John F. Wilson, "Religion at the Core of American Culture," in *Altered Landscapes: Christianity in America, 1935–1985*, ed. David W. Lotz with Donald W. Shriver, Jr. and John F. Wilson (Grand Rapids: Eerdmans, 1989), 373–76; Harry S. Stout, "The Historical Legacy of H. Richard Niebuhr," in *The Legacy of H. Richard Niebuhr*, ed. Ronald F. Thiemann, Harvard Theological Studies 36 (Minneapolis, Fortress Press, 1991), 92; Joseph A. Conforti, *Jonathan Edwards, Religious Tradition, and American Culture* (Chapel Hill: University of North Carolina Press, 1995), 186–96; George Marsden, "Jonathan Edwards, American Augustine," *Books & Culture* 5 (Nov./Dec. 1999), 10; and Zakai, *Jonathan Edwards's Philosophy of History,* 1–26 and *passim*.

21. On the relationship between the rise of modern evangelicalism and the decline of Christendom, see also Andrew F. Walls, *The Cross-Cultural Process in Christian History: Studies in the Transmission and Appropriation of Faith* (Maryknoll, N.Y.: Orbis Books, 2002), 27–48, 194–214.

22. "Profitable Hearers of the Word," in *WJE* 14:264–65.

23. Though much has been written on this spirit of liberal American self-culture, I have found the following works most helpful: Daniel Walker Howe, *Making the American Self: Jonathan Edwards to Abraham Lincoln* (Cambridge, Mass.: Harvard University Press, 1997); Nathan O. Hatch, *The Democratization of American Christianity* (New Haven: Yale University Press, 1989); Gordon Wood, *The Radicalism of the American Revolution* (New York: Knopf, 1992); and Joyce Appleby, *Inheriting the Revolution: The First Generation of Americans* (Cambridge, Mass.: Harvard University Press, 2000). Tellingly, even in James E. Block's more submissive "nation of agents," JE's "proto-agency" perspective is ruled out of the mainstream. According to Block, the national "vision was of individuals freed from lifelong submissiveness within authoritarian hierarchies in every domain of societal life in order to be resubordinated to the emerging institutions of liberal society, and placed *qua* individuals as equal agents capable of undertaking the realization of collective ends." Further, this vision of "agency liberalism struggled against and overcame the traditional models of servitude and Puritan proto-agency (though the latter long lingered) embedded in early religious movements and local hierarchies, in colonial dependency, southern slave society, and early industrial organization." And "Edwards's conservative defense of religious and civil elites who shared with secularizing elites the rejection of uncontained popular religious enthusiasm and its empowerment of women and minorities, and his increasingly marginal pessimism regarding American prospects, represented desperate efforts to sustain the Puritan legacy. . . . Today he remains largely a cautionary voice, Melville's lonely prophet, improbably reminding a human-centered culture of the limits of human action." James E. Block, *A Nation of Agents: The American Path to a Modern Self and Society* (Cambridge, Mass.: Harvard University Press, 2002), 29, 33, 204 and *passim*.

24. On these movements and their influence, see Conforti, *Jonathan Edwards, Religious Tradition, and American Culture*; Douglas A. Sweeney, *Nathaniel Taylor, New Haven Theology, and the Legacy of Jonathan Edwards* (New York: Oxford University Press, 2003); and *Jonathan Edwards at Home and Abroad: Historical Memories, Cultural Movements, Global Horizons*, ed. David W. Kling and Douglas A. Sweeney (Columbia: University of South Carolina Press, 2003).

The Sacred and the Profane Connected: Edwards, the Bible, and Intellectual Culture

Robert E. Brown

Lehigh University

Since my study of Edwards has been concerned largely with his biblical interpretation, it is perhaps fitting that I first perform an act of redactive criticism on the title of my paper. The original manuscript had a parenthetical interrogative "(?)" placed after the word "Connected." Thus, rather than being an affirmative declaration of the connection between the sacred and the profane, the original form of this statement indicates some form of ambiguity on the part of the author. The interrogative was dropped from the conference program and poster, however. Evidently an unknown editor (we'll call him "WJE") understood this punctuation mark as a mistake, perhaps an indication that the author remained uncertain of his choice of title at the point of submission, or, that he had committed a typographical error. The editor thus took it upon himself to clarify the meaning as best he could (for this is what editors do), by eliding the mark in question. An alternative hypothesis holds that subsequent to the initial editing, the publisher of the conference materials (we'll call her "P") simply garbled the editor's faithful transcription, such that the mark in question was dropped inadvertently during the printing process. Thus, as it pertains to the present manuscript, we have what some in the audience might wish to call the "WJEP" documentary hypothesis.

The point of this little tongue-in-cheek exercise is threefold. First, it illustrates the difficulty of maintaining the integrity of texts during the process of transmission, something with which Edwards and his contemporaries were acutely concerned. Second, as revised the title is meant to call into question the success or relevance of Edwards's approach to biblical interpretation. Third, it calls attention to my own ambivalence about the pertinence of Edwards's biblical commentary in any assessment of his significance for American culture.

The organizers of this conference asked participants to be prepared to "think broadly and generally about Edwards's place in American life and letters," and to consider the "sometimes ambiguous and controversial" nature of his legacy. With respect to these parameters, Edwards's biblical interpretation seems to have no place at all. To be sure, some of his earliest admirers esteemed his understanding of the Bible as exceptional and prescient. Sereno Dwight, for example, surmised that in his biblical materials Edwards "had . . . entered on a series of investigations, which, if ultimately found correct, would effectuate [the] most important changes in the opinions of the Christian world."[1] But none of his admirers went so far as to take up the mantle of an "Edwardsean hermeneutic." No schools came forth to advocate opposing visions of how to most faithfully represent his ideas about the nature of the Bible. Higher critics in America never had to contend with the specter of the biblical Edwards in the way that modernist theologians found it necessary to exorcise his Calvinism from their midst. Few if any biblical scholars today would find his commentary instructive, nor do I think it likely that this material, newly published, will experience the kind of devotional admiration his other works have received in the current popular renaissance of his thought. Edwards's biblical interpretation has had virtually no effect on succeeding generations, and thus it has experienced no significant amount of cultural appropriation.

Edwards's potential legacy then as a model of how to articulate the relationship between sacred text and profane knowledge in an integrated discourse seems to have been stillborn in American culture. Lest this paint too bleak a picture, however, let me say that I believe this relatively unappreciated side of Edwards's career is quite important, not only for understanding his place in American culture, but also for understanding the nature of American culture itself. This aspect of his represents a vital component of both, though it may require additional subtlety in our analysis.

In his remarkable book, *Theorizing Myth*, Bruce Lincoln chronicles, among other things, the long-standing ideological contest behind the modern west's separation of "myth" from the rational discourses of history, science, and philosophy, and the subsequent use of the category of myth by some to advance certain political agendas, namely, nationalism and racism. Above all, Lincoln argues, the central question that animated the perceived adversity between these two forms of discourse was one of political authority—what type of (and thus whose) speech would command respect and attention, so as to win ideological and social supremacy? Once successfully characterized by their lack of rationality, narratives that once had been regarded as primordial repositories of truth were reduced in stature to the level of superstition and priest-state propaganda.[2]

It occurs to me that a corresponding analysis of the development of critical biblical interpretation is in order as well (a *Theorizing the Bible*, if you will). Shawn Kelley's recent work, *Racializing Jesus: Race, Ideology, and the Formation of Modern Biblical Scholarship*, moves in that direction, although along very specific lines.[3] Perhaps a more apt model of what I have in mind is something like Louis Menand's recent and wide-ranging work, *The Metaphysical Club*, which traces the development of American pragmatism through the biographical histories of its chief architects: Oliver Wendell Holmes, William James, Charles S. Pierce, and John Dewey. Menand poignantly draws the connection between their social experiences and their subsequent epistemological and pedagogical formulations. It is important, I think, to move beyond the standard historiography of criticism as the progress toward increasingly rational interpretation (which certainly has its place), and try to achieve instead an understanding of why certain ideas about the Bible mattered to certain people—why they found those ideas intellectually plausible and socially useful, and what they perceived as their relevance to real, lived religion. It requires no stretch of imagination to recognize that the "mythologizing" of the Bible in early modernity had potent implications for the religious and social institutions of Christendom, or that it would be politicized.[4] To engage the Bible critically was not simply a journey towards rationality, but was simultaneously a political, social, and moral activity. It represented a new kind of consciousness about religions and their narratives, a consciousness experienced even by those like Edwards, who engaged such ideas in order to resist them, even if to a lesser degree.[5]

Let me cite two instances in Edwards's extensive body of work on critical interpretation that might prove fruitful avenues for investigating its location within a social matrix, namely, his concerns over the application of modern historical method to sacred texts, and their reconciliation to modern natural science.

The development of historical erudition was intimately related to the ideological contest over religious authority in the late seventeenth and early eighteenth centuries, and the new critical approaches to biblical interpretation were readily enlisted in them. As J. A. I. Champion and others have observed, criticism of religion in early modern Europe did not just represent a controversy over the competence of human reason, but one about "the perceived injustice of the distribution of authority in society." Since the authority of the church and state was rooted in historical tradition, criticism offered opponents an opportunity to de-authorize political and ecclesiastical institutions.[6] The hunt was on, therefore, "to find an intellectual strategy which would permit escape from a political theology whose theoretical power and widespread reception walled in the dissident."[7]

By challenging the authenticity of the narratives on which these institutions rested, critics challenged their political supremacy as well. The championing of the autonomy and indeed superior competence of human reason in relation to revelation implied another form of autonomy as well: that society could and would remain pious, moral, and ordered without the sustenance of its regnant religious traditions. By calling into question the historical authenticity of the Bible, critics sought to effect a cultural dis-establishment of their society's foundational narrative, and thereby the hegemony of its religious institutions. Thus, "methodological apparatus . . . was linked to the ideological function of historical discourse. The intellectual disunity of the period meant that participants had to search for some form of authoritative leverage in polemical debate, for a form of knowledge that could be deployed and maintained with a status of certainty and objective truth. [Thus] the past, and the presentation of the past, became a displaced crucible for ideological dispute."[8]

Arbitrating political and religious contests in the context of historical argument produced a considerable impetus toward the development of erudition in method.[9] The shared cultural assumption that truth and reality could be derived from historical representation meant that empirical facts were the coin of the realm for ideological credibility. The new historical mentality, as Joseph Levine observes, valued this "distinction above any other kind." It was thus "necessary to devise some explicit criteria for recovering the historicity of an event," which entailed inventing "a new idea of fact, a notion that the literal representation of past or present could be interesting in and for itself, or for some present purpose, and that it could and should be radically distinguished from a spurious or imaginary description."[10] Moral authority rested on historiographical integrity; this integrity rested on the factuality of a given narrative's account of things. To be exposed as a "false coyner" spelled doom for one's interpretation of history, and thus for one's religious or political positions.[11]

Edwards was, therefore, part of an intellectual drama with potent social implications. That he sensed this can be found, among other places, in his repeated criticism that those who derided the significance of religious narrative undermined the rationale for social cohesion.[12] But it is most evident in his attempts connect biblical narrative with the new history. The epistemological supremacy of the "fact" permeates his biblical commentary. The rubric, "FACTS PUBLICKLY KNOWN," in blocked capitals functions as a fundamental *leitmotif* in this material.

Nowhere did the ideological implications and social consequences of the new history and biblical narrative collide more notoriously during his lifetime than over the seemingly intractable problem of the Mosaic authorship of the

Pentateuch. His effort to explain the genesis of the Pentateuch is probably the most striking example of an almost purely historical approach among his writings, and indicates the degree to which critical issues directed his intellectual agenda. To my mind this material represents one of the most significant achievements in early American religious thought—much more conceptually sophisticated than, say, Ethan Allen's *Reason the Only Oracle of Man* (1784) or Thomas Paine's *Age of Reason* (1794), which deal with many of the same issues—yet it is wholly absent from the annals of American history and literature.[13]

If the Pentateuch was not written by Moses but at some far distant time, then the likelihood that it was an intentionally fraudulent work seemed evident to Edwards and his contemporaries. And the assertion of fraud was a loaded one. Perhaps nowhere was the ideological contest more acutely expressed in early modernity than in the specter of priestcraft. One of the most powerful conceptual and emotional weapons at the disposal of dissidents was the claim that social institutions had been foisted upon the body politic by the clerical imposition of a fraudulent religion based on a forged religious history. As Champion has observed, the charge of priestcraft loomed behind almost every attempt to deconstruct traditional religious beliefs and texts in the eighteenth century, as well as behind attempts to provide an alternative construction of the history of true religion. To the degree that the biblical accounts could be shown to be other than as they had been traditionally represented, the argument that they were the imposture of a tyrannical priesthood could be made more effectively.[14] Was the Bible, in the end, only a monumental "Donation of Constantine"?

Edwards's response to the constellation of issues regarding the question of Mosaic authorship is found chiefly in two documents. The first of these is entry No. 416 in the "Notes on Scripture," a relatively polished essay and by far the longest of any in the four notebooks of this series. The second is a 131-page notebook, begun probably in the early 1750's, in which he elaborated upon the earlier essay.[15] Edwards was particularly concerned to address the question, first raised by Baruch Spinoza, of whether the post-exilic priest Ezra was in fact the one responsible for editing or "authoring" these five books, a historical judgment that proved to be perfectly suited the priestcraft conspiracy theory, and was frequently exploited as such in the 18th century. Edwards marshals a number of historical counter-arguments, which need only to be noted for the sake of the present discussion. The main thrust of his conclusion for Mosaic authorship rests on an appeal to the unitary features of the Pentateuch—that these five books form one continuous narrative indicative of a single author—and to elements indicating that its provenance must have preceded the Jewish captivity in Babylon. It should be observed, however, that the conceptual sophistication of his argument is remarkable, and represents a kind of high water mark for historical erudition in colonial American thought.[16]

The point to be made here is that to read Edwards simply in terms of his final judgments on the issue of authorship is to miss much of what is going on. Edwards is acutely aware that to countenance a later origin for the Pentateuch would be to undermine the very rationale for a society structured according to the Mosaic constitution—the very conclusion reached by the likes of Paine and Allen a half century later. Far from representing an abstract historical judgment about authorship, then, such presumptively methodological debates about the interpretation of empirical data also carried with them an imbedded, coded debate about the religious and social arrangement of British society. Edwards responded to the challenges of the new history by appropriating it almost wholesale. He readily embraced its claims to be able to represent the real past through the marshalling of reliable facts organized into a coherent narrative, and expressed his conviction that the biblical narratives should be measured by their adherence to such a method. In this way he anticipates the sort of rationalist apologetics which was to find its full flowering in nineteenth-century American religious thought, in the confident assertion of the harmony of the Bible and secular knowledge. But this was also for Edwards a characteristically conservative response, intended to forestall the subjection of an ancient sacred text to the full force of modern skeptical inquiry, and prevent its application to religious society.

The problem of the authorship of the Pentateuch is just one of many examples in Edwards's biblical commentary that point to a complex interpretive context. The second example I want to draw from is his interest in the implications of empirical science for biblical interpretation. Edwards lived in an age when empirical knowledge of the physical world was intruding upon traditional interpretations of the surface narrative of the Bible. It was beginning to raise serious questions about the adequacy of ancient descriptions of cosmology and of historical events involving miracles or other forms of divine intervention. This was chiefly a problem related to the more developed disciplines of astronomy and physics, but it also was becoming a difficulty for rudimentary geological and biological disciplines.

Perhaps nowhere did his interest in employing the fruits of scientific study in the service of the Scripture history manifest itself more vividly than over specific issues pertaining to eschatology, namely, the nature of hell and the universal conflagration. Edwards's reputation as a neurotic if not manipulative fire and brimstone preacher is firmly engraved in the mythology of early American religion. What is not appreciated, however, is the degree to which the question of the final consummation of all things had become for him a problem of physics and astronomy as well. Not simply an issue of evangelical persuasion or of maintaining the justice of God, this was as much a matter of assessing the feasibility of the mechanics involved in the eschatological scenario depicted in the Bible. For Edwards, as for almost all intellectuals of the era, "the last day became an object, not merely of theological speculation as to its unfolding, nor merely of millenarian expectation as to its time, but also of scientific reflection as to how it would occur. The last day became part of the new science."[17]

The nature of God's final disposition of things had been a problem in English thought since at least the middle of the seventeenth century.[18] The Socinian objection to the eternity of hell's torments was rather eagerly adopted by a number of leading Anglican thinkers, including Thomas Burnet, Isaac Newton, and William Whiston. Such thinkers argued that the alternative concept of annihilation, besides being more just, was also more consonant with the natural laws governing the dissolution of the universe. Newtonian physics treated the universe like a machine, and as with other machines predicted that it would eventually wind down. Theologians and scientists thus sought to discover ways of reconciling this natural process of entropy with biblical descriptions of a final fiery conflagration.

In his *New Theory of the Earth* (1696) and *Astronomical Principles of Natural and Revealed Religion* (1717), Whiston employed Newton's thesis that comets were responsible for the maintenance of the universe to argue that the earth's history could be explained almost exclusively by cometology. The earth had been created by a comet; a comet had destroyed Eden after the fall; the deluge was caused by a passing comet. Comets, therefore, were the most likely candidates to bring about the conflagration. When they had expended their material they would no longer be able to sustain the stars, which would soon lose their substance; the earth would be restored by the resulting celestial fire to its original state of paradise.

Whiston used his earth theory and general cosmology to argue that the conflagration would end in the annihilation of the wicked rather than their eternal torment. These views were brought together in a separate treatise in 1740, his *Eternity of Hell Torments Considered*.[19] Whiston presented a particularly difficult challenge for traditionalists like Edwards because he argued in the strongest terms that the biblical cosmology could be taken literally and still be reconciled to the best science of the day. He could hardly be accused of arriving at his views of divine punishment by rejecting the authority or literal meaning of the Bible. Thus some manner of interpretation had to be developed that would show that the notion of eternal hell also accorded well not only with sound biblical interpretation but also with modern physics. The "geography of hell" had changed, and it was incumbent upon Edwards to adapt his interpretation accordingly.[20]

Edwards's treatment of these issues is scattered throughout the various strata of his writings—the "Table" to the "Miscellanies" alone lists over one hundred entries on various aspects of hell and the conflagration. He contended that these descriptions were not to be taken literally: they are only "metaphors and similitudes." In his apocalyptic writings he addresses the problem of reconciling the vertically described picture of the universe in the Bible with the relativistic understanding of location in modern astronomy. He rejects the Whistonian contention that "new earth" spoken of in the Bible is simply the present earth restored (the "literal" reading), since "fire by purging" could only bring it to its primitive state, but not to its glorious state. Rather, the promise of a "new heaven and earth" need not be taken to refer literally to those seen now, but could refer to an entirely new arrangement in another part of the universe. This is so because the terms "heaven" and "earth" are to be understood phenomenally. Their meaning is relative to location: if "we were in Jupiter or Saturn, that which would be under our feet would be called earth by us, and that which was over our heads, heaven." Heaven and earth are simply the "vulgar meaning of the words" that refer to what is below and above, not specific planets and stars. Thus it is possible and even probable that the new heaven and earth "will be some glorious place in the universe prepared for this end by God, removed at an immense distance from the solar system." Though "there is nothing said of such a remove in this prophecy," yet it "seems to suppose it in the same place." For "the Scripture does not represent things, especially in prophecy and vision, according to philosophical verity, but as they appear to our eyes."[21]

Edwards's concern for such matters intensified after the appearance of Whiston's *Eternity of Hell Torments* in 1740.[22] Between 1740 and 1745 he produced a string of entries in the "Miscellanies" aimed at answering the central claims raised by Whiston on the nature of hell and its relation to the conflagration.[23] In them one sees just how thoroughly considerations of astronomical mechanics shaped his response, and thus how important natural science, and the culture of physico-theology that was appropriating it, had become for the reformulation of his theology. They reveal the degree to which he found it necessary to accommodate the biblical descriptions and their traditional "literal" interpretation to a modern understanding of the cosmos and to the laws that governed it.

Like Whiston, Edwards was a cometologist.[24] In his schematization, comets are responsible for replenishing the stars, and thus for sustaining the current operations of the universe. They help to prove that the universe will predictably end; as the stars draw off their mass, the comets will eventually dissipate. Having lost the source of their sustenance, the stars and planets will in turn meet their demise. But comets also disturb the motions of other celestial bodies, and so will send them into a phase of universal collapse, the perfect equivalent of Isaiah's description of the heavens being rolled up like a scroll.[25] This immense condensation of matter will produce a fiery cataclysm. "Philosophy tells us that the motions of the several parts of the visible world must, in great length of time, gradually cease; and that if it ceases, it will all run together into a common heap; but if it does so, it must necessarily be involved in a great conflagration. For I suppose ninety-nine parts in an hundred of the visible world are the most fierce liquid fire."[26]

Given that the known laws of physics and the material composition of the universe are adequate to demonstrate the inescapable fact of the final conflagration, what are the mechanics of God's final judgment, and what in them militates against the notion of annihilation? Here Edwards counters Whiston's extreme literalism by asserting that the Bible's vulgar language of appearances must be accommodated to known astronomy. When it speaks of the heavens raining down fire upon the earth, this is due to the position of the human observer. What in fact will happen is that gravitational pull will cause heavenly bodies to collapse upon one another. The heat generated by this event will turn the earth into molten metal, a liquid globe of fire. "What a storm of fire and brimstone will this be, when the innumerable stars of heaven shall come down like rain."[27] It is on this terrestrial hell that the wicked will spend eternity. But this will not lead to their annihilation. Just as the saints receive a resurrected body that is eternal and indestructible, so too will the damned. Since it is not in their present bodies but in resurrected bodies that they suffer judgment, they will suffer a kind of physical torment without being consumed. This is possible because the reconstitution of the universe will produce a change in the elements, the acquisition of a rarified nature that permits constant sensations of pain without consumption. Thus it is "not unlikely that as the senses that will be acted upon by the rays of light and particles of fire will be altered, so the rays of light and particles of fire that will act upon them will be altered."[28]

His acceptance of the new physics led him to conclude that the biblical characterizations of hell were to be understood metaphorically, yet at the same time he insisted that the physical imagery behind the metaphors revealed dreadful portents of divine wrath. Perhaps more significantly, his rejection of the sort of literalism represented by Whiston pushed him to embrace an understanding of the relationship between scientific and biblical descriptions of the natural world that would become prominent in Protestant liberalism. But Edwards's rejection of the identification of scriptural language with "philosophical verity" was intended to defend traditional doctrine. Whiston's extreme literalism was intended to buttress a doctrinal departure. The debate shows that the association often made between progressive hermeneutics and modern theological conclusions is not a necessary one, but was at least in early modernity a somewhat plastic one, determined in part by the ideological considerations at hand. Edwards, at least in his eschatology, reversed the paradigm, insisting on a looser association between the discourses of science and religion, and believing that traditional theology was best supported by such an interpretive strategy.

It is clear then that something much more important and absorbing is revealed by the early American interest in critical interpretation. When anachronistically viewed in relation to present scholarship, it appears quaint and outmoded. When understood as a vital part of the unfolding drama of the religious and social revolution that was modernity, then its relevance becomes immediately apparent. In Edwards we encounter the beginning of an intellectual drama almost unparalleled in American culture—the contest over the status of the Bible as a social authority. Far from being an obscure or arcane element of Edwards's otherwise brilliant intellectual career, it is in fact a momentous development in American religious history. Edwards's biblical interpretation was a "modernizing" enterprise, in which the importance of integration with contemporary philosophical, historical, and scientific knowledge was paramount, even if this meant recognizing to some degree the claims that that knowledge had on the interpretation of the texts themselves. Even though his confidence in ultimate harmony of the text with profane knowledge, and in the vindication of traditional interpretative approaches, is not especially shared in contemporary scholarship, there are more (and more important) connections to the present than one may be accustomed to expect.

I suspect that for this neglected dimension of Edwards to be fully and rightfully appreciated, two things will have to occur.

First, as I have been alluding to here, the historiography of critical thought will have to be revised to include those elements of its development and reception that move beyond the chronicled movement toward rationality. Edwards's interpretive strategy, it should be clear by now, was an intensely rationalized one, if theologically traditional. Edwards's strategies for resolving particular interpretive problems is likely to be less useful to contemporary intellectual culture if it leaves off at asking only "what did he get right or wrong (modern or pre-modern)?" and more instructive if we ask "what made his interpretive strategies seem plausible at the time?" or "what did he perceive to be at stake in adopting them?" Reclaiming Edwards's place in this dimension of American culture will require a greater interest in and sensitivity to the social history of ideas. If nothing else, it will prevent his interpretive strategy from being lifted out of context, or from being judged (prematurely, at least) as "fundamentalist" or "tragic" or "inaccessible."[29] If Edwards appears inaccessible on these matters the fault lies not with him, but with us, in a failure to read this material imaginatively and dispassionately. It was in wrestling with critical approaches to the Bible that Edwards reached the height of his sophistication as a historical thinker and in his comprehension of the new erudition. The fact that Edwards's hermeneutic shared so much in common with so many luminaries of early modernity—Newton, Le Clerc, Boyle, Pascal, Bengel (a list is too long to recount here)—should alert us to the need for a more thorough and integrated assessment.

Second, American religious historiography will also have to be revised, so as to include earlier periods of the engagement with critical historical thought. In its standard formulation that historiography consists of two epochs: the antebellum, pre-critical period in which the interpretation of the Bible remained essentially unchanged from its traditional roots, and the industrial, modernist period in which all hell broke loose, and rationality emerged (or, in which drastic change took place in dramatic fashion). In point of fact Edwards's era was a period of distinct (and sometimes turbulent) transformation in the way that American interpreters viewed the nature of their founding religious narratives. This necessitated new ways of thinking about the relation of those narratives to scientific modes of inquiry, a transformation that anticipates developments in later American religious thought. To recognize this is to understand that American culture has been in an almost perennial conversation about the nature of its sacred texts, their relation to contemporary intellectual achievements, and their cultural authority. Edwards lived on the cusp of a revolution that (together with the secular state) initiated the most radical series of changes in western Christianity, a phenomenon that seized the American imagination about its religious heritage for generations. The complexities of this discourse need to recovered and appreciated for their significance to American history and culture. Edwards will be found to be as important and creative a thinker on such issues as any in early America; his work discovers an age much more like our own than we are accustomed to thinking.

As a metaphor for this lesser known aspect of his career, I keep in my mind an image of Edwards preaching. Not the celebrated image of Edwards, say, in 1741, but rather, one from the last decade of his life. In February of 1754 he preached a sermon on Christ's resurrection to the inhabitants of Stockbridge. The sermon outline is structured according to questions about the historicity of the resurrection. These included the specific details of "how he rose" as well as the "evidence of his resurrection": that he "appeared to many;" that the disciples "had no temptation to lie;" that his antagonists "could not find out that he was not [raised]."[30] Since the sermon survives only in bare outline, we can only surmise what his full embellishments that day might have been. One has to wonder whether such epistemological intricacies were important to his listeners. Thus one can bemusedly entertain the image of Edwards holding forth on issues that the majority of his frontier parishioners, be they Indian or white, were probably unaware of and almost certainly unconcerned with. It will no doubt never rival the image of Edwards at Enfield, nor should it. Yet it is still an image that ought to be entered into the broader consciousness of Edwards as a cultural figure—the brilliant philosopher and theologian who was also if not yet equally an astute historical thinker; the pastor and man of letters who precisely and insightfully anticipated issues that his parishioners would inevitably have to confront in their religious lives. It is an arresting image of the degree to which these concerns had captivated his energy and attention, one that can in some sense symbolize the culminating theological motivations of his life and career. Whether it will continue to serve as a metaphor for that part of Edwards which remains "in the wilderness" of contemporary cultural appropriation remains to be determined.

NOTES

1. See Sereno Dwight, "The Life of President Edwards," in *The Works of President Edwards*, ed. Sereno Dwight (10 vols., New York: Carvill, 1830), 1:57, 58, 108. Edwards's first biographer (1765), Samuel Hopkins, also chose to highlight the importance of the Bible for the course of Edwards's career. In Hopkins's estimation, at least, Edwards's significance as a religious thinker was to be measured in great part by his interpretive acumen: He "cast much light on many parts of the Bible, which has escaped other interpreters." Samuel Hopkins, *The Life and Character of Jonathan Edwards* (1765; Northampton: Andrew Wright, 1804), 88.

2. Bruce Lincoln, *Theorizing Myth: Narrative, Ideology, and Scholarship* (Chicago: University of Chicago Press, 1999), 42 ff. In response to this attempt to diminish the value and authority of myth, the Romantics celebrated myth as the embodiment of the memory, values, character—and thus vitality—of the *Volk*, a portal to a pure, primitive, and emotive past, one superior to the rationalistic evisceration of civilization. It was this notion of myth as the pillar of ethnic identity, along with the search for an *ur-Volk* that helped to fund the rise of hegemonic nationalism in the late nineteenth and early twentieth centuries.

3. Kelley's interests are largely European, and concerned with Bultmann's use of Heidegger. See Shawn Kelley, *Racializing Jesus: Race, Ideology, and the Formation of Modern Biblical Scholarship* (New York: Routledge, 2002). See also the specialized studies of Burke O. Long, *Planting and Reaping Albright: Politics, Ideology, and Interpreting the Bible* (University Park, Pa.: Penn State University Press, 1997); David J. A. Clines, *Interested Parties: the Ideology of Writers and Readers of the Hebrew Bible* (Sheffield, England: Sheffield Academic Press, 1995); Tina Pippin, *Violence, Utopia, and the Kingdom of God: Fantasy and Ideology in the Bible* (New York: Routledge, 1998); and Charles E. Carter, *Community, Identity, and Ideology: Social Science*

Approaches to the Hebrew Bible (Winona Lake, Ind.: Eisenbrauns, 1996). In the main, however, such investigations tend more toward study of the ideology contained in the Bible rather than the ideologies of those interpreting the Bible.

4. Lincoln observes in this connection that the *philosophes* found the criticism of myth "a convenient vehicle for a veiled critique of Bible and church." Since rational philosophy, and not irrational myth, constituted authoritative discourse, Christianity could be dismissed as simply a more recent and more dangerous form of *mythos*. Lincoln, *Theorizing Myth*, 49.

5. See Hans Frei, *The Eclipse of Biblical Narrative: a Study of Eighteenth and Nineteenth Century Hermeneutics* (New Haven: Yale University Press, 1974), 86–92.

6. J. A. I. Champion, *The Pillars of Priestcraft Shaken: The Church of England and its Enemies, 1660–1730* (Cambridge, England: Cambridge University Press, 1992), 11–12. See also Roger Lund, "Introduction," in *The Margins of Orthodoxy: Heterodox Writing and Cultural Response, 1660–1750* (Cambridge, England: Cambridge University Press, 1995), 1–29.

7. J. C. D. Clark, *English Society 1688–1832: Ideology, Social Structure, and Political Practice During the Ancièn Regime* (Cambridge, England: Cambridge University Press, 1985), 277–282.

8. Champion, *Pillars of Priestcraft Shaken*, 34.

9. Among other things, the contest between the establishment and its critics helped to foster the modernization of English historiography. Since history legitimated the status quo, it became necessary for its defenders to present a "cogent and credible version of the past" in their accounts of that arrangement. Arguments and representations by thinkers on both sides of the debate were measured by the factual accuracy of their competing interpretations. Rules of evidence became obligatory in order to give the impression that the ideal of a "credible, true, and good history" had been achieved. Champion observes that debates about religion carried forth on critical historical grounds had a decided effect upon the form in which histories were written; specifically, that the emphasis on factuality produced an increasingly precise apparatus to demonstrate it, through citations, footnotes, and appendices. There was considerable discussion about the appropriateness of these devices, since it interfered with the eloquence of the narrative, a quality that was still valued in many circles. The trend toward source acknowledgement prevailed, however, because the perception about the nature of historical writing had changed. Significantly, Edwards too planned to develop this sort of critical notation in his revision of the "History of the Work of Redemption." See Champion, *The Pillars of Priestcraft Shaken*, 11–12, 30.

10. Joseph M. Levine, *Humanism and History: Origins of Modern English Historiography* (Ithaca, N. Y.: Cornell University Press, 1987), 20.

11. Champion, *The Pillars of Priestcraft Shaken*, 26–41. Though contemporary historians have been inclined to see the distinction of 'modern' history in the disjunction between the factual and hortatory functions of the genre, many of the important historical thinkers of the era continued to assign an important and even primary moral function to historical narrative, and decried factual accumulation as mere antiquarianism. This view pervaded discussions of biblical history as well, such as those of Bolingbroke and Voltaire. Edwards's view that sacred history should have an exem-

plary function is thus in keeping with the critical sentiments of the age. See Champion, *The Pillars of Priestcraft Shaken*, 25–33; Philip Hicks, *Neoclassical History and English Culture: From Clarendon to Hume* (New York: St. Martin's Press, 1996), 4–5; Joel C. Weinsheimer, *Eighteenth-Century Hermeneutics: Philosophy of Interpretation in England from Locke to Burke* (New Haven: Yale University Press, 1993), 72–102; Bertram E. Schwarzbach, *Voltaire's Old Testament Criticism* (Geneva, Switzerland: Droz, 1971), 5–12; and Howard Robinson, "Bayle's Profanation of Sacred History," in *Essays in Intellectual History* (New York: Harper's, 1929), 147–162.

12. Thus, in "Miscellanies," no. 127 (1724), he complains: "When was any social worship performed by deists? And if there should be a society of deists that were disposed socially to express their love to God, and honor of him, which way would they go to work? They have nothing from God to direct them. Doubtless there would be innumerable jangles about [it] and eternal dissensions, except they were all resolved to fall in with the Christian model. We may be therefore convinced, that revelation is necessary in order to right social worship" (*WJE* 13:291).

13. It is seemingly the earliest such effort in colonial religious thought, at least with regard to its nature as a formal treatise, and with the probable end of being published in some manner. "Notes on Scripture," no. 416, was evidently written during the years 1740 to 1745; sometime in 1743 seems a probable date. Stephen J. Stein dates nos. 400–412 before May of 1743, suggesting an approximate time for no. 416 as well. However, as Thomas A. Schafer has shown, the entries in these notebooks were frequently made out of their final sequential order; therefore it is possible that Edwards wrote no. 416 slightly earlier or somewhat later than this date. See *WJE* 15:36–46.

14. Champion, *Pillars of Priestcraft Shaken*, 12–20, 133–168, and 173–179. See also Henning Graf Reventlow, *The Authority of the Bible and the Rise of the Modern World* (Philadelphia: Fortress Press, 1984), 302–374.

15. Other material can be found in his "Rough Notes" and "Subjects of Enquiry." The "Rough Notes" may date from the late 1730s, although if it can be assumed that Edwards's reference to "No. 864 at the end" on the first page is to "Miscellanies," no. 864 (c. 1741–42), this would place these notes closer to the time frame of no. 416. On page one he notes: "Books of the Old Testament Not Forged. . . . The nature of the laws of Moses makes it impossible that they should be palmed upon the people. . . ." The "Subjects of Enquiry" dates from the late 1740s or early 1750s, paralleling the dating of the revision notebook. On pages 14 and 18 Edwards notes his intention "to show largely what evidences there are that the facts of the Mosaic History never could be forged," and "in reading the Old Testament to observe what confirmations there are of the truth of the Mosaic history." These are both subjects that are developed extensively in the Pentateuch notebook.

16. Those interested in a fuller discussion of Edwards's treatment of Mosaic authorship can read my *Jonathan Edwards and the Bible* (Bloomington, Ind.: Indiana University Press, 2002), 111–128. Having already observed that Moses was said to have made written records of historical events as well as revealed law, Edwards's appeals to the seamless quality of the narrative and legal portions of the Pentateuch. This seamlessness is both conceptual and stylistic, a quality he takes to be indicative of a

single hand. History and precept are integrally and inseparably bound together. They are so "connected, interwoven, blended, inwrought, and incorporated" in the narrative, there is "such a connection, and reference, and dependence," that they appear "as it were to grow together as the several parts of a tree." Against Ezra's authorship Edwards proposes several difficulties. One of these is a moral argument from silence. If the Jewish people had had a sacred Mosaic book of laws, however truncated, how could they be induced to accept another book in its stead? Moreover, even if this had occurred, why would they not also maintain a fealty to the original? How could such an important sacred text, preserved for centuries, be so abandoned as to disappear without a trace? Would not at least some extant copies have remained, at least for some time subsequent, presumably making their historical existence recoverable? In addition, he claims, the style of writing in the Pentateuch differs significantly from Ezra's known work, the book of Chronicles. Finally, he observes that the Hebrew text of the Samaritan Pentateuch is comprised of a pre-exilic "Phoenician" (i.e. Canaanite) script, while the Jewish (Masoretic) version consists of a post-exilic "Chaldeac" (i.e. Aramaic) script, a state of affairs inconsistent with a theory of the post-exilic origin of the *ur*-text. Most importantly, the post-exilic community's evident possession of a 'book of the Law' prior to Ezra's return would have made it impossible for him to palm off a new work as Moses' own, ancient text. *WJE* 15:440–442, 457–466.

17. Philip C. Almond, *Heaven and Hell in Enlightenment England* (Cambridge, England: Cambridge University Press, 1994), 111.

18. See D. P. Walker, *The Decline of Hell: Seventeenth-Century Discussions of Eternal Torment* (Chicago: University of Chicago Press, 1964).

19. In addition to Walker and Almond, on the physics of the conflagration see James E. Force, *William Whiston: Honest Newtonian* (Cambridge, England: Cambridge University Press, 1985), 32–63; Stephen Jay Gould, *Time's Arrow, Time's Cycle: Myth and Metaphor in the Discovery of Geological Time* (Cambridge, Mass.: Harvard University Press, 1987), 21–59; and Martin J. S. Rudwick, "The Shape and Meaning of Earth History," in *God and Nature: Historical Essays on the Encounter Between Christianity and Science*, ed. David C. Lindberg and Ronald L. Numbers (Berkeley, Cal.: University of California Press, 1986), 296–321.

20. Almond, *Heaven and Hell in Enlightenment England*, 87.

21. "Notes on the Apocalypse," in *WJE* 5:140–141; see also "Miscellanies," no. 133 (1724), in *WJE* 13:294. Edwards argues against the notion that (like the Greek Hades) the literal location of hell is under the earth. This is but a "metaphor expression" of the state of the dead, the symbolic language of a vision: "when taken for reality, it is childish." "Miscellanies," no. 60 (1723), in *WJE* 13:229–233. See also "Notes on Scripture," no. 274 (1737), in *WJE* 15:230–231, on Jonah's description of hell as being in the bowels of the earth, and at the bottom of the sea.

22. Though he does not mention Whiston's work in the "Catalogue" until the 1750s (MS p. 34), the dating of "Miscellanies," nos. 863–952 (c. 1740–45) probably indicate his early awareness of it, or at least the renewed state of the argument that it provoked. In any case he was no doubt aware of the general argument in the 1720s.

23. See "Miscellanies," nos. 863, 901, 906, 921, 924, 926, 927, 929, 931, 952 (c. 1740–1745), and 1097 (c. 1748) in *WJE* 20: 92, 157, 161, 167, 169, 171, 172, 175,

210, 484. These sorts of considerations no doubt have implications for understanding the genesis and rhetoric of the Enfield sermon, "Sinners in the Hands of an Angry God" (1741), which he wrote and delivered at a time when the reality and vivid imagery of hell as it is described in the Bible was being challenged philosophically.

24. He may well have obtained his views from Whiston: see his notes on "Natural Philosophy" in *WJE* 6:230, 294–295.

25. " Miscellanies," nos. 1038, 1041 (c. 1746), in *WJE* 20:378–79, 380–82.

26. " Miscellanies," nos. 900 (c. 1743) and 867 (1741, in *WJE* 20:156–57, 108–109.

27. " Miscellanies," no. 929, in *WJE* 20:173.

28. "Miscellanies," no. 924, in *WJE* 20:168. He subsequently supplemented his physical account of eternal torment with extensive historical-grammatical and theological answers to Whiston; see "Miscellanies," no. 1348 (c. 1756), in *WJE* 23:391–411.

29. See Miller, *Jonathan Edwards*, 307–330; Peter Gay, *A Loss of Mastery: Puritan Historians in Colonial America* (Berkeley, Cal.: University of California Press, 1966), 88–117; Bruce Kuklick, "An Edwards for the Millennium," *Religion and American Culture* 11.1 (Winter 2001): 114–117.

30. MS Sermon on Matt. 28:6–7 (Feb. 1754). In December of 1756 he also delivered an extensive sermon on the evidentiary basis for Christ's miracles, material he had previously given as public lectures in January and March of 1740. MS Sermons on John 10:37–38 (a) and (b), with the doctrine, "The miracles that Christ wrought when he was here upon earth were divine works."

Jonathan Edwards and the Cultures of Biblical Violence

Stephen J. Stein
Indiana University, Bloomington

The symposium at the Library of Congress on the life and contributions of Jonathan Edwards to American religion and culture struck an appropriate celebratory tone on the occasion of the tricentennial of Edwards's birth. No participant on the program—scholar or disciple, critic or admirer—failed to acknowledge the powerful influence of Edwards during the eighteenth and subsequent centuries. The tricentennial celebration was a moment when many recognized Edwards's significance and identified the variety of ways his impact can be measured. That is also the motivation informing this paper. Each presenter at the conference utilized a unique perspective on Edwards's activities, writings, and accomplishments. That is also the base I am employing to address a topic of interest that has emerged from my editing of his biblical writings for the Yale University Press edition of *The Works of Jonathan Edwards*.[1]

The range and the variety of Edwards's commentary on scripture are astonishing. He was preoccupied with biblical exegesis throughout his professional career; it was his constant concern. In 1722 a young Jonathan Edwards, fresh from two years of graduate study at Yale College, while serving as a supply minister in New York City, penned the following resolution. "Resolved, to study the Scriptures so steadily, constantly, and frequently, as that I may find, and plainly perceive myself to grow in the knowledge of the same."[2] He may not always have been as diligent in his studies as he desired, but nearly twenty years later, when penning his autobiographical reflections, Edwards wrote,

> I had then, and at other times, the greatest delight in the holy Scriptures, of any book whatsoever. Oftentimes in reading it, every word seemed to touch my heart. I felt an harmony between something in my heart, and those sweet and

powerful words. I seemed often to see so much light, exhibited by every sentence, and such a refreshing ravishing food communicated, that I could not get along in reading. Used oftentimes to dwell long on one sentence, to see the wonders contained in it; and yet almost every sentence seemed to be full of wonders.[3]

His "greatest delight" was a lifelong personal and professional preoccupation.[4]

The product of this lifelong intellectual investment is apparent in Edwards's commentaries on the Bible, including especially "Notes on the Apocalypse,"[5] "Notes on Scripture," and the "Blank Bible," the paradoxical name he gave to an unusual manuscript formally titled "Miscellaneous Observations on the Holy Scriptures." The "Blank Bible," which he inherited from his brother-in-law Benjamin Pierpont, was comprised of a small King James Version of the Bible with larger blank sheets interleaved between its pages, the whole bound in leather as a book.[6] Edwards wrote his comments on biblical passages on those blank sheets. But it was not only in his biblical commentaries that Edwards penned exegetical judgments. They also filled his sermons, published treatises, and a variety of occasional notebooks.[7] The theological notebooks called collectively the "Miscellanies" are an especially rich resource filled with manifold observations on scripture.[8]

Edwards's commentary on the Bible includes all kinds of theological and religious judgments. On the basis of his study of and reflection on scripture, he articulated a variety of positive religious themes, many of which still echo powerfully and constructively in Christian theology, in Protestant denominations, in evangelical churches, and in devout family circles. By contrast, he also struck a number of negative themes, some of which have not received the same amount of attention and are unlikely candidates for uncritical complimentary treatment. Some of them also still echo powerfully. Among the latter are his reactions to and observations on the cultures of biblical violence, which I have chosen to explore in this paper. My choice of topics, admittedly, has been influenced by the fact that we live in a world preoccupied with the relationship between religion and violence. It is therefore natural, appropriate, and instructive for historians to ask how we have come to this point.

Jonathan Edwards's commentary on the Bible includes some disturbing reactions to a variety of scriptural accounts of violence. On reflection, it has become apparent to me that the celebration of particular aspects of biblical violence was central to his religious perspective and at the heart of his theology. In what follows I will identify several instances involving biblical violence and describe Edwards's reactions to them. Not surprisingly, in doing so one discovers how central violence was and is to Christian theology and how ambivalent Christians can be about that violence. Edwards is representative of a larger tradition with real ambiguities about such matters.

In his commentaries Edwards responded to several different "cultures of biblical violence." I intend the word "culture" in the broadest sense—to identify the ways of thinking, talking and acting by any given group of people. In this presentation, I follow Edwards's lead in assuming that multiple cultures are represented in the Bible. For example, he found biblical texts bearing on the cultures of the ancient Near East, the cultures of ancient Palestine, the culture of ancient Israel, the culture of the Jews in Palestine at the turn of the eras or during the life of Christ, the Mediterranean culture of the early church, the culture of medieval Christianity, the culture of the post-Reformation world, the culture of Edwards's own eighteenth century, and the culture of a future eschatological age. Each of these cultures involves massive complexity. Admittedly, I am addressing only one aspect of his understanding of these complex cultures, namely, the relationship between religion and violence. The point of my presentation is that Edwards frequently celebrated the violence at the heart of the biblical accounts in ways that perhaps shaped the tradition of which he was a part and still does in our own day, sometimes with not so desirable results.

It will surprise no one who is familiar with the Bible to hear that the Bible is brimful of violence of all kinds. Stories of sin and disobedience result in violent punishment and resulting hardship. The Fall brought unending labor to both men and women, one in the field and the other in childbirth. Antediluvian excesses resulted in the destruction of all humans and animals except eight of the former and selected pairs of the latter. The sexually active inhabitants of Sodom and Gomorrah, with the exception of four, were consumed by fire and brimstone. And then there is the near miss, in which Abraham was told to sacrifice his son as a burnt offering as a test of his commitment to Yahweh, and then allowed to substitute a ram on the altar. Edwards recognized the moral offense involved in this story. His commentary on Genesis 22 was explicit about the violence. Abraham was not only called "to see [Isaac] die, though that would have been a great trial under such circumstances; but he is to cut his throat with his own hands, and when he has done, to burn his flesh on the altar in offering to God, to that God that carnal reason would have said had dealt so ill with him." Imagine, wrote Edwards citing the English commentator Matthew Henry, "How would he ever look Sarah in the face again . . . with the blood of Isaac sprinkled on his garments?" This near-death experience for Isaac, painful as it was to contemplate, became for Edwards "an instance of the harmony between the Old and New Testament," for God orders things "to be acted and spoken . . . with a design to indigitate and represent heavenly things, without the least thought of the actors or speakers." In this case the actions anticipated "the sacrifice by which sins against himself should [be] atoned."[9] Therefore for Edwards, the violence, contemplated but not culminated, was appropriate and religiously meaningful.

I suspect that it will not be necessary to detail all of the biblical accounts that follow that are suffused with physical violence of one kind or another. Jericho is destroyed except for Rahab and her family because it stood in the way of the chosen people. Unending conflicts between ancient Israel and neighboring peoples—the Canaanites, the Philistines, the Moabites—fill the pages of the Hebrew Bible. The era of the judges is a period of unbroken conflict and violence. When the monarchy was established in Israel, warfare and dissension still prevailed much of the time. Edwards recognized the potential scandal that some of this violence—whether it was violence of language or violence of action—represented.

Here is one specific example. Some very unusual circumstances surrounded the battle described in Exodus 17 between the children of Israel in the Sinai desert and the Amalekites, a people called "the first of the nations" (Num. 24:20). This was the battle that when Moses held up his rod, then Israel prevailed; when his arms became tired and dropped, then Amalek prevailed. Ultimately, the forces under Joshua triumphed. Then Moses constructed a celebratory altar, and he said that God "will have war with Amalek from generation to generation" (Ex. 17:16). That curse of perpetual war with the Amalekites became Edwards's justification for a strange and troubling account of violence in the book of Esther. In his earliest commentary on the book of Esther, Edwards equated the figure of Esther with the church, the spouse of Christ.[10] Therefore Esther's request that the ten sons of Haman "be hanged upon the gallows" raised for Edwards questions about Esther's vengeful spirit. He recognized the ethical tension in her request, but he defended her. Edwards declared that Esther's actions and the resulting hangings were to "fulfill the will of God" concerning the Amalekites, since Moses, as recorded in Ex. 17:16, had declared that God was to war with the Amalekites "from generation to generation." Therefore it was "the Spirit of God," he asserted, not Esther, that called for revenge.[11]

Edwards resorted to this same kind of ethical rationalization when explaining the locations in the Psalms where the psalmist prays for revenge on his enemies. The imprecatory psalms have been a scandal to more than one commentator through the centuries. Edwards absolved the psalmist of responsibility by suggesting, for example, in Psalm 59, that when David "seems to pray against his enemies, the enemies that he speaks [of] are not his personal enemies," but rather "enemies of the church of Christ."[12] In Edwards's view, that distinction seemed sufficient justification for the violent language. He mounted a similar argument in his commentary on Job, suggesting in his exegesis of Job 31:30 that "imprecations of curses to enemies" are not "expressions of personal resentments."[13] Therefore such curses or invocations do not violate the religious injunction against wishing evil on those that work injury. To call this ethical rationalization by Edwards casuistical does not seem inappropriate.

It would not be fair to use only the Hebrew Bible for this discussion of the cultures of biblical violence. The gospel records of the life of Christ present multiple occasions when Edwards reflected on violence. The massacre of the young children in Bethlehem by Herod, a strange and tragic tale, is one such episode. In his comment on Matthew 2:16, Edwards justified "Herod's destroying all the young children," declaring it "a just punishment of the people of Bethlehem for their treatment of the blessed virgin and her young child, by inhumanly refusing to entertain her in their houses when her travail came upon her," thus "exposing the life of her child." Edwards continued, because of this lack of hospitality to Mary and the infant Jesus, *God* destroyed the infants and dreadfully afflicted their mothers, a just punishment for their inhumanity and cruelty.[14] Edwards's judgment concerning the massacre is truly unusual and not in line with traditional interpretations of the story.

Edwards repeatedly addressed the recurrent theme of Christ's conflict with the Jews during the years of his earthly ministry. In fact, that theme was not confined to the New Testament. In writing on Deuteronomy, Edwards cited Matthew Henry to the effect that the sin of the Jews "in rejecting Christ and his gospel was more heinous and more provoking to God than idolatry itself, and left them more under the power of Satan." It also brought on them destruction and dispersion at the hands of the Romans. In the same entry, Edwards noted without comment a story in Josephus of a woman who during the Roman siege of Jerusalem killed and ate her own child. Edwards's summary observation was that it is amazing "that a people so long the favorites of heaven should be so perfectly abandoned and cast off," a judgment he found fully fitting.[15] Edwards repeatedly asserted the theme of deserved violence directed against the Jews. On Proverbs 17:13, he wrote, "The Jews rewarded Christ, and his apostles, and other disciples evil for good. Therefore evil never departed from them and their posterity. Their house was left to them desolate, and the guilt of Christ's blood was on them and their children."[16] Today that attribution is regarded by Christians and Jews alike as an incendiary judgment.

Edwards's anti-Jewish perspective was also evident in his negative commentary on Jewish ritual and the ceremonial law. When commenting on a text in the book of Leviticus detailing particulars involved with the offering of "first fruits," he asserted that "first fruits" are not "fit to be offered to God . . . unless sanctified by the Spirit of God and dignified by the merits of Christ."[17] That judgment is, in effect, a dismissal of the value of priestly religion prior to the time of Christ. An even harsher dismissal of the efficacy of the Levitical priesthood occurred in Edwards's interpretation of the story of the destruction of the two sons of Aaron, Nadab and Abihu, "by divine wrath" at the very time of the establishment of the priesthood. Edwards wrote, "Thus it pleased God to show the insufficiency of the Levitical priesthood at the first setting of it up. He showed that they were so insufficient to make atonement for others, that they were liable to the divine wrath themselves for their own sins." Later in the same entry, Edwards added, "they that come to God, and don't trust in the atonement for sin made by Christ's being consumed in the fire of God's wrath, shall be consumed by the fire of God's wrath themselves."[18] Nadab and Abihu, the sons of Aaron, were "devoured" by "fire from the Lord" for their actions (Lev. 10:1–2). In Edwards's view, all ritual acts fall short of the redemptive power necessary to remove sin, including even the actions of the high priest in the Holy of Holies.

The one way Edwards consistently found positive meaning in the stories of the Hebrew Bible, or what he regularly called the "Old Testament," was through typological interpretation of the text. Persons and events in the Hebrew Bible took on special meaning for Edwards insofar as they anticipated the story of Christ's life, death, and resurrection. Typological interpretation rests on an assumption that denies sole or sufficient meaning in the text with respect to the Jewish experience. For example, animal sacrifices in Jewish ritual were established to atone for the sins of the nation. In Edwards's judgment, however, they had no expiatory efficacy and were given primary meaning only insofar as they anticipated the sacrifice of Christ on the cross.[19]

The most violent event recorded in detail in the New Testament was the suffering and death of Christ. The account of Christ's betrayal, trial, and crucifixion form the denouement in the gospels. Violent for certain, the details of that violence occupied Edwards's unending attention. He wrote, for example, several entries dealing with the phenomenon of Christ's sweating blood. In the Garden of Gethsemane, Edwards noted, "The blood, being gradually forced through his [i.e. Christ's] pores, congealed in clotters before it fell to the ground, so that they were *great* drops, not properly drops, but rather clotters." And he suggested that the mingling of blood and water on the cross through the mixing of Christ's "great watery sweat" and the blood "that issued from his vitals" was symbolic of the cleansing nature of Christ's blood.[20] The crucifixion was a story reminiscent of the tale of Abraham and Isaac, but in this case there was no ram sacrificed, but rather a lamb, for Edwards, the Lamb of God. Edwards was repeatedly explicit about the parallels between the two accounts.[21]

Edwards was not unique in glorying in the details of Christ's suffering and death. The Christian story has at its heart a violent tale, one that today would evoke charges of cruel abuse. Yet Edwards joined with fellow Christians in celebrating the love of Christ who willingly sacrificed his life in that violent scene on Golgotha and the graciousness of a heavenly Father who accepted that one death as sufficient for the transgressions of all sinners in the world. Normal mathematical formulas do not explain that salvific transaction. Edwards's fixation on the details of the crucifixion and on the attendant violence is typical of Christian theologians. In the case of the crucifixion, his preoccupation with violence reflects the deepest themes of Christian thought and piety.

For Edwards the suffering of Christ was also instructive for what his followers should and must expect. Writing on Matthew 27:35, Edwards noted, "The manner of Christ's suffering, which was by wounding his hands and feet, is typical of the way in which he suffers in his cause and interest in the world from his enemies. He suffers as it were in his hands with which he works, and his feet which he goes upon. His works and his ways are found fault with, and reproached, and maligned."[22] It is tempting to construe Edwards's comment in a personal manner, for he himself was the target of reproach. He was maligned, and his opponents succeeded in securing his dismissal from the Northampton congregation. Yet there are reasons to glory in Christ's "natural weakness," Edwards affirmed in writing on John 12:27–28, because "the power of God appears the more glorious in the victory that he obtained by that weak instrument, the human nature of Christ. God was pleased to make use of [a] tender plant, a babe to overthrow that mighty, proud enemy, the devil. It was a little babe that bruised his head, that trampled him underfoot, and gloriously triumphed over him."[23] Here Edwards's positive reflections on the violence Christ directed against Satan and its role in the redemptive process carry over to those who join with him in the suffering church.

For Edwards, however, the tale of the cross was of no effect for individuals until they accepted Christ as their Savior, a process manifest as conversion in eighteenth-century evangelical New England. Conversion was often depicted by Edwards as a violent experience. For example, he used the story in the gospel of Matthew which told of the disciples' despairing on the Sea of Galilee at night before Christ appeared to them while walking on the water to speak about "sinners under conviction." They experience "great exercise and distress" because of the danger of their circumstances and their own inability to reach a safe haven. Christ's appearance was initially troubling, as are "the first spiritual discoveries that persons have after great awakenings and distresses of conscience."[24] This same pattern of conversion, often accompanied by violent physical exercises and mental anguish, occurred during the outpouring of the Spirit in Northampton and throughout New England.[25]

Perhaps the one culture of biblical violence that most occupied Edwards's attention throughout his ministry was his preoccupation with the post-Reformation Protestant struggle with Roman Catholicism. He identified Catholicism as an antichristian force subject to the will of the Antichrist, whom he identified as the Pope. The Antichrist was a major topic of concern for Edwards from the earliest years of his biblical study and throughout his ministry. His notebook on the "Apocalypse" may be his most concentrated cluster of writings dealing with the violence perpetrated by antichristian forces on the church. In one entry, for example, he equated the beast of Revelation 13 with the Antichrist whom he likened to a leopard, a bear, a lion, and a dragon. Each of these creatures was violent in a different way: the leopard had a "fierce cruel nature"; the bear kills by "hugging to death"; the lion has a "devouring nature"; and the dragon brings "fire from heaven."[26] On another occasion early in the "Miscellanies," Edwards equated the Church of Rome with "a viper or some loathsome, poisonous, crawling monster."[27] He never wavered in his judgment concerning the Antichrist. For example, in the early 1750's he entitled an entry in the "Miscellanies" he quoted from Thomas Goodwin's *Exposition on the Epistle to the Ephesians*, "How the Pope is Antichrist." The closing sentence in that entry, no. 1273, reads, "Antichrist is the eldest son of Satan, as Christ is the eldest Son of God."[28]

What is perhaps most interesting about this antichristian theme is how Edwards found evidence for it in all parts of the Bible, not simply in the Apocalypse. His commentary on the book of II Samuel, which contains the story of the treasonous actions of Absalom against his father King David, depicted the tale as understandable in terms of the conflict of the church with Antichrist. Absalom became "a type of Antichrist," anticipating in origins, physical appearance, character, pretensions, actions, and outcome the tale of the Pope. Born of a Gentile woman to David, Absalom was similar to the "mixture of Christianity with heathenism" in popery. Absalom's pretensions to his father's throne Edwards equated with Antichrist's claims to be the head of the church. The battle between David and Absalom anticipated the last great struggle of the church with the forces of Antichrist. David's ultimate victory over Absalom signaled the ultimate overthrow of the forces of Antichrist—an event for which Edwards watched for signs.[29]

For Edwards, additional textual evidence of the biblical link between the Antichrist and violence is found in his interpretation of the "abomination of desolation" spoken of in Daniel 9:27. That "abomination" he identified serially with the spoiling of the temple by Antiochus Epiphanes, king of Syria, in the second century B.C.E., with the destruction of Jerusalem and the temple by the Romans in 70 C.E., and with the "setting up the Pope in the church of God, the spiritual Jerusalem." In effect, the first two of these episodes were "lively types" of the Pope, according to Edwards.[30] Therefore the papacy answered most fully to the "abomination of desolation."

But Edwards's vision of the future called for the eventual defeat and destruction of the forces of Antichrist. He foresaw both "a terrible outward destruction of Papists at the time of the downfall of the Antichrist as well as the overthrow of their church and religion by spiritual weapons."[31] The overthrow of the antichristian forces was linked, in Edwards's mind, to the inauguration of the eschatological age, a long-awaited time when the defeat of Antichrist and the resulting prosperity of the church would anticipate an end of the present order. "So when Antichrist is destroyed, then will follow that prosperous and joyful state of the church we are looking for," wrote Edwards in commenting on Genesis 18. This "prosperous state of the church," he noted, "is in Scripture often compared to a woman's bringing forth a child, that she had been in travail with." The "glory, joy, and laughter" of the church will be accomplished "after the destruction of Antichrist, or the Church of Rome, that is spiritually called Sodom."[32]

The last violent struggle between good and evil resulting in victory for the saints and Christ will be followed by judgment and the beginning of an eternity for the saints in the presence of Christ. One might assume that the scene embracing the triumphant heavenly hosts will be free of the violence that has characterized life on earth. Strangely enough, that will not be the case, in Edwards's view. The saints in heaven gathered around the throne of God will "enjoy" one more kind of violence. The resurrected believers in heaven will witness the unending violence wreaked on the damned in hell. They will, Edwards wrote, "rejoice in seeing vengeance executed on their enemies" because they will "see glorious justice executed" on "that wickedness by which they have so extremely suffered." They will also rejoice because "they will see God's love and tenderness towards them in his severity towards their enemies." But there is more, too. "The saints in heaven may and will hate the damned," he wrote; "they may therefore delight in seeing just revenge executed for their injuries to them." Edwards contrasted this heavenly situation with the present world where "we ought not to desire revenge on our fellow creatures . . . because we ought not to hate them" because "love ought to prevail" above hate. "But," he continued, "when these reasons of love cease, and our enemies become proper objects of our hatred, then we may delight to see just revenge executed upon them." At that point, the saints will "rejoice in God's vengeance upon their carnal enemies."[33] In sum, Edwards's vision of eternity includes the prospect of the saints joining the heavenly hosts gathered around the throne, singing the praises of God in heaven and looking with delight on the sufferings of the damned in hell, their hearts filled with revenge.

Jonathan Edwards's lifelong preoccupation with the study of the Bible provided many occasions for him to comment on the cultures of violence contained in the biblical text. The Bible was a rich diverse repository of religious materials for him. Some of that biblical violence had been central to the understanding and interpretation of the process of redemption in Christian theology for centuries. In that respect Edwards was part of a long tradition of theological and exegetical reflection. In other cases, however, his views of these cultures of biblical violence had not been held universally by Christians, or by all morally sensitive individuals. These latter views have received less scholarly attention because they are not necessarily complimentary to Edwards. They underscore the intense hostility he felt and expressed toward other religious traditions and those who were part of them. These exegetical reflections also document the ways in which Edwards took part in the religious conflicts of the eighteenth century.

NOTES

1. I have edited *WJE* 5, 15, and 24. Footnote references to the "Blank Bible" in this paper are to the pages of the manuscript.

2. "Resolutions," no. 28, in *WJE* 16:755.

3. "Personal Narrative," in *WJE* 16:797.

4. Diverse representative scholarship on JE's interests in the Bible includes Conrad Cherry, "Symbols of Spiritual Truth: Jonathan Edwards as Biblical Interpreter," *Interpretation* 39 (1985): 263–271; Stephen J. Stein, "The Quest for the Spiritual Sense: The Biblical Hermeneutics of Jonathan Edwards," *Harvard Theological Review* 70 (1977): 99–113; Stein, "The Spirit and the Word: Jonathan Edwards and Scriptural Exegesis," in *Jonathan Edwards and the American Experience*, ed. Nathan O. Hatch and Harry S. Stout (New York: Oxford University Press, 1988), 118–130; John H. Gerstner, *The Rational Biblical Theology of Jonathan Edwards*, 3 vols. (Powhatan, Virginia: Berea Publications, 1991–1993); and Robert E. Brown, *Jonathan Edwards and the Bible* (Bloomington: Indiana University Press, 2002).

5. "Notes on the Apocalypse" is JE's commentary on the book of Revelation. It is located in *WJE* 5:95–305.

6. On the origins of the "Blank Bible," see Stein, "The Biblical Notes on Benjamin Pierpont," *The Yale University Library Gazette* 50 (1976): 195–218.

7. For example, see *The Sermons of Jonathan Edwards: A Reader*, ed. Wilson H. Kimnach, Kenneth P. Minkema, and Douglas A. Sweeney (New Haven: Yale University Press, 1999); *WJE* 3, esp. 221–349; *WJE* 11; and the "Miscellanies" in *WJE*: 13, 18, 20, 23.

8. JE's "Miscellanies" have appeared in *WJE* 13, 18, 20, and 23.

9. No. 362 on Gen. 22, in *WJE* 15:348–349; Gen. 22:8, "Blank Bible," 23; and no. 53 on John 11:51, in *WJE* 15:65.

10. No. 46 on the Book of Esther, in *WJE* 15, 60–63.
11. Esther 9:13, "Blank Bible," 384.
12. Ps. 59, "Blank Bible," 425.
13. Job 31:30, "Blank Bible," 398. In this location JE also referenced an entry on "Imprecations" in the "Table to the Miscellanies." See *WJE* 13:137–138.
14. Matt. 2:16, "Blank Bible," 659, 662.
15. Deut. 28:45–68, "Blank Bible," 164.
16. Prov. 17:13, "Blank Bible," 469.
17. Lev. 2:15, "Blank Bible," 83.
18. Lev. 10:1–2, "Blank Bible," 89–90.
19. JE's views of the Jews and Judaism were not isolated from the judgments of others in early America. For background on the attitudes of early New Englanders towards the Jews, see Arthur Hertzberg, "The New England Puritans and the Jews," in *Hebrew and the Bible in America: The First Two Centuries*, ed. Shalom Goldman (Hanover, N.H.: University Press of New England, 1993), 105–121. Hertzberg's opening sentence reads, "The Puritans of New England were obsessed by the Jewish Bible, but they were not hospitable to Jews, or to Judaism" (p. 105).
20. Luke 22:44, "Blank Bible," 733, 753.
21. See no. 7 on Gen. 22:8, in *WJE* 15:50. See also Gen. 22:8, "Blank Bible," 23.
22. Matt. 27:35, "Blank Bible," 682.
23. John 12:27–28, "Blank Bible," 758.
24. Matt. 14:24–27, "Blank Bible," 670.
25. See, for example, the "great terror" experienced by Abigail Hutchinson, a parishioner in Northampton whose conversion experience Edwards detailed favorably at length in *A Faithful Narrative of the Surprising Work of God in the Conversion of Many Hundred Souls in Northampton*, in *WJE* 4:191–199. For the larger experiential context of revivals in New England, see Douglas L. Winiarski, "Souls Filled with Ravishing Transport: Heavenly Visions and the Radical Awakening in New England," *William and Mary Quarterly* 3rd ser., 61 (2004): 3–46.
26. "Notes on the Apocalypse," "Exposition of Chapter 13," and no. 35a on "Chapter 13:11," in *WJE* 5:110–112, 138.
27. No. hh, "Antichrist," in *WJE* 13:185–186.
28. *WJE* 23:217.
29. II Sam. 15–18, "Blank Bible," 249, 250–253.
30. No. 413 on Dan. 9:27, in *WJE* 15:419–421.
31. Rev. 13:10, "Blank Bible," 892. JE's entry on this verse also identified Matt. 26:52 as further support for this view.
32. No. 355 on Gen. 18, in *WJE* 15:341.
33. Rev. 18:20, "Blank Bible," 895, 898.

Franklin, Jefferson and Edwards on Religion and the Religions

Gerald R. McDermott

Roanoke College

The three most influential American thinkers in the eighteenth century—Benjamin Franklin, Thomas Jefferson, and Jonathan Edwards—differed more in religion than in politics. Despite his hierarchical authoritarianism,[1] Edwards's politics pointed toward an emerging republicanism. He agreed with Franklin and Jefferson that New World colonials could run their own affairs with more competence than the king and his advisors. All three agreed that colonials had rights that needed to be defended.[2] And it is worth noting that Edwards's theological heirs overwhelmingly supported the American Revolution.[3]

So while there are indications that Edwards would have allied with Franklin and Jefferson in their opposition to the British Empire had he survived the smallpox outbreak at Princeton, there is also every indication that they would have been inveterate opponents on what Edwards considered the greater questions of the nature of God and how God has communicated with his intelligent creatures. The purpose of this paper is to compare these three thinkers on the issues that *most* divided Americans in the eighteenth century.

BENJAMIN FRANKLIN (1706–90) ON RELIGION AND THE RELIGIONS

John Adams once charged that Franklin belonged to the ranks of "atheists, deists and libertines."[4] The French *Dictionnaire des athées anciens et modernes*, published in 1800, listed Franklin as an atheist.[5] The truth of the matter is that Franklin was neither an atheist nor a Christian, but a complex religious thinker who was deeply influenced by both Calvinism and deism.

Raised in a Calvinist church and home, the teenage Franklin read the deists Shaftesbury and Collins, who convinced him to reject orthodox Christian faith as harsh and illogical.[6] At the age of eighteen he published *A Dissertation on Liberty and Necessity, Pleasure and Pain*, which "in spite of Franklin's later repudiation . . . reflects one of the major themes of his more mature religious position: the notion of God as the distant, unapproachable First Cause."[7] Four years later, in his "Articles of Belief and Acts of Religion," Franklin denied communication in either direction between God and his human creatures: "I imagine it great Vanity in me to suppose, that the *Supremely Perfect*, does in the least regard such an inconsiderable Nothing as Man. . . . I cannot conceive otherwise, than that He, *the Infinite Father*, expects or requires no Worship or Praise from us, but that He is even INFINITELY ABOVE IT."[8]

In his recent book on Franklin's religion, Kerry S. Walters argues convincingly that for Franklin all religion is anthropomorphic and relatively defective. The same basic revelation through reason and instinct is given to all, there is no special revelation given to one race of humanity, and so all doctrine and theology are relative responses to a basic religious imprint embedded in the human condition.[9]

Hence it is no surprise that at the core of all religions is belief in a Prime Mover.[10] By the end of his life Franklin had come to affirm all but one of Lord Herbert of Cherbury's five characteristics of essential religion. Herbert was the so-called "father of deism" who declared that all human beings know a priori that there is a God, that he ought to be worshipped, that moral virtue and piety are necessary, that sin is to be expiated with repentance, and that there is reward and punishment after death.[11] For sin's expiation by repentance Franklin substituted the "immortality of the soul."[12]

Franklin's basic religious perspective was what Walters calls "theistic perspectivism." By this is meant the notion that most religion consists of symbols and metaphors intended to mitigate the cold, forbidding reality of a First Cause that is impassable and aloof. Some call their god "Yahweh," and others "Shiva" or "Allah," but all three monikers are more accessible to the mind and more comforting to the heart than the abstract "Supreme Architect." These are useful fictions but not illusions because there is in reality an objective referent, the divine originator. Humans can know very little about this divinity, but that is not the point. What is important in religion is mythos not logos. The gods and beliefs about them are cultural artifacts with two important functions: existential comfort and social utility. They enable us to deal with what might seem to be an indifferent cosmos, and they keep us from tearing each other apart.[13]

For that reason the doctrine of particular providence is (and should be) at the foundation of every religion. Philosophy, which teaches the same religious truths, is not enough for the uneducated masses who are "weak and ignorant men and women," especially the "inexperienced and inconsiderate Youth of both Sexes." They need religious motivation to restrain them from vice and support their virtue.[14] Only religion can effectively restrain the self-serving passions of those unable to read philosophy.[15]

True religion, then, concentrates not on apologetics but moral good works. For this reason Franklin urged his sister to read Edwards's *Some Thoughts Concerning the Revival*. In that work, Franklin happily noted, Edwards wrote that acts of moral rectitude were more important than merely external religiosity.[16]

Since the heart of true religion is morality and everything else believed about God (except that there is a First Cause) is relatively unknowable, Franklin avoided "distinguishing Tenets of any particular sect."[17] Theology and creeds breed dogmatism and persecution, so it is best, Franklin concluded, to be a minimalist on organized religion. He preferred the Church of England because of its latitudinarian theology and emphasis on morality, and disdained Presbyterian predilection for doctrine.[18] He could also be anticlerical. His "Letter from China," written in 1785 and published three years later, was probably intended to poke fun at paid clergy by ostensibly ridiculing Chinese who paid money to have prayers said for them.[19]

Nevertheless, Franklin believed that some religions were better than others, and used two criteria with which to evaluate them: internal coherence and social utility. In 1749, when he was 43, Franklin wrote that Christianity is the most excellent, "above all others antient or modern."[20] But in a backhanded criticism of American colonial Christianity, Franklin praised Muhammad and Muslims for their generosity to enemies. In a treatise written to influence public opinion after two massacres of Indians by "Christian" colonials in Pennsylvania, Franklin told two stories. In the first Muhammad rebuked one of his captains for murdering captured enemy soldiers, and in the second a Moorish father protects his own son's killer (a Spanish cavalier) because of the Muslim custom of protecting captives after one has eaten with them. In this context, Islam seemed far more humane than Christianity.[21]

If Franklin's deism kept him from ever becoming a Christian "orthodox or otherwise,"[22] his Calvinist upbringing prevented him from endorsing some elements of what is typically considered "standard" deism.[23] His most famous deviations from the deist mainstream were his speech at the Constitutional Convention in which he declared "that GOD governs in the Affairs of Men," and his statement in his autobiography that "the Deity ... made the world and govern'd it by his Providence."[24]

Unlike other deists, Franklin was also pessimistic about human nature. Although he regarded the idea of original sin "ridiculous," he did not believe that virtue comes naturally or that reason is neutral. Like Edwards, Franklin held that human beings are typically driven by self-interested motives, and that we use reason to whitewash those motives. Hence it would be foolish, he surmised, to trust reason as a foundation for virtue. On one occasion Franklin said he doubted the human species was worth preserving.[25]

But if Franklin differed from most deists in their hope that reason could create a religious and social alternative to traditional religion, he nevertheless agreed with Collins and other deists that reason was competent to disprove the authority of the Bible. After first reading Collins as a teenager, Franklin never departed from his conclusion that the Bible was self-contradictory, fraudulent, and plagiaristic, having borrowed many of its accounts from other religious traditions. Philosophical reason was not strong enough to convince the masses to be virtuous, but apparently it was capable of keeping Poor Richard and other educated citizens on the straight and narrow. If Franklin's heart convinced him of the social utility of religious symbols, his reason nevertheless reminded him that these symbols were "useful fictions."[26]

Franklin, then, was torn between his Calvinist heritage, which left its traces in some of his deepest inclinations, and the influence of his deist mentors, who convinced him intellectually that Calvinism as a whole was untenable. This was a tension which he retained throughout his life, and without ever satisfactorily resolving it.[27]

THOMAS JEFFERSON (1743–1826) ON RELIGION AND THE RELIGIONS

Like Franklin, Thomas Jefferson was deeply influenced by deist writers when a young man. Perhaps because Jefferson read more broadly in deist literature,[28] he reflected more systematically on religious epistemology, or how we know what is religiously true. Jefferson discussed two sources of religious knowledge, both of which are given by nature: "reason," by which he meant "the testimony of sense and intellect,"[29] and innate moral sense.[30]

Reason, asserted Jefferson, is "the only oracle which God has given us to determine between what really comes from him, and the phantasms of a disordered or deluded imagination." It is the "umpire of truth" which, he declared confidently, "I have followed . . . faithfully in all important cases."[31]

Jefferson believed that reason points unambiguously to a designer of the cosmos who continually sustains it: "Were there no restoring power, all existences might extinguish successively, one by one, until all should be reduced to a shapeless chaos."[32] At the same time, Jefferson's reason convinced him that the deity maintains the cosmos by fixed, mathematically-precise laws. Therefore the biblical story of Joshua's commanding the sun to stand still must be mistaken.[33]

If reason teaches metaphysics, the moral sense teaches ethics. Jefferson, like his fellow benevolists in the eighteenth century, believed that human nature naturally discerns and leans toward the good: Nature "implanted in our breasts a love of others, a sense of duty to them, a moral instinct in short, which prompts us irresistibly to feel and succour their distresses."[34] It renders virtue pleasing and vice displeasing to the common man and woman. Jefferson understood that the moral sense is interpreted differently in different cultures, and requires education and example to keep it pointing in the right direction.[35] Sometimes he suggested that Jesus' teaching was simply an expression of a universal moral law evoked by this moral sense given to all.[36]

Like other deists, Jefferson was disturbed by the "scandal of particularity," the notion that God had restricted special revelation to a small portion of the world's populations. He complained to John Adams that according to the orthodox understanding "one sixth [of the world's population] are supposed to be Christians . . . and five sixths are without knowledge of God."[37] To Jefferson and all other deists, this seemed patently unfair and therefore untrue of the god whom they knew would distribute knowledge of himself universally.

Besides, the God of the Jews, who supposedly chose one tiny nation over all the others, was "cruel, vindictive, capricious and unjust." He "had bound the Jews to many idle ceremonies, mummeries and observances of no effect towards producing the social utilities which constitute the essence of virtue." It is no wonder that Jewish ethics is "vicious"—its God "delights in blood, commends assassinations, massacres and even exterminations of people."[38]

Jefferson's revulsion for the Hebrew Bible and its culture was typical of deist attitudes toward Jews and their tradition. Voltaire, for example, always called them the "execrable Jews," and once wrote that a Jew is someone who should have engraved on the forehead, "Fit to be hanged."[39] It was also typical of his intellectual mentor, Henry St. John, Viscount Bolinbroke, from whom Jefferson copied sixty manuscript pages into his commonplace book—by far the longest single entry in his notebooks.[40] In one passage that Jefferson copied, Bolingbroke claimed the Bible is full of "gross defects and palpable falsehoods."[41] Jefferson, as we shall see in our discussion of the gospels, was only slightly less critical of the New Testament. The Book of Revelation, for example, was for Jefferson "merely the ravings of a Maniac, no more worthy, nor capable of explanation than the incoherences of our own nightly dreams."[42]

Jefferson also agreed with Franklin and other deists that the essence of religion is morality, and that most theology is therefore superfluous and presumptuous "priestcraft" constructed for clerical interests. "For it is in our lives, and not from our words," he wrote a correspondent in 1816, "that our religion must be read. . . . The artificial structures they have built on the purest of all moral systems, for the purpose of deriving from it pence and power, revolts those who think for themselves."[43] Hence Jefferson was interested only in "the moral branch of religion, which is the same in all religions."[44] If he had his way, all the churches would substitute "morals for mysteries."[45]

Unfortunately, however, the history of Christianity had been corrupted by human theologies which led "millions of innocent men, women, and children" to be "burnt, tortured, fined, imprisoned," and "made one half the world fools, and the other half hypocrites."[46] Most Christian worship was simply "demonism."[47] Christian doctrines such as the Trinity, atonement and original sin were just so many corruptions of the original simplicity delivered by Jesus, and more reminiscent of "paganism" and "polytheism" than true religion.[48] He wrote John Adams that "the virgin birth will one day be seen to be in the same class as the claim that Minerva was generated in the brain of Jupiter."[49] And for the "insanities" of "Calvin and Hopkins" the only "proper remedy" was the "strait-jacket."[50]

The "maniac ravings of Calvin" were particularly odious to Jefferson. Calvin's soteriology was precisely the opposite of what reason would suggest: "My fundamental principle would be the reverse of Calvin's, that we are to be saved by our good works which are within our power, and not by our faith which is not within our power." Calvin's and others' "metaphysical insanities" have "made a Babel of a religion the most moral and sublime ever preached to man, and calculated to heal, and not to create differences."[51]

Before the 1790s Jefferson considered Epicurus a better moral teacher than Jesus, and therefore Epicurean and Stoic philosophy superior to Christianity as a stimulant for social virtue. He agreed with Bolingbroke, that "a system of ethics . . . collected from the writings of antient heathen moralists of Tully, of Seneca, of Epictetus, and others, would be more full, more entire, more coherent, and more clearly deduced from unquestionable principles of knowledge" than an ethical system based on the teachings of Jesus.[52] The teachings of Epicurus—which insisted on matter and void alone in an eternal universe under deities that do not meddle in human affairs, and where virtue is the foundation of happiness and utility the test of virtue—was "the most rational system remaining of the philosophy of the ancients."[53] In contrast, Jesus was an ordinary man "who set out without pretensions to divinity, ended in believing them, and was punished capitally for sedition by being gibbeted according to the Roman law."[54] In short, Jesus wrongly believed he was on a special mission from God and his teachings were inferior to the best Greek philosophers.

But beginning in the last decade of the eighteenth century, Jefferson took a more positive view of both Jesus and Christianity. This was, ironically, "at the very time public attacks on him as an enemy of Christianity were mounting."[55] Two developments were responsible for this change. First, the sharp partisan conflicts of the 1790s convinced Jefferson that the ancient Greek moral system was not sufficient to sustain public virtue. The ancients taught admirable self-discipline, but failed to teach "peace, charity and love to our fellow men" or embrace "with benevolence, the whole family of mankind." Jesus, on the other hand, taught universal philanthropy and focused in addition on intentions rather than simply external deed.[56]

The second influence on Jefferson was Joseph Priestley, whose two-volume *An History of the Corruptions of Christianity* argued that the one God had indeed sent Jesus on a mission to reveal his true nature, and to show human beings how to live virtuous lives so they would be rewarded rather than punished in the life to come. Priestley argued that Jesus never claimed to be a member of the godhead, but that God showed his approval of Jesus by performing miracles through him and raising him from the dead.[57] So Jesus was the greatest moral teacher ever, and all human beings are obliged to worship the one God and follow Jesus' moral teachings.

Jefferson was persuaded by Priestley that Jesus was indeed sent by God for a special work, but he rejected Priestley's belief in miracles and the resurrection since these would violate the laws of nature, which he knew to be uniform. He was also inspired to launch his own quest for the historical Jesus— or, as he put it, "The Philosophy of Jesus." With remarkable self-confidence, Jefferson separated Jesus' authentic words and deeds from what he considered both the innocent mistakes and deliberate deceptions committed by the "groveling [gospel] authors." A one-man precursor to the Jesus Seminar, Jefferson declared, "I separate therefore the gold from the dross; restore to him the former, and leave the latter to the stupidity of some, and roguery of others of his disciples." The true passages were "as easily distinguishable as diamonds in a dunghill."[58] The result was what has become known as the "Jefferson Bible," completed in two stages, first "The Philosophy of Jesus" and then "The Life and Morals of Jesus of Nazareth."

After 1800 Jefferson believed that Jesus' teaching was "the most sublime morality which has ever fallen from the lips of man."[59] But it was flawed nonetheless: "It is not to be understood that I am with [Jesus] in all his doctrines. I am a materialist; he takes the side of spiritualism: he preaches the efficacy of repentance towards forgiveness of sin, [but] I require a counterpoise of good works to redeem it &c. &c."[60]

Jesus was also mistaken in believing that he was "inspired from above," but this was little different from Socrates' belief that he "was under the care and admonitions of a guardian daemon." This mistake can be forgiven, however, since even some "of our wisest men still believe in the reality of these inspirations, while [remaining] perfectly sane on all other subjects."[61]

Despite Jesus' naïve "enthusiasm," the Galilean used the proper rational approach to describing God, taking the best human virtues and enlarging them. As if to anticipate Feuerbach's notion of projection, Jefferson wrote that Jesus took "for his type the best qualities of the human head and heart, wisdom, justice, goodness, and adding to them power, ascribed all of these but in infinite perfection, to the supreme being, and formed him really worthy of their adoration."[62] For Jefferson, then, Jesus was a deist, and Jesus' god was a larger and more perfect version of Jefferson's ideal man. Jesus was a man who deduced God from his own better inclinations, and imagined this god to be the apotheosis of his own desires for himself.

Jefferson was convinced that this proto-Unitarianism would gradually displace traditional Christianity in America. In 1822 he predicted, "The pure and simple unity of the creator of the universe is now all but ascendant in the Eastern states, it is dawning in the West, and advancing towards the South; and I confidently expect that the present generation will see Unitarianism become the general religion of the United States."[63]

Jefferson's prophetic powers were obviously limited, but his prescription for the relations of church and state proved powerful in at least its long-term impact. He envisioned a "free marketplace of religion that was self-regulating, as multiple, competing sects checked each other." His work on Virginia's Statute for Establishing Religious Freedom (passed January 1786) was based on the principle that the freedom to believe according to one's conscience is a natural right, and those beliefs should not affect civil liberties. Its premise was that truth will finally triumph. In Jefferson's memorable words, "Truth is great and will prevail if left to herself; . . . she is the proper and sufficient antagonist to error, and has nothing to fear from the conflict unless by human interposition disarmed of her natural weapons, free argument and debate; errors ceasing to be dangerous when it is permitted freely to contradict them."[64]

JONATHAN EDWARDS ON RELIGION AND THE RELIGIONS

Jonathan Edwards was born three years earlier than Franklin and forty years before Jefferson, but he was as just as familiar with deist ideas as Franklin and nearly as conversant with them as Jefferson. Because Edwards believed that deism was a major, perhaps the principal, ideological enemy of Reformed Christianity in the eighteenth century, he constructed his aesthetic revision of Christian faith in ways that often challenged deist proposals.[65] As a result, important aspects of his theological enterprise were often unwitting rejoinders to arguments we have seen in Franklin and Jefferson.

For example, Edwards expended considerable effort wrestling with the deist claim—and therefore Franklin's and Jefferson's proposal—that reason alone can show humanity the most basic religious truths. Edwards agreed that reason alone can teach a considerable range of religious truth, but only when connected rightly to a heart that is open to the beauty of God. Reason that is rooted in aesthetic vision can prove the existence of God, tell us what God is like, disclose the purpose of creation, and even perceive God's excellency.[66]

But Edwards charged that reason that is not aesthetically grounded—which is what the tradition called "fallen" reason—had shown itself impotent to discover on its own the unity of God, life after death, the author and purpose of the world, the length of the sabbatical week, the final judgment, the nature of heaven, and sacrifice for sin.[67] These things had been shown by God to Adam and Noah, who passed them down by tradition to their descendants. Just because they appear reasonable in hindsight, does not prove that reason originally discovered them.

Most importantly, reason was never able to show how sinful humans could be reconciled to their Creator. Locke and the deists may have been right to say that reason could show the necessity of repentance after sin, but they were wrong to believe that reason could show sinners how to achieve true repentance. So assurance of salvation was also impossible to find by reason alone. Since God is just as well as good, reason can never assure us that God is ready to forgive. What if he has greater regard for justice than mercy? Reason could never prove that he would forgive all sins, no matter how great. Nor could it prove how much repentance is necessary. Therefore the light of nature may show us the general shape of true religion, but it is unable to provide a religion of restoration. In other words, nature reveals God, but humans have not come to know the true God through nature. Even if they had come to this knowledge, they still would not know if God wanted to save them or damn them.[68] Apart from grace humans typically misuse the natural knowledge of God for self-justification rather than self-mortification.

Besides failing to provide a religion of restoration, fallen reason has been unable to show God's excellency or beauty, which is seen only in Christ. This means that even if a person by reason discovered all Christian doctrines and all the moral and natural attributes of God, she still would not have saving knowledge of God. For that knowledge comes through a vision of God's beauty, which is found most clearly in Christ. Reason abstracted from history and sin is capable of seeing God's beauty in Christ, but fallen reason as known in this world has proved itself incapable of this aesthetic vision.[69] As Wilson Kimnach has noted, Edwards came to the conclusion that while fallen reason can prove religious propositions to be *true*, it cannot make them seem *real*.[70]

Such vision is impossible without knowledge of Christ that comes through revelation in scripture. In fact, without knowledge of how it relates to Christ, *no* doctrine is known rightly. Hence "the whole of Christian divinity depends on divine revelation" because even truths taught by the light of nature are not taught

> in that manner in which it is necessary for us to know it, for the knowledge of no truth in divinity is of any significance to us any otherwise than it some way or other belongs to the gospel scheme, or has relevance to Christ the Mediator. It signifies nothing for us to know anything of any one of God's perfections unless we know them as manifested in Christ, and so it signifies nothing to us to know any part of our duty unless it will [bear] some relation to Christ. It profits us not to have any knowledge of the law of God, unless it be either to fit us for the glad tidings of the gospel or to be a means of our sanctification in Christ Jesus and to influence us to serve God through Christ by an evangelical obedience and therefore we stand in the greatest necessity of a divine revelation.[71]

Hence deist knowledge of God is not true knowledge because it denies the revelation of Christ. Even their knowledge that God is one and not many is somehow distorted because it does not acknowledge that the one God was in Christ reconciling the world to himself. If God the Redeemer is not known, God the Creator is not known truly.

This also means that all knowledge of God short of regeneration, though that knowledge is propositionally correct, is nevertheless fundamentally distorted. For without a vision of Christ's beauty, which comes in regeneration, nothing is seen truly. In a passage that may represent the canon within the Edwardsean canon, the New England theologian insisted on the centrality of this vision to all true religious knowledge.

> He that sees the beauty of holiness, or true moral good, sees the greatest and most important thing in the world, which is the fullness of all things, without which all the world is empty, no better than nothing, yea, worse than nothing. Unless this is seen, nothing is seen, that is worth the seeing, for there is no other true excellency or beauty. Unless this be understood, nothing is understood, that is worthy of the exercise of the noble faculty of understanding. This is the beauty of the Godhead, and the divinity of Divinity (if I may so speak), the good of the Infinite Fountain of God; without which God himself (if that were possible to be) would be an infinite evil: without which, we ourselves had better not have been; and without which there had better have been no being. He therefore in effect has nothing, that knows not this.[72]

For Edwards, failure to know and see these things was the reason deists such as Franklin and Jefferson rejected the "satisfaction" theory of the atonement.

Only those with "sensible" (as opposed to "speculative") knowledge of God's excellency can imagine the "dreadfulness of the wrath of such a Being" and therefore understand the "natural agreement between affronts of such a majesty and the suffering of extreme misery; it appears much more credible to them that there is indeed an extreme misery to be suffered for sin." This lack of sensible knowledge explains why many are "blind to the suitableness of Christ's satisfaction." They don't see that this is a "divine contrivance."[73]

Nor do they understand transcendence. As a result, they reduce it to human proportions: all the repentance humanity is capable of "is no repentance at all. . . . it is as little as none in comparison of the greatness of the injury, for it cannot bear any proportion to it." If God were to pardon simply on the basis of human repentance, it would be "dishonorable to God, just as dishonorable if he pardoned without any repentance at all"[74]

For Edwards, then, reason can show many religious truths, but they are not known properly unless they are seen in relation to Christ and his redemption. The problem, according to Edwards, was not reason itself, but minds which lack the "simple ideas" which are necessary to perceive certain divine things outside the mind. Hence the first explanation of why reason fails is that understanding of divine things requires the presence of certain mental conditions that the unregenerate do not possess. Without those simple ideas, reason cannot function as it ought. Its proper operation depends on a certain disposition of the mind; without that holy disposition, reason is stymied, and cannot see the highest and most essential religious truths. These truths therefore cannot be communicated in simply propositional form to the unregenerate; they are "incommunicable" and "ineffable" because they depend on the presence of simple ideas and a resulting vision that issues from "ten thousand little relations and mutual agreements."[75]

Edwards's second way of explaining reason's failure was to point to prejudice, which arises from education and custom. The greatest demonstration of human prejudice, for Edwards, was a natural human propensity away from the true God. The fallen human mind, he declared, is "naturally" full of arguments against the gospel. It is prone to idolatry, with a disposition to act contrary to reason.[76] The result is "a multiplicity of deceits . . . thousands of delusions."[77] Human beings "rack their brains" to devise arguments that will stop their consciences and make them feel justified in their sin.[78] They do not act rationally, and are incapable of seeing the beauty of divine things, which alone can free reason to work properly.[79]

Hence for Edwards, reason is capable of knowing God, but only when one's cognitive faculties are rightly disposed. God cannot be known by "objective" reason that has not been enlivened by spiritual experience. As William J. Wainwright has put it, "A suitably disposed natural reason is thus capable of establishing God's existence and general nature. Truths which depend on the ideas of holiness and true beauty can also be established by rational arguments, but the force of these can be appreciated only by people with spiritual frames."[80]

Therefore reason is not enough. According to Edwards, it can tell many true things about God. But without aesthetic vision it can never get at the reality it was meant to show. For that reason, revelation is necessary.

More than anything else, it was their rejection of the Bible as written revelation that distinguished deists such as Franklin and Jefferson from all their religious adversaries.[81] They contended that God had already spoken all human beings need to hear through nature and reason, and that special revelation in the Bible was not only unnecessary but patently fraudulent.

Edwards began his defense of biblical revelation with a series of arguments for its necessity. Since he believed that reason was prevented by sin from leading human beings to the true God, he was convinced that revelation was necessary to supply what fallen reason could not. Only revelation had been able to provide true knowledge of God's nature and unity, God's works, creation, government, his great designs, his will, rewards and punishments, the nature and end of human happiness, morality, life after death, the origin of sin, the future state, and the way of redemption.[82]

Besides, God is a moral governor. In moral government there is always communication between ruler and ruled, so that the ruled understand the moral rules by which they are to live. Hence it was reasonable that the mind of a ruler should declare his rules to his subjects.[83]

If reason tells us that revelation is necessary because of the need for communication, it also tells us that God's mercy requires revelation to his intelligent creatures. God has infinite concern for them, and so would not leave them alone to reason. For it was painfully clear that fallen reason had failed to show the way to true religion.[84]

Edwards also attacked the deist slogan, "One must doubt revelation because it does not agree with reason." Edwards argued that this reveals human prejudice. It is analogous to doubting a reliable friend's report after he has returned from a long journey because what he reports is strange and unfamiliar to us.

But the real problem with the deist slogan is that it ignores the critical distinction between reason as a faculty and reason as a rule. Edwards used another analogy. To accept the deist slogan is like saying, "I'll never believe a telescope if it shows things different from what my naked eye sees, because my eye is the rule by which I see." This statement ignores the different senses in which the word "eye" is used: as a bodily organ and a faculty of seeing. To say that it is a rule is only to make the ridiculous assertion that I will refuse to accept as true anything I cannot see with my naked eye. No one actually intends that, but because of their sloppy use of the word "reason" the meaning of their words actually amounts to that.

In the case of the telescope, an acceptable *rule* could be to accept as true what the best instruments (including the eye and the best telescopes) affirm. This rule would also include correcting a perception of the eye with the best judgment of astronomers (for instance, discounting the eye's perception that the sun rises and sets). The eye, then, is not a rule but a faculty governed by the use of a rule.

Similarly, deists fail to make a proper distinction between the faculty of reason and the rule of reason. They fail to realize that the faculty of reason is a faculty of judgment—not only our highest but our only faculty of judgment. However, it is not and cannot be our highest *rule* of judgment. For the judge, and the rule by which he judges, are two different things, as are the judge and the faculty by which he judges. The eye is not a rule but a faculty governed by a rule. So too, the faculty of discerning truth, and a rule to regulate and determine the use of that faculty, are quite different things.

Now if by reason is meant the *faculty* of reason, Edwards continued, or the power of the mind to see the *force* of arguments, the statement is even more nonsensical. It is the same as saying that the mind's ability to see the force of arguments is a surer rule for judging truth than that particular argument: experience. Or, a man's understanding is a better rule to understand by than a particular means or rule of understanding. This is an "abuse of language"![85] In sum, Edwards concluded, to say that reason is a superior rule to revelation is as foolish as to say that human reason is a test of truth superior to experience.[86]

Edwards also attacked the deist presumption (which means Franklin's and Jefferson's assumption) that morality should replace mystery in religion. Edwards argued, first, that since religion involves the use of language, religion will necessarily contain mystery. For language uses signs taken from material reality while religion deals with immaterial realities. Second, mysteries in religion should not be surprising because there are so many mysteries in philosophy and nature. There are many things in nature, such as the union of body and soul, which are more difficult to fathom than some things in the spiritual world. There are many contradictions in mathematics and science which are just as great or greater than the supposed contradictions in the Trinity. For instance, the effects of electricity and magnetism are very mysterious. But their mysteries were not objections to his faith in the accounts of the *Philosophical Transactions* of the Royal Society.[87]

Edwards said that mystery is to be expected in religion because religion is concerned with spiritual things that are not the objects of our senses. We can easily imagine that a revelation about the invisible God, and a future state when we are separated from the body, would contain mystery. Things of that world would be very different from things of this world, things of sense, and all that earthly language is meant to express.[88]

At this point Edwards conducted a thought experiment. Imagine what it would be like, he wrote, if we were born without eyes or optic nerves. Suppose we were then told that some things can be perceived at a distance, and better than close up when touched. And that some things can be seen "that it would take millions of ages to travel to them." Undoubtedly this would seem incredible, just as descriptions of color would be utterly incomprehensible and mysterious. So would the statement that we can perceive at once the extent and shape of a tree, whose size and shape would take us many days by touch to perceive. All these would be impossible to reconcile with reason, without "very long and elaborate instruction." If we were rational, we would give full credit to the testimony of those who had experienced these things more directly. In other words, we would come to know these things "by the revelation of the word of them that see."

Edwards's *coup de grace* was to point out that even deist notions were full of mystery and paradox. Think first, he reminded them, of the deist notion that there exists an unmade and unlimited Being. It is absolutely certain that this Being exists, yet it is full of mystery, and the very idea involves incomprehensible paradox and inconsistency. For this is a Being without a cause, omnipresent yet without extension, who experiences duration without succession. This last point is particularly difficult. "It seems as much as to say, an infinitely great or long duration all at once; or all in a moment; which seems to be saying, an infinitely great in an infinitely little; or an infinitely long line in a point without any length."

If Edwards could not abide deism's stripping religion of mystery, he was equally insistent that morality is not the essence of religion. While for Franklin and Jefferson all religion was subordinated to morality, for Edwards morality served the higher end of worship. He argued in the *Religious Affections* that moral practice was among the best demonstrations of true religion. But at the same time personal "devotion" to God, or "beholding" and "admiring" and "contemplating" divine glories, is "the highest end of man" and his "principal business." "Mutual love, charity, justice [and] beneficence" are subordinated to the higher end of devotion to the divine in worship. "For all justice, beneficence, etc. are good for nothing without [devotion] and are to no purpose at all." All morality and justice "are only for the advancement of the *great* business, to assist mutually each other to it." Morality in the absence of worship is finally immoral because it ignores true moral standards and the source of personal strength. And worse, it is blasphemous because it flouts the one who founded and sustains true morality.[89]

While Edwards conceded the importance of morality but privileged participatory worship, he implicitly accepted the deist premise that it would be unjust for God to withhold his revelation from the majority of the world. This is why he consistently employed the *prisca theologia* in his creative interpretation of the meaning and significance of non-Christian religions. The *prisca theologia* was a tradition in apologetic theology, resting on misdated texts (the Hermetica, Chaldean oracles, Orpheia, and Sybilline oracles), that attempted to prove that vestiges of true religion were taught by the Greeks and other non-Christian traditions. Typically it alleged that all human beings were originally given knowledge of true religion (monotheism, the Trinity, *creatio ex nihilo*) by Jews or by tradition going back to Noah's good sons (Shem and Japheth) or antediluvians such as Enoch or Adam. Then it passed down to Zoroaster, Hermes Trismegistus, Brahmins and Druids, Orpheus, Pythagoras, Plato and the Sybils.

By this move Edwards rejected the deist notion of a common religious substratum at the heart of all the world religions. But he also denied the Reformed scholastic contention that only in the Christian religion can be found marks of true religion.[90] Edwards seemed convinced by the end of his life that many of the religions contained the condition for the possibility of saving knowledge, despite his simultaneous conviction that no nation as a whole had ever taken advantage of these "relics of truth."[91]

CONCLUDING REMARKS

The culture war of the eighteenth century, typified by disagreements between religiously orthodox thinkers Edwards on the one hand and deist thinkers Franklin and Jefferson on the other, can be viewed as a grand debate over what it means for God to be just and good. The real disagreement was not about whether or not God existed, or whether or not belief in his existence was essential to a healthy polity (all three agreed it was), but about the nature of goodness and justice—and, consequently, the nature of God.

The debate was occasioned by two fundamental presuppositions. Franklin, Jefferson and all deists assumed one could start with abstract reason and then proceed from abstract ("self-evident") principles to conclusions about goodness, justice and God—in that order. Edwards and all orthodox assumed, to the contrary, that one should start with traditions rooted in the testimonial experience of preeminent religious progenitors.

Franklin and Jefferson applied the deist method by stripping the religions of what they considered their extraneous trappings and reducing them to a basic core. This became the essence of religion *qua* religion and therefore of all the religions: reasonable by their lights, non-mysterious, with morality at its center and no need for special revelation. Edwards countered that unregenerate reason was incapable of seeing the aesthetic center of true religion and therefore misunderstood the nature and purpose of true moral virtue. Fallen reason could know certain things about God, but history had proven its inability to assure sinners of a way to union with the personal God. Thus the need for special revelation, whose validity could be seen only by those willing to look beyond the narrow confines of deist reason.

At issue for the two competing definitions of religion were the role of morality and the relative centrality of the human. Franklin's and Jefferson's religions consisted in humanocentric devotion to morality; for Edwards true religion was a theocentric devotion to a transcendent God, at whose service morality was probative not constitutive.

Neither the Franklin-Jeffersonian nor the Edwardsean religious vision prevailed in the centuries after Edwards's death. There were plenty of orthodox divines in America who declaimed against deism, both from the pulpit and the press, and some perpetuated the *prisca theologia* tradition, but none was able to reverse the movement of cultural leaders to the Scottish moral philosophy that was at odds with Edwardsean ethical theory. It didn't help that Franklin and Jefferson's concentration on self-determination was welcomed by Americans who thought they knew how to make themselves free, or that in late eighteenth-century America there "never arose an Edwards to take the measure of [the] republican political ideology"[92] that like a juggernaut swept even theology under its wheels, or that later New England theologians became "self-absorbed, expending most of their energy on internal struggles" while "fail[ing] to respond effectively" to new challenges such as urban ministry, German idealism, and Darwinism.[93] On the other hand, most Americans came to conclude that the deist portrait of humanity and nature had been shallow and alienating. Transcendentalist and revivalist appeals to human experience were more appealing.

But if American religious culture followed a road not traveled by any of the three thinkers described in this paper, their influence nevertheless remains. Their debate over the meaning and roles of tradition, reason and morality helped set the agenda for American theology in the next two centuries. That debate is critical to understanding not only the intellectual and political disputes of the eighteenth century but also their reverberations in the twenty-first.

NOTES

1. JE believed that God's original design was for there to be a class of rulers to whom deference was owed. On the other hand, he never elaborated on the gradations

among humans as liberal parsons did, and waxed eloquent instead on the beauty of equality. He believed in a hierarchical structure for society, but pleaded on behalf of those marginalized by the structure and exposed the moral corruption of society's elite. George Marsden, *Jonathan Edwards: A Life* (New Haven: Yale University Press, 2003), 3, 259, 370; McDermott, *One Holy and Happy Society: The Public Theology of Jonathan Edwards* (University Park: Penn State Press, 1992), 153–71.

2. On JE's politics, see McDermott, *One Holy and Happy Society*, esp. 172–76.

3. McDermott, *One Holy and Happy Society*, 173.

4. *Diary and Autobiography of John Adams*, ed. L. H. Butterfield, 2 vols. (Cambridge, Mass.: Belknap Press, 1961), 2:391; cited in Kerry S. Walters, *Benjamin Franklin and His Gods* (Urbana: University of Illinois Press, 1997), 3.

5. Alfred Owen Aldridge, *Benjamin Franklin and Nature's God* (Durham: Duke University Press, 1967), 231.

6. *The Autobiography* of *Benjamin Franklin*, ed. Leonard W. Labaree, Ralph L. Ketcham, Helen C. Boatfield and Helene H. Fineman (New Haven: Yale University Press, 1964), 64; see also Walters, *Benjamin Franklin and His Gods*, 32.

7. Walters, *Benjamin Franklin and His Gods*, 45. Walters persuasively argues that while Franklin later softened this view of the divine, he never finally abandoned it. Walters, *Benjamin Franklin and His Gods*, 44.

8. *The Papers of Benjamin Franklin* (New Haven: Yale University Press, 1959–0000), 1:102. Emphasis is original. Alfred Owen Aldridge notes that Franklin was indecisive about the notion of providence (God's intervention in human affairs, including answering prayer). Even though he famously said at the Constitutional Convention "that GOD governs in the Affairs of Men," even here "he did not hold out the hope that specific prayers or petitions would be answered." Aldridge, "Enlightenment and Awakening," in *Benjamin Franklin, Jonathan Edwards, and the Representation of American Culture*, ed. Barbara B. Oberg and Harry S. Stout (New York: Oxford University Press, 1993), 38.

9. Walters, *Benjamin Franklin and His Gods*, 6–8, 10–14, 86–93.

10. Walters, *Benjamin Franklin and His Gods*, 132.

11. Herbert, Lord of Cherbury, *On Truth in Distinction from Revelation, Probability, Possibility, and Error*. 3rd ed. Trans. Meyrick H. Carre. (Bristol: J.W. Arrowsmith, 1937), 56.

12. Letter to Madame Brillon, April 1781, *Writings*, vol. 10, 419. Cited in Walters, 133.

13. Walters, *Benjamin Franklin and His Gods*, 84–89.

14. *Papers of Benjamin Franklin*, 7:294–95.

15. Letter to unknown correspondent, 3 July 1786, *Papers of Benjamin Franklin*, 7:294–95.

16. Edwin S. Gaustad, "The Nature of True—and Useful—Virtue: From Edwards to Franklin," in *Benjamin Franklin and Jonathan Edwards*, ed. Oberg and Stout, 47.

17. *The Autobiography of Benjamin Franklin*, 157

18. Walters, *Benjamin Franklin and His Gods*, 141.

19. Aldridge, *Benjamin Franklin and Nature's God*, 140.

20. Franklin, "The Education of Youth," in *Papers of Benjamin Franklin*, 3:413.

21. *Papers of Benjamin Franklin,* 11: 53–60.
22. Walters, *Benjamin Franklin and His Gods,* 9.
23. Deism was far more diverse than is commonly recognized, encompassing both those who believed in providence and those who rejected the notion. See McDermott, *Jonathan Edwards Confronts the Gods: Christian Theology, Enlightenment Religion, and Non-Christian Faiths* (New York: Oxford University Press, 2000), 19–21.
24. Quoted in Robert N. Bellah, "Civil Religion in America," in *Church and State in American History,* 2nd ed., ed. John F. Wilson and Donald L. Drakeman (Boston: Beacon Press, 1987), 296; *The Autobiography of Benjamin Franklin,* 146.
25. Walters, *Benjamin Franklin and His Gods,* 119, 125, 120, 125, 120.
26. Walters, *Benjamin Franklin and His Gods,* 126.
27. Walters concludes that at times Franklin's Calvinist upbringing trumped his deist reasoning: "He [often] followed his heart and not his head." *Benjamin Franklin and His Gods,* 6–8, 111, 112. Perhaps his long friendship with evangelist George Whitefield prevented him from completely dismissing that Calvinist upbringing. On their friendship, see Harry S. Stout, *The Divine Dramatist: George Whitefield and the Rise of Modern Evangelicalism* (Grand Rapids: Eerdmans, 1991), 125, 220, 222–33, 286–87.
28. Jefferson read principally from Bolingbroke (1678–1751) and Anthony Ashley Cooper, third earl of Shaftesbury (1671–1713), but also from Toland, Tindal, Chubb, Blount, Hobbes, Mandeville, Middleton, Bayle, Diderot, Voltaire, Volney, Price, Priestley, Hume and others who were either deists or significantly influenced by deism. Edwin S. Gaustad, *Sworn on the Altar of God: A Religious Biography of Thomas Jefferson* (Grand Rapids: Eerdmans, 1996), 22–25.
29. *The Literary Bible of Thomas Jefferson,* ed. Gilbert Chinard (Baltimore: Johns Hopkins Press, 1928), 49.
30. TJ to Thomas Law, 13 June 1814. This and most other Jefferson letters cited in this paper are printed in the appendix to *Jefferson's Extracts from the Gospels: "The Philosophy of Jesus" and "The Life and Morals of Jesus,"* ed. Dickinson W. Adams, introduction by Eugene R. Sheridan (Princeton: Princeton University Press, 1983). For other sources on Jefferson's understanding of moral sense, see Sheridan, 8n.
31. TJ to Miles King, 26 September 1814, in *Jefferson's Extracts from the Gospels.*
32. Letter to John Adams; cited in Gaustad, *Sworn on the Altar of God,* 37.
33. Letter to Peter Carr; cited in Gaustad, *Sworn on the Altar of God,* 33.
34. TJ to Thomas Law, 13 June 1814, in *Jefferson's Extracts from the Gospels.*
35. Sheridan, in *Jefferson's Extracts from the Gospels,* 8.
36. For example, see TJ to James Fishback, 27 September 1809, in *Jefferson's Extracts from the Gospels.*
37. TJ to John Adams, 11 April 1823, *Jefferson's Extracts from the Gospels.*
38. TJ to William Short, 4 August 1820; *Literary Bible,* 64.
39. Frank Manuel, *The Changing of the Gods* (Hanover: Brown University Press, 1983), 112–16.
40. Sheridan, in *Jefferson's Extracts from the Gospels,* 6.
41. *Literary Bible,* 70.
42. TJ to Alexander Smyth, 17 January 1825, in *Jefferson's Extracts from the Gospels.*

43. TJ to Mrs. M. Harrison Smith, 7 August 1816, in *Jefferson's Extracts from the Gospels*.

44. TJ to John Adams, 12 October 1812, in *The Adams-Jefferson Letters: The Complete Correspondence between Thomas Jefferson and Abigail and John Adams*, ed. Lester J. Cappon, 2 vols. (Chapel Hill: University of North Carolina Press, 1959), 2: 385.

45. Gaustad, *Sworn on the Altar of God*, 132–38.

46. TJ, *Notes on the State of Virginia*, ed. William Peden (Chapel Hill: Univ. of North Carolina Press, 1955), 159–60.

47. TJ to Richard Price, 8 Jan. 1789, in *Jefferson's Extracts from the Gospels*.

48. TJ to William Short, 4 August 1820, in *Jefferson's Extracts from the Gospels*. Jefferson was influenced by the 1793 ed. of Joseph Priestley's *Corruptions of Christianity* (2 vols.), which argued that most Christian dogma was a corruption of the primitive moral message of Jesus. Sheridan, in *Jefferson's Extracts from the Gospels*, 14–15.

49. TJ to John Adams 11 April 1823, in *Jefferson's Extracts from the Gospels,*.

50. TJ to Thomas B. Parker, 15 May 1819, in *Jefferson's Extracts from the Gospels,*.

51. TJ to John Adams 11 April 1823; TJ to Thomas B. Parker, 15 May 1819; TJ to William Short, 4 August 1820; TJ to Ezra Stiles Ely, 25 June 1819, in *Jefferson's Extracts from the Gospels*.

52. *Literary Bible*, 50.

53. TJ to William Short, 31 October 1819, in *Jefferson's Extracts from the Gospels*.

54. TJ to Peter Carr, 10 August 1787, in *Jefferson's Extracts from the Gospels*.

55. Sheridan, in *Jefferson's Extracts from the Gospels*, 14.

56. Sheridan, in *Jefferson's Extracts from the Gospels*, 14; TJ to Benjamin Rush, 21 April 1803, enclosed "Syllabus," in *Jefferson's Extracts from the Gospels*.

57. Joseph Priestley, *Corruptions of Christianity*, 2 vols. (London, 1793), 2: 440–66. Cited by Sheridan, in *Jefferson's Extracts from the Gospels*, 14–15.

58. TJ to William Short, 4 August 1820; TJ to William Short, 13 April 1820; TJ to John Adams, 12 Oct. 1813, in *Jefferson's Extracts from the Gospels*.

59. TJ to William Short, 31 Oct. 1819, in *Jefferson's Extracts from the Gospels*.

60. TJ to William Short, 13 April 1820, in *Jefferson's Extracts from the Gospels*. Jefferson's materialism extended even to God: "[Jesus] told us indeed that 'God is a spirit,' but he has not defined what a spirit is, nor said that it is not *matter*. And the antient fathers generally, if not universally, held it to be matter: light and thin indeed, and ethereal gas; but still matter." TJ to William Short, 4 Aug. 1820, in *Jefferson's Extracts from the Gospels*.

Jefferson followed Lucretius in holding that nothing has existence independent of the stuff of nature. According to Charles A. Miller, from his student days until the end of his life Jefferson doubted the existence of an immaterial soul or spirit. The future state was a doctrine of Jesus which he never praised directly and the only one he described as "strictly instrumental." Miller, *Jefferson and Nature: An Interpretation* (Baltimore: Johns Hopkins University Press, 1988), 25. Nevertheless, when John

Adams lost Abigail, Jefferson comforted his friend with the knowledge that there would be that "ecstatic meeting with the friends we have loved and lost and whom we shall still love and never lose again." Quoted in Gaustad, *Sworn on the Altar of God*, 142. For more on Jefferson's doubts about an immaterial soul, see Miller, *Jefferson and Nature*, 25n.

61. TJ to William Short, 4 August 1820, in *Jefferson's Extracts from the Gospels*.

62. TJ to William Short, 4 August 1820, in *Jefferson's Extracts from the Gospels*.

63. TJ to James Smith, 8 December 1822, in *Jefferson's Extracts from the Gospels*.

64. Frank Lambert, *The Founding Fathers and the Place of Religion in America* (Princeton: Princeton university Press, 2003), 227, 234; for a description of Jefferson's work on the Virginia statute, see Gaustad, *Sworn on the Altar of God*, 49–75.

65. McDermott, *Jonathan Edwards Confronts the Gods*, 34–51.

66. McDermott, *Jonathan Edwards Confronts the Gods*, 56–63.

67. "Miscellanies," no. 519, 514, in *WJE* 18:64, 57–58; *The End for Which God Created the World*, in *WJE* 8:419; "Perpetuity and Change of the Sabbath," in *Works of President Edwards*, ed. Edward Hickman, 2 vols. (London, 1834), 2:95; "The Final Judgement," in *Works*, ed. Hickman, 2:192; "Nothing on Earth Can Represent the Glories of Heaven," in *WJE* 14:134–60 ; *WJE* 9:134, 137.

68. "Miscellanies," nos. 1304, 1239, 1304, in *WJE* 23: 253–64, 175.

69. "Man's Natural Blindness in Things of Religion," in *Works,* ed. Hickman, 2:252.

70. Wilson H. Kimnach, "General Introduction to the Sermons," in *WJE* 10:201.

71. "Miscellanies," nos. 519, in *WJE* 18:64; and no. 837, in *WJE* 20:52–53.

72. *WJE* 2:274. This vision of divine beauty is Christological, as can be seen elsewhere in *WJE* 2:258–59, 274, 344–57, and *passim.*

73. "Miscellanies," no. 782, in *WJE* 18:452–66.

74. "Miscellanies," no. oo, in *WJE* 13:188. Curiously, there is some indication that deists may have influenced JE's understanding of the atonement, which eventually included aspects of the governmental theory to supplement his more Anselmian satisfaction theory. At Stockbridge Edwards quoted Thomas Chubb on the atonement without refuting him. The Chubb selection in "Miscellanies, no. 1213 (*WJE* 23:145–46), states that an innocent person cannot be punished for the sake of the guilty; God is not thereby required to forgive the sins of the guilty. Therefore God's pardon of sinners is wholly free. The passion moved God to forgive, but not by satisfying God's wrath. For more on JE's atonement theory, see Dorus Paul Rudisill, *The Doctrine of the Atonement in Jonathan Edwards and His Successors* (New York: Poseidon Books, 1971).

75. "Miscellanies," no. 201, in *WJE* 13:338.

76. *WJE* 2:307; *WJE* 3:147, 153.

77. "Man's Natural Blindness," 251.

78. "Christian Cautions," in Hickman, 2: 176.

79. *Original Sin*, in *WJE* 3: 157; "Divine and Supernatural Light," in Harold P. Simonson, ed., *Selected Writings of Jonathan Edwards* (Prospect Heights, IL: Waveland Press, 1970), 85.

80. Wainwright, "The Nature of Reason: Locke, Swineburn, and Edwards," in Alan G. Padgett, ed. *Reason and the Christian Religion* (Oxford: Clarendon Press, 1994), 106–07.

81. McDermott, *Jonathan Edwards Confronts the Gods*, 21–33. To be sure, Jefferson accepted a small portion of the New Testament as a faithful record of Jesus's life and teaching. But even these parts were not "revelation" from God insofar as there was no Holy Spirit to reveal, the gospel authors were unreliable, and Jesus' authentic teachings were partly wrong. Even when they were right, they were merely illustrative of truths available to all human beings.

82. "Miscellanies," no. 128, in *WJE* 13:291–92; and no. 582, in *WJE* 18:118.

83. "Miscellanies," no. 1338, in *WJE* 23:345–55; and no. 864, in *WJE* 20:95–106.

84. "Miscellanies," no. 544, in *WJE* 18:89–90; and no. 249, in *WJE* 13:361–62.

85. MS, "Book of Controversies," 195–96.

86. MS, "Book of Controversies," 196.

87. "Miscellanies," nos. 1233, 1234, 1340, in *WJE* 23:166–67, 167–68, 359–76.

88. "Miscellanies," no. 1340, in *WJE* 23:359–76.

89. "Miscellanies," nos. gg, kk, in *WJE* 13:185, 186; *Nature of True Virtue*, in *WJE* 8: 560, 609–18.

90. Richard A. Muller, *Post-Reformation Reformed Dogmatics* (Grand Rapids: Baker, 1987), 1: 116.

91. McDermott, *Jonathan Edwards Confronts the Gods*, 130–45.

92. Mark Noll, *America's God: From Jonathan Edwards to Abraham Lincoln* (New York: Oxford University Press, 2002), 50.

93. Douglas A. Sweeney, *Nathaniel Taylor, New Haven Theology, and the Legacy of Jonathan* Edwards (New York: Oxford University Press, 2003), 143.

Lost and Found: Recovering Edwards for American Literature

Philip F. Gura

University of North Carolina at Chapel Hill

On two different occasions in the past twenty years I have undertaken lengthy assessments of the scholarship in early American literature. In the first essay I treated the period from 1966–86, the first twenty years during which the journal *Early American Literature* was published. In the second I covered the following fifteen years, with an eye to future directions for scholarship in the new millennium.[1] Adding to my confusion, the seeming reduction of interest in Edwards by scholars of early American literature was in inverse proportion to the appearance of more and more volumes in the magnificent Yale edition, scholarship virtually unmatched in volume and importance for any other American writer, save perhaps for Emerson. But the publication of Emerson's *Journals and Miscellaneous Notebooks*, and of his sermons and other manuscript materials, resulted in an explosion of work by scholars of American literature, something very different from what has occurred with Edwards, at least in literature.

I want to begin with some larger questions this observation raises. If Edwards recently has lost a position in American literature that he previously held with such distinction, should he be reinstated, and, if so, on what grounds? Or, has the canon revision in which the literature profession recently has engaged written Edwards out of a position of centrality? In short, does Edwards—and did he ever—belong in the canon of American literature?

First, we do well to recall how limited his eighteenth-century reputation was, despite the attention that he drew as an apologist for the revivals subsequently known as the Great Awakening. In a letter to Thomas Foxcroft in 1749, for example, Edwards's disciple Joseph Bellamy observed that "To this day I believe not half the country have even so much as heard of Mr. Edwards piece on the Scotland Concert [that is, his *Humble Attempt*]," and noted that, in order to insure its publication he had found five men who would guarantee to purchase fifty copies each. As to Edwards's other recent book, *A Treatise Concerning the Religious Affections*, Bellamy reported "many books still to be sold." Seven years later, as Edwards was producing his great philosophical works, Bellamy wrote to Edwards's other chief disciple, Samuel Hopkins, with an idea about how to make Edwards more popular and accessible. He suggested that Hopkins and he write a catechetical text that would simplify Edwards's ideas. "Let 2 or 300 hundred questions be stated," he explained. "You write on one, I on another, for the press, to assist young students in the study of Divinity." "Mr. Edwards Books will be the better understood," he explained, for "at present [even] the learned do not understand him."[2] We know, too, that after Edwards's death in 1758 attempts to republish his works in the colonies met with little success, although across the Atlantic, specifically in Scotland, where a strong revival tradition continued to flourish, there was a bit more interest.

Thus, when in his diary in 1787 Yale president Ezra Stiles observed that in another generation Edwards's works "will pass into as transient notice perhaps scarce above oblivion," he spoke for many people. He did not realize, however, that, even as he wrote these words, the initial fires of the Second Great Awakening were burning in New Hampshire, Vermont, and, finally, even in his own Connecticut, and that these new champions of revival anointed Edwards their spiritual godfather. Thus, in 1808 the famous printer Isaiah Thomas began to publish what became an eight-volume edition of Edwards's collected works. Further, through their widespread circulation by the American Tract Society by the late 1820s Edwards's works (specifically those on revivalism) had acquired a new and far more important status than they had had even in the early 1740s. By 1830 Stiles's prophecy that in the future when someone came upon Edwards's works "in the rubbish of Libraries," the "rare character who may read and be pleased with them will be looked upon as singular and whimsical," looked foolish.[3] The people who read and appreciated Edwards indeed were legion.

This is the context for Samuel Lorenzo Knapp's inclusion of Edwards in his pioneering *Lectures on American Literature* (1828), the first book-length publication devoted to the topic. In the little space he devoted to Edwards, though, Knapp did not speak to Edwards's writings as literature, nor did he mention his pietistic works then circulating in such large numbers through the efforts of the Tract Society. Instead, he focused on his *Freedom of the Will*, a book that much engaged contemporary theologians, particularly more liberal ones who saw it as the chief impediment to the promulgation of their own ideas about free will. Acknowledging the book's still considerable influence in theological debate, Knapp concluded, "it is no common mind that can produce any thing worthy of notice on such a mysterious subject."[4]

Knapp wrote when the New Nation was working hard to prove its intellectual equality to things European, and this probably accounted for his emphasis on a work that showed Edwards sparring in an international arena. Such a figure was of particular importance to Knapp's sense of the country's growing intellectual sophistication. Two decades later Rufus Griswold, best known for his unrelenting character assassination of his erstwhile friend Edgar Allan Poe, was still in thrall to this notion. In his *Prose Writers of America* (1846), he, too, praised Edwards's international reputation as a logician, "the first man of the world during the second quarter of the eighteenth century," as he termed him. But he also moved on to literary ground, admiring Edwards's "uncommonly good" style. "It is suitable to his subjects," he continued, for "he seldom has been surpassed in perspicuity and precision." And if Edwards was "deficient in harmony" and occasionally had faults "of a mechanical sort," his wit still "was of the Damascus sort, shining and keen."[5] Six years later, Evert Duyckinck, editor of another early anthology, agreed but noted that if Edwards had been interested primarily in belles-lettres, "he would have shown as an acute critic and poet." As it was, however, Edwards had been born "of the ghostly line of Puritanism," and thus "all his powers were confined to Christian morals and metaphysics."[6]

These antebellum literary historians were reticent to make any claims for Edwards's significance to American literature because they regarded his primary subject matter as outdated theology. Such criticism of Edwards on the grounds of his donée persisted through the second half of the nineteenth century. Which of us does not recall, for example, Oliver Wendell Holmes's witty deconstruction of Edwardsean Calvinism in "The Deacon's Masterpiece: or the Wonderful 'One-Hoss Shay'"? Yet elsewhere Holmes praised Edwards as a philosopher, pairing him with Franklin as one of the only two colonists who "had established a considerable and permanent reputation in the world of European thought."[7]

Moses Coit Tyler, author of the first scholarly study of early American literature, agreed. Edwards, he wrote in 1878, was "the most acute and original thinker" the country had yet produced. But Tyler, with belles-lettres as his province, struggled to find a way to praise Edwards's style. He "had the fundamental virtues of a writer," that is, "abundant thought, and the utmost precision, clearness, and simplicity in the utterance of it." Moreover, to Tyler's mind his pages held "many examples of bold, original, and poetic imagery." That said, however, Tyler's summary is telling: "As a theologian, as a metaphysician, as the author of *The Inquiry into the Freedom of the Will*, as the mighty defender of Calvinism, as the inspirer and the logical drill-master of innumerable minds in his own country, and in Great Britain, he, of course, fills a large place in ecclesiastical and philosophical history."[8] But not, of course, in literary history per se.

Tyler's contemporary Mark Twain could not have disagreed more. In the winter of 1902 Twain wrote his friend and pastor Joseph Twichell about his recent encounter with just the book Tyler would praise, though it boggles the mind to figure out why he had ever picked it up. "Continuously until near midnight," he wrote, "I wallowed and reeked with Jonathan in his insane debauch; rose immediately refreshed and fine at 10 this morning, but with a strange and haunting sense of having been on a three days' tear with a drunken lunatic." "All through the book," he explained, was "the glare of a resplendent intellect gone mad—a marvelous spectacle." "No, not all through the book," Twain explained. "The drunk does not come on till the last third, where what I take to be Calvinism and its God begins to glow and shine red and hideous in the glows from the fire of hell." "By God," Twain concluded, "I was ashamed to be in such company."[9]

In the early twentieth century, such evaluations persisted among those who saw in Puritanism and its legacy all that had been wrong with American culture. Thus, Edwards's absence in those two great iconoclastic works, D. H. Lawrence's *Studies in Classic American Literature* (1923) and William Carlos Williams's *In the American Grain* (1925), books that codified what Modernism found of value in earlier American writing. Lawrence famously devotes a chapter to Franklin but has nary a word for Edwards, and Williams uses Cotton Mather to interrogate the country's Puritan heritage.[10]

In his influential *The Golden Day* (1926), for example, Lewis Mumford agreed, naming Edwards as the last great expositor of Calvinism." Edwards, he observed critically, "wrote like a man in a trance, who at bottom is aware that he is talking nonsense."[11] So, too, Mumford's contemporary, Vernon Louis Parrington, who in his *Main Currents in American Thought* (1927) celebrated the rise of liberal democracy through three centuries of American history and whose champions from the colonial period included such renegades as Roger Williams and Thomas Jefferson. As for Edwards, admittedly he was "a theologian equipped with the keenest dialectics, a metaphysician endowed with a brilliantly speculative mind, [and] a psychologist competent to deal with the subtlest phenomena of the sick soul." But, like Cotton Mather before him, Parrington noted, Edwards suffered as "the unconscious victim of a decadent ideal [that is, divine sovereignty] and a petty environment."[12]

In the 1930s the tide began to rise in Edwards's favor, particularly with the appearance in 1935 of Clarence Faust and Thomas H. Johnson's *Jonathan Edwards: Representative Selections*, in the prestigious "American Writers

Series" edited by Harry Hayden Clark.[13] Edwards was one of only two writers from the colonial period chosen for the series; Franklin, of course, was the other. Typically, however, in his section on "Edwards as a Man of Letters," co-editor Johnson did not attempt to sell Edwards as a belletristic writer but rather praised him in a tradition of English polemicists, both religious and philosophical. Further, Johnson argued Edwards's inclusion in the series primarily on his "eminence or popularity," attested to by the frequency with which his polemical works were published in Europe and America between 1731 and 1800, and not on any literary merit. Despite the name of the series in which the book appeared—a series published by the American Book Company, no less— in this volume Faust and Johnson still presented Edwards primarily as theologian and philosopher, as thinker rather than writer.

So what was he even doing here, in the company of Cooper, Bryant, Emerson, Melville, and other undeniably belletristic authors? The answer lies in what other academics had a hand in the volume. Johnson, for example, had written his doctoral dissertation on "Edwards as a Man of Letters" at Harvard, and his director was none other than F. O. Matthiessen, then preparing his seminal *American Renaissance*. (Faust had worked with R. S. Crane at the University of Chicago, on "Edwards as a Thinker.") And both editors thanked two other professors of literature at Harvard for help on the book's lengthy introduction: Kenneth Murdock, the author of an important biography of Increase Mather and other works on Puritanism, and a young professor named Perry Gilbert Eddy Miller, who like Faust had taken his doctorate at Chicago.

Thus, the making of Edwards's modern reputation was linked to Miller and his cohort's larger revisionary project, the emergent master-narrative about the development of American culture that Miller had begun to adumbrate, of how European ideas were indelibly transformed once they were transplanted across the Atlantic into the free air of the New World. With his grand philosophical and theological vision, Edwards stood as a significant transitional figure into the age of the American Revolution and beyond, as Miller, and then his student Alan Heimert, argued.

The fascination Edwards held for the two subsequent generations of scholars in literature—between say, 1940 and 1975—thus lay in his championing by this group of scholars and their acolytes, scholarship that achieved its greatest stimulus in 1949 with the publication of Miller's biography of Edwards in the "American Men of Letters" series. But the assessment of Edwards's import still was not made on his writing per se, despite the title of the series. Recall, for example, Miller's striking statement in the preface to that work, how Edwards was "one of America's five or six greatest artists who happened to work with ideas instead of in poetry or fiction."[14] Thus, Miller's *Jonathan Edwards* is certainly not about literature in the way that his contemporaries, the "New Critics" Cleanth Brooks and Robert Penn Warren, conceived it. Edwards entered American literary anthologies on the strength of his significance in American intellectual history, not for his writing *per se*. But he was undeniably there as a great presence because Miller made him so.

What happened in the mid-1970s to make Edwards begin to fall out of fashion? Metaphorically, the key lies in Miller's passing and in the subsequent eclipse of the school of intellectual history that he epitomized, for the 1970s and 1980s brought not only social history—whose practitioners one of Miller's disciples curtly dismissed as "demographers and other plumbers"— but in literary study the movement into post-structuralism and the "linguistic turn." With very few exceptions, scholars *au courant* in these new methodologies did not find Edwards, and very few others in early American literature save Edward Taylor, very interesting. Better the linguistic complexity— indeed, ambiguity—of an Emerson or Melville, than the relentless logic of Edwards or the self-righteousness of a Franklin.

Edwards remained important to one literature scholar in this period, however, Sacvan Bercovitch, whose path-breaking work on typology and early American literature spawned a minor industry as students scrambled to locate and dissect the use of scriptural analogy in a range of religious writers (including Edwards), is more relevant here.[15] In his influential work, *The American Jeremiad* (1978), Bercovitch allots Edwards a central role in the extension into the eighteenth century of the "rhetoric of consensus" that for this ideological critic explains the persistence of the "American way" through four centuries. By focusing on rhetoric instead of theology, Bercovitch engaged Edwards's language, but only to find it typical of what Bercovitch saw everywhere else in American literature, promulgation of a middle-class hegemony. For Bercovitch, Edwards's confirmation and continuation of the rhetoric of American exceptionalism that derived from the first generation of Puritan settlers marks his chief significance in American cultural history.[16]

By the mid-1990s the action in early American literature shifted to new arenas, literally and metaphorically. There was, for example, an effort to enlarge greatly the geographical boundaries of the discipline, literally to all the lands that comprised Europe's imperium from the sixteenth through the eighteenth centuries. Thus, the field virtually became one of comparative history and literature, and the whole Atlantic Rim, including Africa and the Caribbean, now in the purview of serious early Americanists. Concomitantly, as the triumvirate of race, class, and gender remained ascendant in many centers of graduate training, scholars' interests shifted to those figures in whom one best saw an engagement with such matters. In early American studies, the writers of the "Black Atlantic" became significant, for example, and women whose poetry and novels explored the implications of liberty to a still-subjugated sex rose to the surface. The time was still not propitious for newly minted graduate students in literature to take on Edwards.

By the late twentieth century there were yet other obstacles to the reclamation of Edwards into the literary canon. Consider the comment of *Early American Literature*'s current editor David Shields, in a "Forum" in the *William and Mary Quarterly*, that "no one reading the manuscripts submitted to the academic presses and journals during the past decade can escape the conviction that theological literacy among early Americanists has declined." "The controversies," he continues, that "fired the greatest intellects of the Reformed movement seem scarcely fathomable to many."[17] This probably accounts in part for the fact that the Yale edition has only two scholars from a literature department on the board, thus implicitly delivering Edwards to the historians and seminarians, putting out of the loop the kinds of professors of literature who, thirty years earlier, had kept him prominent in their journal articles and books. Let us recall, too, that in the 1950s Miller himself, an English professor, headed this project.

Another impediment to the rehabilitation of Edwards is the nature of his presence in our literary anthologies, for the texts by which he is represented to the unwashed undergraduate masses also bears on how we frame and understand his achievement. The main action in these texts remains two-fold: to set up Edwards for comparison to Franklin (as we saw Holmes do one-150 years ago) and to place him in the Great Awakening as a fire-and-brimstone preacher. Thus, after all these years, every anthology still must include Edwards's "Personal Narrative" and his *Sinners in the Hands of An Angry God*. I have no quarrel with the first, for I believe it genuinely important, but why we still need the second selection is anyone's guess. In Edwards's lifetime not much was made of it. Samuel Hopkins, Edwards's first biographer, never mentions it, nor does Sereno Edwards Dwight in his study of 1829. Benjamin Trumbull was the first to bring this piece to wide attention, in 1818, in his *Complete History of Connecticut*, a central artifact of the Second Great Awakening.[18] Like a burr that will not be shaken, the notion that this sermon somehow represents the apogee of Edwards's art has persisted. What better way to turn off readers to this thinker than to stress this atypical work? We should not be surprised that to most of our students he seems a curious artifact of a lost century, not a vital part of America's literary tradition.

So, is Edwards indeed a vital part of our literary heritage? Or is he merely an interesting *thinker*, as he has been to most of those who have included him as a representative of our national literature over the past two centuries? Why should he be included in the canon if, say, someone such as Charles Grandison Finney, arguably as important a religious thinker for the nineteenth century, or Theodore Parker or Henry Ward Beecher, is not? Have we included Edwards in our census only because there are so few others before 1800 who wrote and published? Do we claim him only because in our chauvinism we need to believe in the existence of a sophisticated intellectual genealogy, and so enlist an Edwards, or a Cotton Mather, to develop it?

What we have lived with at least since Knapp's pioneering study in 1829 is literary historians' seeming unwillingness to make a convincing case for Edwards's inclusion in the canon on the basis of his writing. Given the sheer monumentality of the Yale edition, its restoration of millions of the words that over a lifetime Edwards wrote, it is time to interrogate Edwards's *oeuvre* as we would that of any literary figure who "influences" subsequent writers and a culture's general direction. We speak of the influence of Emerson in this way, and Hawthorne.

We need, for example, to pay particular attention to his self-consciousness about language and as well to his deep appreciation for what we can only call the aesthetic. With regard to his interest in words themselves, I find particularly significant what he has to say on this topic in his *Treatise Concerning the Religious Affections* when he draws the distinction between the "affections" and mere passions. "It must be confessed," Edwards observes, "that language is here somewhat imperfect, and the meaning of words in a considerable measure loose and unfixed, and not precisely limited by custom, which governs the use of language."[19] Throughout his career he struggled with this problem of the relation of words to the ideas they represent, and sought a verbal precision that effectively tied his opponents in knots as they tried to parry the thrusts of his verbal logic.

In his notes on "The Mind," for example, he complained that "we are used to apply the same words a hundred different ways," so that "ideas being so much tied and associated with the words, they lead us into a thousand real mistakes."[20] Or, as he put it in his *Freedom of the Will*, too often "due care has not been taken to conform language to the nature of things, or to any distinct clear ideas."[21] Born in part of his early appreciation of John Locke's writings and buttressed with his own language experiments, from the pulpit as well as on the page, Edwards crafted a prose style hypnotic in its cadence and seductive in its persuasive power because of his sensitivity to the inherent imprecision of words, a writer's main tools.

Then there is the matter of Edwards's interest in aesthetics. This emphasis on beauty is found throughout Edwards's work. His tenth sign of truly gracious affections, for example, directly engages the aesthetic, for "another thing," he explained, "wherein those affections that are truly gracious and holy, differ from those that are false, is [in their] beautiful symmetry and proportion."[22] The saint, in other words, sees the world aright and thus has an aesthetic appreciation of its utter harmony and beauty. As the literary critic Emory Elliott recently has written, Edwards believed that, "when illuminated with grace, every human act of love and virtue becomes a gracious work of art, spreading God's beauty in the world." In this way, he continues, "Edwards celebrates the human capacity for artistic creativity and spiritual transcendence—the human power to give something back to God." [23]

But if his fascination for language and its reflection of divine beauty make Edwards a writer of merit, is he an *American* writer? Is he different, say, from Francis Hutcheson or Locke himself? He most certainly is not American in the way, say, that Hawthorne, or Twain or Faulkner is an American writer, for Edwards would not have thought of himself primarily as "American" but English. He was not writing American literature but instead participated in a transatlantic discourse of letters. With his first writings on the revivals in the mid-1730s, Edwards played to an international audience, for his *Faithful Narrative* circulated virtually simultaneously in English, Scottish, German, and Massachusetts editions. Moreover, when in the 1750s he published his great philosophical treatises, he was in dialogue not with other Americans but with chief English and Continental figures on subjects of mutual interest.

So, if Edwards was a British American writer who participated in a mid-eighteenth century transatlantic discourse community—in the same way, say, that William Byrd or Benjamin Franklin did—why does he matter in what subsequently became American literature and culture? The answer lies with his rehabilitation and reconstruction in the late eighteenth and early nineteenth centuries, a story that Joseph Conforti has brilliantly outlined in terms of Edwards's influence in American religious history but which we have not fully appreciated in the realm of literature.[24] Fully to claim Edwards as an American writer involves consideration of what literary historian Lawrence Buell has characterized as this nation's "Calvinist literary culture," of which Harrier Beecher Stowe is the prime example.[25] Similarly, Douglas Sweeney, in his recent book on Nathaniel William Taylor, has described an "Edwardsean enculturation of Calvinist New England during the first third of the nineteenth century." As he explains, nineteenth-century Edwardseanism included "not only those approved by self-appointed Edwardsean gatekeepers, but all who participated in and took their primary religious identification from the expanding social and institutional network that supported and promoted Edwardsean thought."[26]

If scholars like Buell and Sweeney are right about Edwards's immense presence in antebellum culture, how can we describe this legacy in terms of his literary significance? Edwards's true legacy, I believe, resides in his contribution to what literary and cultural historians term the discourse of sentimentalism, particularly as it was conceived, utilized, and modified in its literary exfoliation by writers as varied as Stowe, Maria Cummins, and Susan Warner as well as by Hawthorne, Melville, and Whitman. In particular, Edwards's emphases on emotion as a central component to the religious life and on disinterested benevolence as one of the signs of true spirituality came indelibly to mark antebellum culture and its literature in particular.

The center of his influence as a writer, then, is not located in his lengthy theological treatises, which had their greatest currency among other theologians and philosophers. Rather, it was located precisely in those works that had their widest circulation in antebellum America, such works of practical divinity as his *Religious Affections*, and *Life of David Brainerd*, as well as the "Conversion of President Edwards" (taken from his "Personal Narrative") and the "Account of Abigail Hutchinson" (excerpted from his *Faithful Narrative*), both reprinted by the American Tract Society. In these works we return over and over to his insight, that, "if the great things of religion are rightly understood, they will affect the heart." [27] The vibration of one heart to the stirrings of another, the sympathy which flows among souls, benevolence to being in general, is what more than anything else defined sentimentalism, and derived in good measure from Edwardsian principles and language.

In the nineteenth century, Edwards's ideas about goodness and virtue had become so internalized that they were, finally inescapable, precisely the "enculturation" that Sweeney describes. Edwards's influence is clear and highly visible in Stowe's *Minister's Wooing* or in Cummins's *The Lamplighter*, but it also is found in those authors whom Matthiessen enshrined as the torchbearers of the American Renaissance. How can anyone come to terms with the moving passage in Emerson's great essay "Experience," for example, when he describes the loss of his son, without understanding the sentimental conventions that accrued around the death of a child? Or interrogate Hawthorne's understanding of interpersonal relationships in his *Blithedale Romance* without considering sentimental attitudes toward self and other?

Or think of the poetry of Whitman, for whom the bonds of sympathy are sacred between all beings, male and female, black and white, rich and poor? Hitherto we have leapt when we have come upon moments when we have seen Edwards named explicitly in some work of nineteenth-century literature — as when, in Melville's "Bartleby the Scrivener" the narrator invokes "Edwards on the Will and Priestley on Necessity." But the secret is that nineteenth-century sentimentalism, *pace* Ann Douglas who viewed it as the hallmark of an eviscerated or emasculated culture, in fact received vigor and currency from Edwardsian language and metaphor. [28]

Thus, in our anthologies of American literature we need to include precisely those pieces that show his theorization of what became the discourse of sentimentalism. Second, we need a sourcebook that treats the origins of sentiment in

America that puts aside the central nineteenth-century contributors to its promulgation relevant, cognate selections from Edwards and his disciples. And we need to understand that, as Richard Brodhead has shown us in *The School of Hawthorne*, influence is exerted in a myriad of ways and is not always as immediately discernible as we would like it. As he puts it, "the pasts writers proceed from are much more variable than familiar theories of tradition formation allow." Further, while authors help to create "the literary past," that history is "also composed by cultural institutions" that writers "learn to inhabit . . . by memorizing and internalizing the versions of history they orchestrate."[29]

If we are going to discern the school of Edwards in all its power and influence, we have to think of influence in this expansive way. I am convinced that his influence is there, everywhere. For this reason alone, we need to keep Edwards in the canon. If we literature students take our cue from Miller's generation and again learn to read theological ideas in literature, we will have reason enough to find a place for Edwards in American literary history.

NOTES

1. Philip F. Gura, "The Study of Early American Literature, 1966–1987: A Vade Mecum," *William and Mary Quarterly*, 3rd ser., 45:2 (April 1988), 305–341; and "Early American Literature at the New Century," *Ibid.*, 57:3 (July 2000), 599–620.

2. Cited in Donald Weber, "The Recovery of Jonathan Edwards," in *Jonathan Edwards and the American Experience*, ed. Nathan O. Hatch and Harry S. Stout (New York: Oxford University Press, 1988, 52–53.

3. Ezra Stiles, *The Literary Diary of Ezra Stiles, D. D., LL.D.*, ed. Franklin B. Dexter, 3 vols. (New York: Charles Scribner's Sons, 1901), 3: 275.

4. Samuel L, Knapp, *Lectures on American Literature, with Remarks on Some Passages in American History* (New York: Elam Bliss, 1829), 82.

5. Rufus Wilmot Griswold, *The Prose Writers of America* (1846), (Philadelphia: A. Hart, 1852), 53, 56.

6. Duyckinck, Evert A. and George L. *Cyclopedia of American Literature*, 2 vols. (New York: Charles Scribner, 1855), 1:92.

7. Oliver Wendell Holmes, *Passages from an Odd Volume of Life* (Boston: Houghton, Mifflin & Company, 1886), 362.

8. Moses Coit Tyler, *A History of American Literature*, 2 vols. (New York: G. P. Putnam's Sons, 1879), 2: 177, 191.

9. Cited in Henry F. May, "Jonathan Edwards and America," in *Jonathan Edwards and the American Experience*, ed. Nathan O. Hatch and Harry S. Stout (New York: Oxford University Press, 1988), 23–34.

10. D. H. Lawrence, *Studies in Classic American Literature* (1923; New York: The Viking Press, 1964), 9–22; and William Carlos Williams, *In the American Grain* (Norfolk, Conn.: New Directions, 1925), 111.

11. Lewis Mumford, *The Golden Day: A Study in American Experience and Culture* (New York: Boni & Liveright, 1926), 32–33.

12. Vernon Louis Parrington, *Main Currents in American Thought*, 3 vols. (New York: Harcourt, Brace and Company, 1930), 1:148, 162–63.

13. Clarence Faust and Thomas H. Johnson, ed. *Jonathan Edwards: Representative Selections* (New York: American Book Company, 1935), cxi.

14. Perry Miller, *Jonathan Edwards* (New York: William Sloane Associates, 1949), xii.

15. Sacvan Bercovitch, ed., *Typology and Early American Literature* (Amherst: University of Massachussetts Press, 1972),

16. Sacvan Bercovitch, *The American Jeremiad* (Madison: University of Wisconsin Press, 1978).

17. David Shields, "Joy and Dread Among Early Americanists," *William and Mary Quarterly*, 3rd ser., 57: 3 (July 2000): 639.

18. Benjamin Trumbull, *Complete History of Connecticut, Civil and Ecclesiastical*, 2 vols. (New London: Maltsby, Goldsmith and Company, 1818), 2: 145.

19. *WJE* 2:97.

20. *WJE* 6:345.

21. *WJE* 1:349.

22. *WJE* 2:365.

23. Emory Elliott, "Reason and Revivalism," in *The Cambridge History of American Literature*, ed. Sacvan Bercovitch, vol. 1 (New York: Cambridge University Press, 1994), 305.

24. Joseph Conforti, *Jonathan Edwards, Religious Tradition, and American Culture* (Chapel Hill: University of North Carolina Press, 1995).

25. Lawrence Buell, *New England Literary Culture: From Revolution through Renaissance* (New York: Cambridge University Press, 1986), 268–75.

26. Douglas A. Sweeney, *Nathaniel William Taylor, New Haven Theology, and the Legacy of Jonathan Edwards* (New York: Oxford University Press, 2003), 141–42.

27. Edwards, *Religious Affections*, 120.

28. Ann Douglas, *The Feminization of American Culture* (New York: Knopf, 1977).

29. Richard Brodhead, *The School of Hawthorne* (New York: Oxford University Pres, 1986), vii–ix.

Jonathan Edwards's *Freedom of the Will* Abroad

Mark Noll

Wheaton College

In the substantial strand of American intellectual history defined by attention to Jonathan Edwards's famous treatise of 1754 on the freedom of the will, the most interesting commentary has come from those who rejected Edwards's arguments. So it was among later theologians like Edwards's near contemporary, James Dana of Wallingford, Connecticut, who offered the first and one of the best refutations, and also from later theologians like Charles Grandison Finney who once dismissed one of the key notions in Edwards's book with studied nonchalance: "The Edwardean notions of natural ability and inability have no connection with moral law or moral government, and, of course, with morals and religion."[1] The reaction of American thinkers who were not theologians has been even more colorful. With specific reference to the theology of this book, Oliver Wendell Holmes once wrote that "Edwards's systems seem, in the light of to-day, to the last degree barbaric, mechanical, materialist, pessimistic. If he had lived a hundred years later, and breathed the air of freedom, he could not have written with such old-world barbarism."[2] And after Samuel Clemens, alias Mark Twain, spent a long evening reading *The Freedom of the Will*, he called the book an "insane debauch" marked by "the glare of a resplendent intellect gone mad."[3]

Americans who tried to maintain Edwards's convictions against such negative comment are also of considerable interest, but for a different reason. Such ones, beginning with Edwards's own students, have often affirmed what he had to say about the will, but with such ingenious, belabored, nervous, or hair-splitting reservations that they doomed Edwards's views to death by a thousand qualifications.[4]

Beyond American shores it has been a different story. With surprising frequency and among commentators of surpassing stature, Edwards's opinions were often warmly welcomed and then put immediately to use. In this short paper, I would like to highlight four distinguished British thinkers who in the second half of the eighteenth century found Edwards's close reasoning on the will persuasive and inspiring. By also describing the very different purposes to which they put Edwards's insights, it is possible to see more clearly the unusual character of Edward's achievement as a thinker, but also the curious character of his influence beyond American shores.

First, however, we must sketch the main arguments in Edwards's volume. Its full title highlights his great concern: *A careful and strict enquiry into the modern prevailing notions of that freedom of will, which is supposed to be essential to moral agency, vertue and vice, reward and punishment, praise and blame*.[5] Edwards, in other words, recognized that many eighteenth-century thinkers, including many Christian thinkers, had come to agree that for a human action to be judged either moral or immoral, it had to proceed from a choice not predetermined by any other cause except the exercise of the will itself. With other observers of his day, Edwards called this opinion "Arminian," which had become the eighteenth-century's catch-all word for moderately serious disagreements with traditional Calvinism. To Edwards, this increasingly widespread assumption was both foolish and dangerous. It was foolish because it violated common sense in two important ways. First, in normal human discourse we talk of actions as always linked to motives: people always act in accord with what they perceive to be most advantageous at the time of choosing. Or in Edwards's phrases, "the will always *is* as the greatest apparent good, or as what appears most agreeable" (144) and "the will always follows the last dictate of the understanding" (148). Precisely this link between motives and willed action makes moral praise or censure possible, since judging the morality of any action always requires assessment of the character of those who acted and the nature of what was done. In other words, to be able to speak of morality at all, we must see the closest possible connection between actions and the motives that lie behind action. So the modern idea that moral judgment requires a choice unconnected to motives is nonsense.

It is, second, just as self-evidently nonsensical to think that choice can be self-determining, that it can proceed with a cause. Rather, in Edwards's words, "the first dictate of the common and natural sense which God implanted in the minds of all mankind, and the main foundation of all our reasonings about the existence of things, past, present, or to come" (181-b) is the belief "that nothing ever comes to pass without a cause." (181a). As is true in general, so also it is true for human action. All of our choices are caused, or at least occasioned, by our motives. To think otherwise is to be led into hopeless confusion.

With these matters clarified, Edwards offers a better, more commonsensical definition of freedom, not the self-delusion of self-determination, but the actual ability to do what you have chosen to do: "The plain and obvious meaning of the words 'freedom' and 'liberty,' in common speech, is power, opportunity, or advantage that anyone has, to do as he pleases. Or in other words, his being free from hindrance or impediment in the way of doing, or conducting in any respect, as he wills" (163).

Viewing human choice as it really is then allowed Edwards to make a critical distinction. Unless humans are incarcerated or incapacitated by some other physical force, they possess a "natural ability" to carry out the actions they want to carry out. But because humans always act in accordance with the motives that seem to them the best, it is proper to say that they exhibit a "moral inability" to act against their strongest motives. In this sense, it is also natural to speak of a "moral necessity" whereby all people act according to their strongest motives. In Edwards's view, this "moral necessity" is "not at all repugnant to moral agency, and the reasonable use of commands, calls, rewards, punishments, etc." (431).

In a long work filled with thick casuistry, one of Edwards's most impressive claims against the opposing contention—that "moral necessity" is incompatible with true freedom—was his reference to God and Jesus Christ. Jesus, in Edwards's view, was the perfect moral agent who always acted with perfect freedom, and yet "his holy behavior was necessary; . . . it was impossible it should be otherwise, than that he should behave himself holily, and that he should be perfectly holy in each individual act of his life" (281).

Edwards, it is important to stress, made these arguments, not primarily to score philosophical points, but because he felt that his conception of human willing was integral to the maintenance of true religion, that is, of properly understood Calvinism. And so in the conclusion of his book he was at pains to show how his account of "natural ability" linked to "moral necessity" reconfirmed a host of traditional Calvinist teachings, including "the total depravity and corruption of man's nature" (432), "the doctrine of *efficacious grace*" (433), "God's *universal* and *absolute* decree" (434), "the doctrine of *absolute, eternal, personal election*" (434), Christ's "particular . . . redemption of a certain number . . . and of a certain number only" (435), and "the infallible and necessary *perseverance* of saints" (435).

To Edwards's own satisfaction, his arguments concerning the will, which so conclusively supported these main teachings of historic Calvinism, represented "the demonstrable dictates of reason, as well as the certain dictates of the mouth of the most High [i.e., Scripture]" (438).

The first important foreign use of Edwards occurred almost as soon as his *Enquiry* appeared. Henry Home, Lord Kames (1696–1782), was a notable

Scottish jurist, critic, church member, friend of David Hume, and constant scribbler.[6] As he grew older, his writing grew more convoluted, so much so that Oliver Goldsmith once opined about Kames's *Elements of Criticism* that it was "easier to write that book than to read it."[7] Kames's engagement with Edwards came earlier and in a book written quite clearly. That engagement is important because it represented the first important intellectual response to Edwards's volume, and also because Kames's receptivity to the details of Edwards's argument was *not* matched by commitment to Edwards's larger purpose.

Three years before the appearance of Edwards's *Enquiry*, Kames in 1751 published a book on free will and moral necessity that paralleled Edwards's slightly later volume in a number of remarkable particulars. In his *Essays on the Principles of Morality and Natural Religion*, Kames argued as Edwards would also argue that all human actions arose from motives.[8] In a phrase similar to what Edwards would publish three years later, Kames held that "the determination [to act] must result from that motive, which has the greatest influence for the time; or from what appears the best and most eligible upon the whole" (167). But then, in opposition to what Edwards would later argue, Kames suggested that humans did retain a definite conviction that they could choose against their motives if they wanted to. Strictly considered, this sense of liberty to choose against motives was "illusive" (217) or "for want of a more proper term, may be called deceitful" (152). Human actions, in other words, were actually part of a necessitarian scheme, but they appeared to be undertaken as free actions.

To Kames, this apparently anomalous situation was in fact a most remarkable demonstration of God's intelligent design of the universe. God had deliberately made things this way. "This universe," according to Kames, "is a vast machine, winded up and set going" (188). But for man to fulfill his purpose as a rational, moral agent within this scheme, "It was necessary that he should have some idea of liberty, some feeling of things possible and contingent, things depending upon himself to cause, that he might be led to a proper exercise of that ability, for which he was designed" (188–89). Once modern observers grasped what was going on in the apparent contradiction between delusive liberty and actual necessity, they could only marvel at the great wisdom that had designed the system. "Nothing carries in it more express characters of design; nothing can be conceived more opposite to chance, than a plan so artfully contrived, for adjusting our impressions and feelings to the purposes of life" (216). In sum, the purpose of what at first glance may have seemed a problem was itself rather intended so that humanity's "admiration of nature, and the God of nature, may be increased." (218).

Shortly after Edwards published his *Enquiry* in 1754, he heard from Scottish friends that associates of Kames were using his book as a testimony to support Kames's position.[9] When Edwards was able to read Kames's volume, he was appalled. In mid 1757, he fired off two letters to his Scottish friend, John Erskine, the longer of which was immediately published. It took strong exception to Kames's argument that humans enjoyed a natural, but delusive sense of freedom. Edwards, by contrast, repeated his contention from the 1754 work that the modern notion of an indeterminate liberty being necessary for moral judgment was absurd. Apparently this message got through, for although Kames in the second edition of his work from 1758 did not acknowledge Edwards by name, he changed what he had earlier written to bring his argument into alignment with Edwards's *Enquiry* and with Edwards's published letter to Erskine. Specifically, in this second edition Kames retracted his opinion about a delusive sense of freedom; in his revised opinion, Kames agreed with Edwards that a false sense of perceived self-determination was *not* in fact required for humans to act rationally and virtuously.[10] Yet although he adjusted the details of his argument, Kames still reaffirmed the more general point of his original edition: what was most important about the way that humans thought about their own actions was the testimony that thought rendered to the moral design of nature and to "the God of nature" who was responsible for that design.

Kames, thus, bent to the specifics of Edwards's argumentation, but he remained in 1758 far removed from the purposes that Edwards pursued in his volume. The enduring clash of larger purpose was manifest in Edwards's second letter to Erskine of 1757 when he reiterated even more succinctly than at the end of his 1754 *Enquiry* why he had gone to such pains to examine this subject. Not a clearer picture of the god of Nature, but the eternal destiny of human beings was at stake. Holding the Arminian, view "tends to prevent any proper exercises of faith in God and Christ, in the affair of our salvation. . . . The nature of true faith implies a disposition to give all the glory of our salvation to God and Christ. But this [erroneous Arminian] notion is inconsistent with it, for it in effect gives the glory wholly to man."[11] Edwards almost certainly did help Lord Kames make a stronger argument in praise of nature and nature's God, even though Edwards himself hoped his argument would turn people away from what existed by nature to what was given only by grace.

The next Briton to adopt Edwards's arguments from the *Enquiry* put them to use in a manner much closer to Edwards's own concerns. Andrew Fuller (1754–1815) was a Baptist minister who had been troubled since his youth by the Hyper Calvinism prevalent in the orthodox segment of British Nonconformity.[12] Fuller's theological uncertainties were coming to be widely shared among English Baptists, but his own wrestling with this issue arose from a concrete incident: shortly after he had been baptized into the membership of his local Baptist church, one of the other youthful members drank himself into a stupor but then claimed that he was not responsible for what he had done since his will was subordinated to his character.[13] Fuller's effort to sort out the relationship between God's sovereignty and human responsibility began with this incident but did not end until he received assistance from America.

That assistance was mediated by Baptist ministers who in 1764 had founded the Northamptonshire Association as a clearinghouse for theological study and personal encouragement. In that group, as it happened, were several who were reading Edwards and passing on his works. They included Caleb Evans (1737–1779), principal of the Baptist Academy in Bristol; John Ryland, Jr. (1753–1825), Baptist pastor in Northampton to whom John Erskine passed on copies of Edwards's works and who was in 1784 inspired by Edwards's *Humble Attempt to Promote Visible Union of God's People in Extraordinary Prayer for the Revival of Religion* (1747) to organize a cell for the purpose of praying for the evangelization of England and the world; and Robert Hall, Sr. (1728–1791), who was the one who specifically recommended Edwards's *Freedom of the Will* to Andrew Fuller.

In terms well-established among British Dissenters, Fuller was wrestling with "The Modern Question," so-called after a pamphlet from 1737 by Matthias Maurice, a Congregationalist pastor who contended that it was "the duty of poor unconverted sinners, who hear the Gospel preached or published, to believe in Jesus Christ."[14] To Baptist traditionalists, this proposition seemed to negate the force of God's sovereign call of election, since how could it be the duty of an ordinary sinner to repent if God was the sole agent in bringing unbelievers from spiritual death to spiritual life? Yet more and more Calvinist Dissenters in the half century of debate that followed the publication of Maurice's work were coming to believe that he was right—the Christian gospel should be preached freely to all, and, even while preachers upheld full divine sovereignty, all hearers of the gospel should be implored to turn to Christ. Still, the suspicion lingered that to take this step was to set aside what seemed to most Particular Baptists clear biblical teaching about God's electing grace and the true path of salvation.

Andrew Fuller was struggling with this issue when he first read Jonathan Edwards. The evidence of influence from that reading was manifest in the substantial volume that Fuller published in 1785, where once again the full title neatly précises the burden of the book: *The gospel of Christ worthy of all acceptation: or the obligations of men fully to credit, and cordially to approve, whatever God makes known. Wherein is considered the nature of faith in Christ, and the Duty of those where the gospel comes in that matter.*[15] What most impressed Fuller in Edwards was "the distinction of *natural and moral ability, and inability*" and how Edwards had used that distinction "to disburden the Calvinistic system of a number of calumnies with which its enemies have loaded it, as well as to afford clear and honourable conceptions of the divine government" (iv). In the exposition of his argument, Fuller did not quote Edwards as frequently as he did British Dissenting theologians, especially the Puritan John Owen and the leading Baptist of the preceding generation, John Gill, but Fuller was clearly following Edwards's reasoning when he provided an account of why sinners did not come to Christ: "The *cannot* itself consists in a *will not*, or in other words, in the want of a *heart* to come to Christ, with a settled *aversion* to him" (71). When Fuller took up the question of moral ability and moral inability, he cited Edwards and his *Enquiry* specifically by name, for this was "A book which has been justly said to go further toward settling the main points in controversy between the Calvinists and the Arminians, than any thing that has been wrote" (192).

Following Edwards and his own teachers among the English Baptists, Fuller came to embrace the conviction that all people should and could turn to God if they would do so. In turn, this obligation justified free and full preaching of the gospel. But in addition, Edwards also showed Fuller how he could continue to believe that redemption required God's gift of "a new sense of the heart" to change the character lying behind all human choices. At least to Fuller's satisfaction, and also the satisfaction of many other Baptists, Edwards had solved the conundrum of how to believe in the scriptural teaching of predestination while also following the scriptural mandate for world-wide evangelism.

And world-wide it certainly was, for the circle of Northamptonshire Baptists nurtured a growing number of individuals who felt an increasing burden to take the gospel message to unbelievers wherever they might be found. One of these individuals was William Carey (1761–1834), a shoemaker, schoolteacher, and pastor who, after being inspired by accounts of Captain Cook's voyages in the Pacific, began to think seriously about the mandate for Christian witness in such parts of the world.[16] After several years of discussion with Baptist colleagues, Carey published in 1792 a short tract that exerted a huge impact: *An enquiry into the obligations of Christians, to use means for the conversion of the heathens: in which the religious state of the different nations of the world, the success of former undertakings, and the practicability of other undertakings, are considered.* Spurred on by Carey, who soon departed for India, Baptist leaders in 1792 founded the Particular Baptist Society for Propagating the Gospel Among the Heathen (or Baptist Missionary Society).[17] The first secretary and ceaseless promoter of this critical agency spurring missionary efforts in the English-speaking world was Andrew Fuller.

Another energetic, innovative, bright, and foundationally thinking Englishman who was reading Edwards on the will at the same time that Fuller was reading him, but who read him to a completely different purpose, was the radical political theorist William Godwin (1756–1832).[18] Like Fuller, Godwin had been raised among theologically minded Nonconformists. Although Godwin's circle represented the part of Dissent that was moving toward Unitarianism, it still included many who read Edwards with appreciation. Perhaps from his Dissenting minister father, or more likely under the instruction of Rev. Andrew Kippis at the Presbyterian Academy at Hoxton, Godwin studied carefully a number of Edwards's works. Godwin himself became a Dissenting minister in 1778, but by 1783 he had lost his Christian faith and embarked on a career as a free-lance radical writer. What he did not lose, however, was the view of human freedom that he had learned from Jonathan Edwards.

The result was that when in 1793 Godwin published *An enquiry concerning political justice and its influence on general virtue and happiness*, the work that marked him out as the architect of anarchy, Godwin paid explicit tribute to Edwards for providing some of his strongest intellectual support.[19] In carrying the radicalism of the French Revolution to dispassionately logical conclusions, Godwin built his idea of a perfect society—free from constraint, free from inherited political institutions, free from the degradations of inequality—upon a thoroughly utilitarian and thoroughly deterministic view of the human person. Through education that enabled humans to see things as they really were, the state and all other coercive institutions would wither away and humans would find beatitude in following the uncorrupted instincts of minds truly informed. For his purposes, Godwin cited Edwards approvingly because of the distinction Edwards had made in *The Nature of True Virtue* between the lesser good of personal gratitude and the greater good of devotion to general benevolence. (43n) Even more directly, Godwin credited Edwards with treating "the argument from the impossibility of free will" with "great force" (175n).

As Godwin set out to describe the proper view of human nature that would make for a truly just society, he began with "the doctrine of moral necessity," because that doctrine provided "a comprehensive view of man in society." (166). Like Edwards, Godwin held that there existed a "certainty of conjunction between moral antecedents and consequents" (161), and then he justified that assertion by referring to the general human approach to "matter and motion" as excluding "the supposition of chance or an uncaused event" (164). In further concord with Edwards, Godwin claimed that commonsense ruled out motive-less action. Rather, continuing along with Edwards, "Our external actions are then said to be free when they truly result from the determination of the mind." (172) Finally, Godwin repeated Edwards's insistence that the being of God—absolutely virtuous, absolutely free, and yet acting always under moral necessity—conclusively settled the argument: "The virtuous man, in proportion to his improvement, will be under the constant influence of fixed and invariable principles, and such a being as we conceive God to be can never in any one instance have exercised this [false idea of] liberty" (176).

Yet the Godwin who walked so closely in Edwards's footsteps as he reasoned on the will did anything but follow Edwards in his prescription for a just society. For mankind, in Godwin's view, "nothing further is required but the improvement of his reasoning faculty to make him virtuous and happy" (176). Not recognition of original sin, not reliance on the Holy Spirit, not humble gratitude for the saving work of Christ, not resignation to the will of God, and certainly not confidence in the religious authority of biblically-trained clergymen. Godwin, in other words, was not in the least interested in the greater purposes to which Edwards had devoted the casuistry in his book on the freedom of the will.

The fourth notable Briton of this era who drew unusual insight from Edwards on the will was much more in the stream of Andrew Fuller than of William Godwin. Yet Thomas Chalmers (1780–1847), an evangelical Scottish Presbyterian minister, theologian, apologist, and activist, was actually led as a young man to Edwards *after* he had been captivated by Godwin's *Enquiry Concerning Political Justice*.[20] Chalmers eventually became one of the most widely admired public leaders in all of Britain during the first half of the nineteenth century. At different times, he was lionized for proposing innovative solutions to the desperate problems of urban poverty in Glasgow, for showing how traditional Christian faith could be interpreted in line with the age's new discoveries in astronomy, for inspiring a corps of able young Scots to take up missionary service in Africa and the Far East, and for leading intrepid protestors against the system of patronage in the Scottish state church to found a rival Free Church of Scotland. The geologist Hugh Miller thought that Chalmers "may be said rather to have created than to have belonged to an era," while William Gladstone, Britain's most important political leader of the century, called him "a man greatly lifted out of the region of mere flesh and blood." He was the first Presbyterian ever to receive the Doctorate in Common Law from Oxford.[21]

Chalmers was serving as pastor in the village of Kilmany when around 1810 he underwent something like an evangelical conversion, but this experience came almost fifteen years after he had read and been profoundly moved by reading Edwards's treatise on the will. In a later report written in 1844 to the minister then serving in Edwards's Northampton, Massachusetts, pulpit, Chalmers dated to 1797 this life-changing encounter: "There is no European divine to whom I make such frequent appeals in my class-room, as I do to Edwards—no book of human composition which I more strenuously recommend, than his 'Treatise on the Will,' read by me forty-seven years ago, with a conviction that has never since faltered, and which has helped me, more than any other uninspired book, to find my way through all that might otherwise have proved baffling and transcendental and mysterious in the peculiarities of Calvinism."[22]

The exact shape of Edwards's impact on Chalmers is suggested by the theological lectures he delivered in his later years and that were then published after his death.[23] In a broader discussion of "the Extent of the Gospel Remedy," Chalmers followed Edwards in arguing that the uniformity of cause and effect was just as applicable in the moral world as in the material world (303–304), that liberty should be defined by reference to humans carrying out what they chose to do rather than by the choosing of what they did (310), and that in discussing such matters it was always necessary to distinguish moral necessity from physical necessity (341). Chalmers began his discussion of human and divine responsibility by saying that "my convictions are as entire as [Edwards's] were on the side of a rigid and absolute predestination" (292). Later in the lecture he inserted a long encomium to Edwards that, among many other tributes, praised the *Freedom of the Will* as "an undying testimony to the superiority and unrivalled strength of his metaphysical talents" (325–26).

Yet for all the superlatives he heaped on Edwards and his *Freedom of the Will*, Chalmers's own interests were not the same as Edwards's. In his theological lectures he wondered aloud, immediately after first praising Edwards on predestination, whether it was wise to insist upon the distinctions that Edwards labored too intensely to make. Then he reminded his students that the key thing about Edwards was the "safety" rather than the "truth" of his position (295). By this distinction, Chalmers meant that he did not want young ministers to become so caught up in metaphysical reasoning that they lost the capacity for action. "We do not care so much for your being strict and sturdy necessitarians, as for you being sound and Scriptural and withal practical divines, not stiffened and frozen out of all your activities, and more especially such as belong to the duties of your vocation, by the withering influence of any dogma whatever" (295).

Thus, as much as he revered Edwards, Chalmers was more concerned that the next generation of Scottish ministers be the right kind of Christian activists than that they be the right kind of precise theologians.[24] Chalmers' general concerns certainly resonated with Edwards's general concerns, but Chalmers manifested a different spirit by being willing to subordinate the details of theological truth to the imperatives of evangelical action.

We have in Lord Kames, Andrew Fuller, William Godwin, and Thomas Chalmers a singular set of testimonies to the genius of Edwards's *Freedom of the Will*. More than any Americans, these four Britons were drawn to, overwhelmed by, or confirmed in varieties of moral necessitarianism by their exposure to

Edwards's book. Fuller, Godwin, and Chalmers expressed their gratitude frankly and fully for the persuasive clarity of his reasoning, and Lord Kames paid a different kind of compliment by, in effect, stealing Edwards's arguments.

Why the specifics of Edwards's arguments on the will exerted a greater direct influence in Britain than in America poses an intriguing historical puzzle. To solve it, context might be the answer. At least after about 1755, the din in America for liberty, and for liberty construed as the essential prerequisite for virtue, was so insistent that any necessitarian scheme, however expertly argued, stood almost no chance at all.[25] Because in Britain beliefs about human functioning moved only slowly away from the assumptions of traditional European Christendom, while Americans gave up those assumptions with revolutionary abandon, the appeal of Edwards's arguments may have been heard more easily at a distance than close at hand.

Yet the way in which Britons put Edwards to work for their own purposes poses another puzzle. The conclusions that Edwards considered the logical outcomes of his reasoning were not necessarily embraced by these British admirers of his work. Only Andrew Fuller joined Edwards in thinking that the correct understanding of morality, necessity, and freedom directly confirmed a modern version of high Calvinism. And Fuller was a Baptist and Dissenter whom Edwards could never have admitted into the membership of his Northampton or Stockbridge churches. To Thomas Chalmers, Edwards was right on the big points, but despite his high praise for Edwards, Chalmers wanted his students to admire rather than to emulate Edwards. Kames and Godwin, who as polar opposites in their conceptions of society and politics would have seen eye to eye with each other on very little, nonetheless agreed with respect to Edwards. These two thought Edwards was brilliant on the will but irrelevant on everything else.

To Edwards, solid logic as well as divine revelation affirmed that people were far better off trusting in the freedom of God than in their own freedom. It is a mark of his spiritual profundity that Edwards so long influenced Americans who mostly thought that the logic of his *Freedom of the Will* contradicted divine revelation. It was a mark of the radical intellectual dislocation of the age that four such supremely talented Britons as Kames, Fuller, Godwin, and Chalmers could agree with Edwards's view of the human will, but not be carried by that agreement to parse the world as it was parsed by Edwards's painstakingly theocentric mind.

NOTES

1. On Dana's work, see especially Allen C. Guelzo, *Edwards on the Will: A Century of American Theological Debate* (Middletown, Conn.: Wesleyan University

Press, 1989), 155–64. Finney, *Lectures on Systematic Theology*, ed. J. H. Fairchild (New York: George H. Doran, n. d. [orig. 1878]), 323.

2. Oliver Wendell Holmes, "Jonathan Edwards" (1880), in *Papers from an Old Volume of Life*, in *The Works of Oliver Wendell Holmes*, 13 vols. (Boston: Houghton, Mifflin, 1892), 8:395.

3. *Mark Twain's Letters*, ed. A. B. Paine, 2 vols. (New York, 1917), 2:719–20, as quoted in Henry F. May, "Jonathan Edwards and America," in *Jonathan Edwards and the American Experience*, ed. Nathan O. Hatch and Harry S. Stout (New York: Oxford University Press, 1988), 23.

4. A distinguished line of scholars, though differing among themselves in evaluations of the later history, have treated that history superbly. It includes Frank Hugh Foster, *A Genetic History of the New England Theology* (Chicago: University of Chicago Press, 1907); Joseph Haroutunian, *Piety Versus Moralism: The Passing of the New England Theology* (New York: Henry Holt, 1932); Bruce Kuklick, *Churchmen and Philosophers: From Jonathan Edwards to John Dewey* (New Haven: Yale University Press, 1985); James Hoopes, *Consciousness in New England: From Puritanism and Ideas to Psychoanalysis and Semiotic* (Baltimore: Johns Hopkins University Press, 1989); Guelzo, *Edwards on the Will*; and Douglas A. Sweeney, *Nathaniel Taylor, New Haven Theology, and the Legacy of Jonathan Edwards* (New York: Oxford University Press, 2003).

5. I have used the superbly edited version prepared by Paul Ramsey, in *WJE* 1. Page numbers in the text are to this edition.

6. I have been oriented to Kames by Richard B. Sher, *Church and University in the Scottish Enlightenment: The Moderate Literati of Edinburgh* (Princeton: Princeton University Press, 1985); William C. Lehmann, *Henry Home, Lord Kames, and the Scottish Enlightenment: A Study in National Character and in the History of Ideas* (The Hague: Martinus Nijhoff, 1971); and Elmer Sprague, "Henry Home," *The Encyclopedia of Philosophy*, ed. Paul Edwards, 8 vols. (New York: Macmillan, 1967), 4:60–61.

7. George F. B. Barker, "Henry Home," *Dictionary of National Biography*, 9:1127.

8. Henry Home, Lord Kames, *Essays on the Principles of Morality and Natural Religion* (Edinburgh, 1751). Page references in the text are to this edition.

9. The Kames-Edwards relationship is admirably covered in *WJE* 1:443–70.

10. *WJE* 1:446.

11. *WJE* 1:468–69.

12. For orientation to Fuller, I have relied on Arthur Henry Kirkby, "The Theology of Andrew Fuller and its Relation to Calvinism" (Ph.D. diss., University of Edinburgh, 1956); Phil Roberts, "Andrew Fuller," in *Theologians of the Baptist Tradition*, ed. Timothy George and David S. Dockery (Nashville: Broadman & Holman, 2001), 34–51; M. A. G. Haykin, "Andrew Fuller," in *Biographical Dictionary of Evangelicals*, ed. Timothy Larsen (Downers Grove, Ill.: InterVarsity Press, 2003), 241–44; and much appreciated personal tutoring from David Bebbington.

13. E. F. Clipsham, "Andrew Fuller," in *Dictionary of Evangelical Biography*, ed. Donald M. Lewis, 2 vols. (Oxford: Blackwell, 1995), 1:414.

14. Quoted in Michael R. Watts, *The Dissenters*, vol. 1: *From the Reformation to the French Revolution* (London: Oxford University Press, 1978), 457. The pamphlet was entitled *A Modern Question Modestly Answered*.

15. Fuller, *The Gospel of Christ Worthy of All Acceptation* (Northampton, 1785). My thanks to Sang Hyun Lee for supplying a copy of this work. Page numbers are to this edition.

16. For a reliable recent treatment, see Timothy George, *Faithful Witness: The Life and Mission of William Carey* (Worcester, Pa.: Christian History Institute, 1998).

17. For authoritative treatment, see Brian Stanley, *The History of the Baptist Missionary Society, 1792-1992* (Edinburgh: T. & T. Clark, 1992).

18. For orientation, I have relied on Leslie Stephen, "William Godwin," *Dictionary of National Biography*, 8:64–68; D. H. Monro, "William Godwin," *Encyclopedia of Philosophy*, 3:358–62; and John P. Clark, *The Philosophical Anarchism of William Godwin* (Princeton: Princeton University Press, 1977).

19. Godwin, *An Enquiry Concerning Political Justice*, ed. Raymond A. Preston, 2 vols. (New York: Knopf, 1926). References in the text are to the first volume of this edition.

20. William Hanna, *Memoirs of the Life and Writings of Thomas Chalmers*, 2 vols. (Edinburgh, 1851), 1:14–15. Works that have shaped my interpretation of Chalmers are noted in Mark A. Noll, "Thomas Chalmers (1780–1847) in America (ca. 1830–1917)," *Church History* 66 (Dec. 1997): 762-77.

21. Quotations from Boyd Hilton, *The Age of Atonement: The Influence of Evangelicalism on Social and Economic Thought, 1785–1865* (New York: Oxford University Press, 1988), 55. On the Oxford D. C. L., Owen Chadwick, "Chalmers and the State," in *The Practical and the Pious: Essays on Thomas Chalmers (1780–1847)*, ed. A. C. Cheyne (Edinburgh: St. Andrews Press, 1985), 68.

22. Chalmers to D. Stebbins, 30 May 1844, in *A Selection from the Correspondence of the Late Thomas Chalmers*, ed. William Hanna (Edinburgh, 1853), 443–44.

23. Chalmers, *Institutes of Theology*, 2 vols., in *Posthumous Works of the Rev. Thomas Chalmers* (vols. 7 and 8 of 9), ed. William Hanna (Edinburgh: Thomas Constable, 1849). Page references are to volume 2.

24. In this interpretation, I am following John Roxborogh, "Thomas Chalmers," *Biographical Dictionary of Evangelicals*, 138–41.

25. This, at least, is the argument spelled out in Mark A. Noll, *America's God, from Jonathan Edwards to Abraham Lincoln* (New York: Oxford University Press, 2002).

Jonathan Edwards and the Politics of Sex in Eighteenth-Century Northampton

Ava Chamberlain

Wright State University

Prior to the communion controversy of 1748–1750 that resulted in Jonathan Edwards's dismission, the two most salient sources of conflict in Northampton were money and sex. Edwards and his congregation bickered and fought with each another, first, over his desire to receive a fixed salary and, second, over his efforts to police the boundary separating licit from illicit sex. In a series of lectures preached in June 1748, Edwards himself emphasizes the latter. "[O]ur way of managing church discipline," he observes, "has been the greatest wound." "No one thing has been the occasion of so many and great wounds [and so much] contention," leading the people to quarrel "with their minister" and quarrel "one with another." It has been, he concludes, "worse than all the scandals."[1]

Samuel Hopkins agreed with this assessment when he identified as first in the chain of events leading to Edwards's dismissal from his Northampton pastorate his censuring several young men in his congregation for reading illicit books and harassing young women. Scholars have followed Hopkins's lead in identifying the so-called "bad book affair" as the circumstance that "seemed in a great Measure to put an end to Mr. Edwards's Usefulness in Northampton," but in addition to this minor infraction, which occurred in 1744, Edwards initiated disciplinary action for at least three more-serious sex-related offenses during this time period.[2] The church censured Samuel Danks in 1743, Thomas Wait in 1747, and Elisha Hawley in 1748, each for their persistent refusal to confess to a charge of fornication and for their overt contempt for the authority of the church.[3] The last and best documented of these controversial fornication cases occurred in closest proximity to the crisis that occasioned Edwards's dismissal. It reveals, perhaps more clearly than the bad book affair, why sex had become a source of such conflict in eighteenth-century New

England. It also exposes more directly the link between Edwards's efforts to enforce moral discipline in his congregation and his decision to close communion to the visibly unregenerate.

Sometime in the fall or winter of 1746 Elisha Hawley, the twenty-year-old son of one of Northampton's most prominent residents, and a young unmarried woman named Martha Root, committed what according to Massachusetts law was a crime and according to Congregational church rule was a sin.[4] They had sex, probably on more than one occasion. Recent studies of sexual behavior in the colonial period have shown that even in New England this small act of rebellion was not uncommon. Puritans were passionate lovers, and with some frequency they allowed these passions to express themselves not only within but also without the marriage bed. County court records reveal that bastardy rates steadily grew in the colonial period, with bridal pregnancies rising from a low of 8.1% in the seventeenth century to a high of 33% in the second half of the eighteenth century.[5] Martha and Elisha's sexual escapades reflect this demographic trend, which was viewed by both magistrates and ministers alike as evidence of the increasing immorality of the younger generation.

For couples like Elisha and Martha, the choice to have sex without the sanction of marriage certainly expressed their disregard for the dominant moral value structure, but they, and the many other couples like them, were probably not simply flaunting the rules. Elisha may have been a cad, who sought sexual pleasure as an end in itself, and Martha may have been a scheming spinster, who used sex to ensnare one of the town's most eligible bachelors. More likely, however, their choice reflected their acceptance of an alternate value structure, which flourished in English popular culture and was transported to New England by the colonists. As Richard Godbeer has persuasively demonstrated, there was no consensus in England or the colonies on what constituted the boundary between licit and illicit sex. The law defined this boundary to be marriage, and this definition was supported not only by social elites, such as magistrates and clergy, but also by a majority of the population. It competed, however, with an alternate view that identified commitment—expressed either publicly in the formal declaration of banns or privately in promises to marry and professions of love—as the boundary. And many "who saw themselves as devout and respectable members of the community combined principles handed down to them from the pulpit with beliefs that diverged from official teaching."[6]

Like many couples who put the cart before the horse, as it were, Martha got pregnant, but unlike most couples Martha and Elisha did not marry. The high rate of bridal pregnancies in this period, that is, women who gave birth within seven months of marriage, indicates most couples honored the commitment they believed justified their premarital sexual activity. But Martha and Elisha, if they had made such a commitment, failed to fulfill it.[7] The most likely impediment to their marriage was Elisha's mother, Rebekah Hawley.[8] As Solomon Stoddard's daughter, Rebekah belonged to one of the most prominent families in the town oligarchy. Unlike her five sisters Rebekah did not marry a minister, but she made a good match at the relatively late age of thirty-six with the forty-year-old bachelor and wealthy businessman, Joseph Hawley.[9] The marriage, however, came to a premature end in 1735 when Hawley slit his throat in despair "about the state of his soul."[10] In colonial Massachusetts suicide was considered a heinous crime and a damnable sin, and although the inquest judged Hawley delirious or *non compos mentis* and so not liable, either criminally or spiritually, for his act, certainly for Rebekah and her two young sons the manner of her husband's death was not only a tragedy but a humiliation.

Rebekah was 49 at the time of her husband's suicide. She did not remarry, but chose instead to retain control of the family's wealth, property, and businesses. And she proved to be a skilled businesswoman, quickly acquiring a reputation for making the best butter and cheese in the valley.[11] According to Mary Beth Norton, wealthy widows occupied an anomalous place in colonial society. Neither daughter nor wife, a widow stepped outside accepted gender roles when she took "her dead husband's place at the head of the family." And widows like Rebekah Hawley, who inherited from their dead husbands a significant estate, acquired with their wealth the individual autonomy and community power generally reserved only for men. Having no male superior within their own families to control them and being socially superior to all lower status men, wealthy widows like Rebekah Hawley occupied liminal positions in colonial society and so could cause great problems. As Norton notes, "the mere presence of high-ranking widows in their communities could . . . confront officials and other colonists with complex conceptual issues. And if high-status widows openly challenged the structure of authority, the problems became even more pressing."[12]

It is unlikely that much happened in the Hawley household without Rebekah's knowledge and approval. And in such an important matter as her two sons' marriages, evidence suggests she kept a tight reign. When her older son, Joseph the third, chose Mercy Lyman, she opposed the match, declaring the girl "had a face like a toasting-iron." But Mercy was the daughter of one of the town's most prominent residents, and not pregnant, and after a long courtship they were married in November 1752. Her younger son, Elisha, chafed even more strenuously under his mother's authority. Even before his affair with Martha Root, she ended his courtship of an apparently unsuitable girl by following him one night to the girl's home, calling him out, and escorting him home.[13] So if Rebekah had blessed the match, it is probable Elisha and Martha would have married. It was a suitable match. She was a church member like Elisha, and although the Roots were not the Hawley's social equals they occupied only a slightly inferior position on the social hierarchy.[14] But the couple did not marry; instead, Elisha was commissioned a lieutenant in the colonial militia by his uncle, Col. John Stoddard, and sent in March 1747, when Martha was only a few months pregnant, to Ft. Massachusetts, a dangerous outpost on the western frontier, to wait out the scandal.[15]

We cannot know why, finally, Rebekah Hawley did not encourage or even force her son to marry his pregnant lover—really the most respectable course for two elite church members. But informing this choice was surely the understanding that refusal would not significantly damage the family's social standing. In the first century of settlement, Massachusetts laws treated fornication as a serious offence; a 1642 statute stipulated that the appropriate punishment for a man convicted of fornication with a single woman was "Marriage, or Fine, or Corporal punishment, or all, or any of these" at the court's discretion. In 1665, disenfranchisement was added to this list of possible punishments.[16] But in practice men routinely confessed their crime and married their pregnant lovers, which allowed judges to impose more lenient sentences. When men refused to confess, however, this law—and others like it proscribing various forms of private sexual conduct—contained an inherent inequality.

In colonial courts standards of proof were high, especially in capital cases, but also for other criminal offenses. Full conviction could not be obtained on the basis of circumstantial evidence alone, but required either a confession or the testimony of two reliable eyewitnesses. In fornication cases, two witnesses were rarely available, making prosecution possible only for a small percentage of the total number of actual violations. Single pregnant women were routinely presented for fornication because their bodies visibly displayed their guilt. Men who refused to confess, however, could not be convicted on their pregnant lover's testimony alone. To compensate for this inequity, and to relieve local communities of the burden of supporting bastards born to single indigent women, a new statute was adopted in 1668 stipulating that a man could be held liable for a bastard child's maintenance if the mother consistently identified him as the father, especially during the labor of childbirth.[17]

Martha Root gave birth to twin girls. One, named Esther, died on 14 Sept. 1747, while the other lived.[18] Martha identified Elisha Hawley as the father probably well before what was no doubt a difficult delivery. But despite this birth and declaration, only Martha faced a criminal fornication charge. She appeared at the November 1747 sitting of the Hampshire County Court of General Sessions, "Confess'd herself Guilty of the Crime of Fornication," and was "ordered to pay a fine of 25 [shillings] . . . and costs."[19] She did not name Elisha the father in court, an act necessary to initiate criminal child support proceedings. Like many other pregnant single women in the eighteenth century, she was silent in court, and Elisha was absent.[20] She assumed the whole guilt for their criminal action. Perhaps she threatened to name Elisha publicly to force a settlement, a tactic sometimes used by women abandoned pregnant by their lovers, for unrecorded negotiations between the two families did eventually produce a result. In May 1748 Martha signed an agreement accepting "One Hundred and fifty five pounds Old Ten^r in full Satisfaction for and towards ye Support and maintenance of a Bastard Child born of my Body Now living."[21]

Elisha escaped prosecution for fornication not because the court considered him an exception or judged him by a different standard. His ability to avoid criminal liability reflected a more general transformation of the legal system occurring throughout New England in the eighteenth century. The Anglicization of court procedures and the growth of the legal profession made for a more litigious society, while an increasingly complex economy filled the courts' dockets with financial disputes. Less concerned with moral regulation, judges became more concerned with standards of evidence. As Cornelia Hughes Dayton has shown, men commonly refused to confess their crimes, preferring instead to hire a lawyer to contest the charges or to formulate grounds for an appeal. Most often, men contested fornication charges by portraying themselves as the innocent victims of unscrupulous women's lies and schemes. Judges, who had once tried to "implement a single standard" of conduct for both men and women, a standard that held "that godly behavior should be the measure for *all* inhabitants" and that punished both men and women equally for their sexual and moral transgressions, became increasingly skeptical of a woman's word.[22] Without this foundation, criminal prosecutions of men for fornication virtually disappeared from the courts, so that by the mid-eighteenth century a double standard had emerged that shielded male impunity with women's sole culpability. As Ulrich notes, "fornication had become a woman's crime."[23]

Despite this de facto decriminalization of fornication for men, families remained committed to the regulation of young people's sexual behavior. Evidence suggests Rebekah Hawley took seriously her role as the moral governor of her family. But she, like a growing number of her contemporaries, apparently believed private and informal means of regulation were preferable to a public courtroom. As Dayton notes, the transformation of the legal system was facilitated by a reconfiguration of the boundary separating public from private space, which increasingly protected middle class and elite families like the Hawley's from "public scrutiny, humiliation, and penalty," and allowed them to claim "the right to keep private the premarital sexual lapses of their young people."[24] And although the Hawleys surely were not successful in keeping Elisha's indiscretion secret—such newsworthy gossip would have quickly spread throughout the town—they did keep it private. Joseph Hawley, Elisha's brother and a young lawyer eager to make a reputation for himself, negotiated privately the settlement with Martha for the child's maintenance. A local justice of the peace apparently arbitrated this settlement, but no trace remains in the court documents.[25] Only Martha's crime and only Martha's confession are visible in the public records.[26]

When Martha accepted the Hawley's settlement offer, the court's interest in this routine fornication case came to an end. In the first century of settlement, the judicial system in Massachusetts cooperated with the churches in policing the moral and sexual behavior of the population. By the mid-eighteenth century, however, the court's interests had begun to diverge from those of the churches. In fornication cases the dominant legal concern was no longer moral but economic. By this time proceedings against "reputed" fathers, either through civil child maintenance suits or privately arbitrated financial settlements, had become "a way of allocating the costs of illegitimacy," thereby protecting town governments from the burden of providing for indigent mothers and their bastard children.[27] The £155 payment to Martha Root achieved this end, but the matter did not end there. Although the Hampshire County Court was getting out of the business of moral regulation, the Northampton Congregational church remained—like many evangelical churches at the time—strongly committed to it.

A letter written by Joseph Hawley to his brother Elisha on 23 December 1748, more than six months after the private settlement, indicates the Northampton church had disciplined Elisha, apparently excommunicating him for his persistent refusal not only to confess his sin but to marry Martha.[28] The church's demands clearly display how far Elisha Hawley's rights as a legal subject had diverged from his responsibilities as a church member. Men had once routinely confessed their sin and married their pregnant lovers, and if they did not the courts convicted and punished equally both the man and the woman, sometimes even enjoining an errant couple to marry, as the law allowed. But by the time Elisha and Martha violated the colony's fornication law, a double standard had emerged that allowed men to escape legal responsibility for their actions. Edwards objected to this new double standard, which brought the colony's ecclesiastical establishment into conflict with its legal system. He, like other evangelical pastors after the Awakening, "wished to return to a single standard akin to that of the seventeenth century—a standard insisting on chastity for both sexes and proper public contrition from all sinners, no matter their social rank."[29] And he was willing to use the power of his office to achieve this end.

Edwards, however, did not unilaterally impose this power upon a uniformly hostile church. As James F. Cooper has demonstrated, a dichotomous model of clergy-laity conflict does not adequately represent Congregational church government in colonial New England. Well into the eighteenth century, he observes, "the right of lay consent continued to prevent ministers or clerical associations from forcing their wills upon reluctant congregations."[30] When dissention occurred over contentious matters like disciplinary cases, the laity were often divided among themselves, with one faction supporting and another opposing the minister's position. Edwards's efforts at social control angered many of his parishioners, but he could not have initiated disciplinary action against Samuel Danks in 1743, the bad book boys in 1744, Thomas Wait in 1747, or Elisha Hawley in 1748, without the support of a church majority. During the proceedings against Elisha Hawley the church even formed, at Edwards's urging, a fifteen-member disciplinary committee charged "to assist the Pastor in taking care of the order and Purity of the Church, and in the Trial and Judgment of sin."[31] Formed of the town's leading men, a majority of the members of this committee must have supported Elisha's excommunication, although the vote surely was not unanimous, for Joseph Hawley himself had been named to the committee, and he may have been joined in his opposition by another member, named Eleazar King.

In March 1731, not long after Edwards became full pastor of the church in Northampton, Hannah Graves of Hatfield was presented for fornication in Hampshire County Court, and in her confession she named Eleazar King the father of her child. King was a member of Edwards's congregation, but he pled not guilty to the charge and was convicted and ordered by the court to pay Hannah four shillings a-week maintenance.[32] Edwards, however, was uncertain how to proceed, for at a meeting of the Hampshire County Ministerial Association in October 1731 he apparently asked his colleagues to address three questions related to his church's disposition of the King case. At this time the ministers agreed that the scripture rules (Ex. 22:16–17; Deut. 22:28–29) requiring a man to marry a virgin who he has humbled are "moral" rules, and so "of perpetual obligation"; that a man who confesses to the sin of fornication cannot be judged truly repentant by his church so long as he refuses to marry; and that these rules applied to Eleazar King. Not long after this meeting King married Hannah Graves, presumably at the insistence of Edwards and the church.[33]

Nearly twenty years later, Edwards proceeded against Elisha Hawley as he had Eleazar King. The circumstances were almost identical, but the times had changed. Appealing the church's judgment to a council of ministers, Joseph Hawley employed in the ecclesiastical context the legal maneuvering that had proved unnecessary for him to use in the courtroom. Convening in the Northampton meetinghouse on 29 June 1749, the council heard arguments from both sides. Hawley apparently argued that the scripture rules requiring a man to marry a virgin who he had humbled did not apply in this case because Martha Root had been "of a grossly lascivious character" before her acquaintance with his brother, and had been the aggressor, enticing him into the entanglement.[34] By his own later admission, Hawley exaggerated the evidence against Martha, but his arguments were evidently successful at the time.[35] Although the council of ministers judged Elisha guilty of fornication and believed he was "bound in conscience" to marry Martha—judgments the court had been unwilling to make—they ruled it not his "duty" to marry her. The church should receive him back into their fellowship "upon his making a penitent confession of the sin of fornication," and, unlike Eleazar King, Elisha's unwillingness to marry Martha should not impugn the sincerity of this confession.[36]

In the 1740s Edwards used his church's power to discipline its members to fill the void created as the Massachusetts legal system disengaged itself from moral regulation. Gender roles were changing, and Edwards objected not to the new image of woman, which he promoted in some of his most popular writings, but to the new construct of masculinity. In the Puritan past, manliness had meant a robust profession of faith, a sincere repentance for sin, and a willingness to accept responsibility.[37] If the courts would no longer enforce this image, Edwards at least could act to keep his congregation pure. But even as he tried to force Elisha Hawley to live like a real Christian man, Edwards revealed to his congregation a new more radical strategy to achieve the same end. He closed communion to all but the visibly regenerate.

The communion controversy erupted during the final months of the Elisha Hawley affair. According to Edwards's *Narrative of the Communion Controversy*, in December 1748, the same month Joseph Hawley informed his brother of the church's action against him, "a young man who was about to be married came and offered to come into the church." When Edwards responded to this new applicant, the first in Northampton since 1744, that he could not "come into the church without a profession of godliness," Edwards's change of mind became common knowledge in the town. He explained his position to the church the following February, and by June—the month the council of ministers determined that Elisha was not obligated to marry Martha—he had finished the manuscript of *An Humble Inquiry* and sent it to Boston for publication.[38] In this final conflict, furthermore, many of the same figures who had blocked Edwards's action against Elisha Hawley reemerged to force him to relinquish his pastorate. Joseph Hawley himself was a leader of the opposition and was chosen to argue the case for dismissal before the council that would ultimately decide Edwards's fate. And when Edwards appeared before this council, in June 1750, he took substantially the same position he had maintained against Joseph Hawley the prior June when a council was called to hear Elisha Hawley's appeal.

Before this council Edwards argued, as he had in *An Humble Inquiry*, that only those who make a sincere profession of godliness and are judged by the church to be visibly gracious persons are qualified for communion. None, he writes, "ought to be admitted to the communion and privileges of membership in the visible church of Christ in complete standing, but such as are in profession, and in the eye of the church's Christian judgment, godly or gracious persons."[39] As he explains in *Religious Affections*, grace is made visible in two ways: first, by a sincere profession of faith and, second, by Christian practice, that is, "a practice, which is universally conformed to, and directed by Christian rules."[40] And the latter is the means by which the sincerity of the profession is judged, for "we are by their fruits to know," Edwards insists, "whether they be what they profess themselves to be."[41]

In taking this position, Edwards applied to new church members the same condition he had used to readmit scandalous members to church fellowship. As he notes in *An Humble Inquiry*, "when a delinquent has been convicted of scandal, 'tis repentance in some respect sincere . . . that is the proper foundation of a right of him to offer himself for forgiveness and restoration."[42] Because Elisha Hawley had failed to sincerely repent his sin he should remain under church censure. And any act of repentance, Edwards argued to the council entertaining his appeal, should not be judged sincere as long as he and Martha remained unwed. Citing the same texts the Hampshire County Ministerial Association had applied to the case of Eleazar King, he insists that the scripture rules "relating to the obligation of a man to marry a virgin that he hath humbled" are "moral" rules and so "of perpetual obligation." Hawley's "refusing to marry a woman with whom he has committed fornication" is, therefore, a sin "heinous enough to deserve church censure."[43] Until he signifies true humiliation for these sins, and visibly displays his inner grace through his outward acts, he should not come to the Lord's Supper. To readmit him on easier terms would be to admit a hypocrite.

In the years following the Awakening, as David Hall notes, "Edwards came to think of most of his congregation as hypocrites."[44] To address this problem, he withdrew access to the sacraments from those church members who professed their counterfeit faith by willfully violating the church covenant. He also refused to admit to the sacraments those persons who did not in word and deed visibly display their godliness. Like many of his Puritan forbearers,

Edwards considered marriage to be a "type of the union between Christ and the church."[45] This typological relation clearly illustrates the unified strategy underlying his two-pronged attack on hypocrisy. Elisha Hawley was morally obligated to marry Martha, he argued, for it is "fit and suitable" for couples who have "united and become one flesh" to be legally joined. They are "one flesh *de jure*, or in obligation," he writes, and so it is unsuitable for them "to see one another from time to time and be seen by others remaining separate, not united as one flesh."[46] Similarly, it was unsuitable for church members, who are *in foro ecclesiae* espoused to Christ as their heavenly bridegroom, to be in reality separate from him. The Lord's Supper, Edwards argues in *An Humble Inquiry,* is a sign of that "which is spiritually transacted between Christ and his spouse in the covenant that unites them." When a person takes the bread and wine, it "is as much a professing to accept of Christ . . . as a woman's taking a ring of the bridegroom in her marriage is a profession and seal of her taking him for her husband."[47] Hypocrites, who join the church without an experience of saving grace, wear the ring but have not consummated the marriage. Fornicators consummate their union but do not wear the ring. In both cases the offending parties are engaged in a fraudulent marriage. The bride is either legally separate from him to whom she is actually joined in physical union or spiritually separate from him to whom she is visibly joined in gracious union. Edwards objected to this gap between appearance and reality, but in neither case could he sustain within his church a unity the wider society was no longer willing to support.

NOTES

1. Sermon on Deut. 1:13–18 (June 1748), L. 21r.

2. Samuel Hopkins, *The Life and Character of the Late Reverend Mr. Jonathan Edwards*, (Boston, 1765), 55.

3. The excommunication of Samuel Danks is in the records of the First Church of Northampton (First Churches of Northampton Archive); for the action against Thomas Wait, see Thomas Wait to JE, 9 March 1746/7 (in Sermon on Matt. 12:41 [May 1747] and Titus 3:2 [22 May 1747]), and JE to Robert Breck, 7 April 1747 (*WJE* 16:221–22); the materials documenting the Elisha Hawley fornication case are located in the Hawley Papers, New York Public Library, and the Jonathan Edwards Papers, Trask Library, Andover Newton Theological School, Newton Centre, Massachusetts.

4. One of Martha's twin girls died on 14 Sept. 1747. If this infant died not long after birth, conception would have taken place sometime the prior fall or winter (See below, n. 18).

5. Daniel Scott Smith and Michael S. Hindus, "Premarital Pregnancy in America, 1640–1971: An Overview and Interpretation," *Journal of Interdisciplinary History* 4 (Spring 1975): 561.

6. Richard Godbeer, *Sexual Revolution in Early America* (Baltimore: Johns Hopkins Univ. Press, 2002), 116.

7. Joseph Hawley himself suspected that Elisha may have privately committed himself to marry Martha, for he advised his brother: "As to Matrimy I would Do what I knew was right in Conscience and before God, if there was anything [that I] knew of, that was particularly binding that Nobody else knew of" (Joseph Hawley to Elisha Hawley, 23 December 1748 [Hawley Papers]).

8. Joseph Hawley reports in a letter to his brother that Martha and her family also objected to the marriage, stating that "the woman declares against asking you, in ye form ye Church talk of, as also her father and mother" (Joseph Hawley to Elisha Hawley, 23 Dec. 1748 [Hawley Papers]). But this statement, if true, reflects Martha's sentiments more than a year after the twins were born and six months after the settlement agreement was made and does not indicate that she never desired to marry Elisha.

9. James Russell Trumbull, "History of Northampton, vol. 3, Northampton Genealogies," Forbes Library, Northampton, typescript, 213.

10. *WJE* 4:206.

11. James Russell Trumbull, *History of Northampton*, 2 vols. (Northampton: Gazette, 1902), 2:82.

12. Mary Beth Norton, *Founding Mothers and Fathers: Gendered Power and the Forming of American Society* (1996; New York: Vintage Books, 1997), 139–40.

13. E. Francis Brown, *Joseph Hawley: Colonial Radical* (New York: AMS Press, 1966), 73, 71; Trumbull, *History of Northampton*, 2:82.

14. The 1749 Northampton census valued Hezekiah Root's estate at £112 and Elisha Hawley's at £117 (Trumbull, *History of Northampton*, 2:188, 185). See also Kathryn Kish Sklar, "'To Use Her as His Wife: An Extraordinary Paternity Suit in the 1740s," *Women and Power in American History: Volume I to 1880*, 2nd ed., ed. Kathryn Kish Sklar and Thomas Dublin (Upper Saddle River, N.J.: Prentice Hall, 2002), 78–79.

15. Brown, *Joseph Hawley*, 70.

16. *The General Laws and Liberties of Massachusetts* (Cambridge 1672), 54–55; in *The Colonial Laws of Massachusetts, Reprinted from the Edition of 1672* (Boston, 1890).

17. *General Laws and Liberties*, 55.

18. Perhaps because they were illegitimate, Northampton Town Hall Records contain no record of the birth of Martha Hawley's twin girls, but they do state that on 14 Sept. 1747 "Esther Root Daught of Martha Root died, it being one of her twins" (Births, Deaths and Marriages, 1654–1853 [Forbes Library]).

19. Court of General Sessions of the Peace, 11 Nov. 1747, (Hampshire County, Court Records, 1677–1859 [Forbes Library]).

20. See Cornelia Hughes Dayton, *Women Before the Bar: Gender, Law, and Society in Connecticut, 1639–1789* (Chapel Hill: University of North Carolina Press, 1995), 195.

21. Settlement Agreement, Hawley Papers.

22. Dayton, *Women Before the Bar*, 31, 60, and *passim*.

23. Laurel Thatcher Ulrich, *A Midwife's Tale: The Life of Martha Ballard, Based on Her Diary, 1785–1812* (New York: Knopf, 1990), 148.

24. Dayton, *Women Before the Bar*, 12, 215.

25. In February 1748 Joseph Hawley reported to his brother, "As to yr Affair yt I was to manage I tried for an agreement before Court, they insisted on £150. down which I thought was too much, Considering what risque there is of ye Chds life . . . (Joseph Hawley to Elisha Hawley, 16 Feb. 1747/48, [Hawley Papers]). In May they eventually settled for five pounds more than this initial offer.

26. At the 17 May 1748 session of the Hampshire County Court "Elisha Hawley of Northampton was discharg'd from his recognizance by which he stood bound to appear at this Court," but the circumstances requiring this recognizance bond are not identified (Hampshire County, Court Records, 1677–1859 [Forbes Library]).

27. Hendrik Hartog, "The Public Law of a County Court: Judicial Government in Eighteenth Century Massachusetts," *American Journal of Legal History* 20 (Oct. 1976): 301.

28. Joseph Hawley to Elisha Hawley, 23 Dec. 1748 (Hawley Papers).

29. Dayton, *Women Before the Bar*, 208.

30. James F. Cooper, *Tenacious of Their Liberties: The Congregationalists in Colonial Massachusetts* (New York: Oxford Univ. Press, 1999), 180.

31. This entry is dated 26 July 1748; First Church Records, vols. 1 and 3, 1661–1924, Northampton, Massachusetts (First Churches of Northampton Archive).

32. Court of General Sessions, 2 March 1731 (Forbes Library).

33. Hampshire Association of Ministers A (1) Records, 1731–1747, Forbes Library, Northampton, Massachusetts; Trumbull, "History of Northampton, vol. 3, Northampton Genealogies," 266.

34. These statements are taken from JE's "Notes for a Council Meeting," June 1749 (Trask Library), and cannot be directly attributed to Joseph Hawley.

35. Joseph Hawley to Martha Root, 8 August 1750. Hawley Papers.

36. Decision of a Council of Ministers, 29 June 1749, Hawley Papers.

37. See Dayton, *Women Before the Bar*, 226–27.

38. *WJE* 12:508, 507, 62, 511.

39. *WJE* 12:174.

40. *WJE* 2:383. See also *WJE* 12:189.

41. *WJE* 2:415.

42. *WJE* 12:177–78.

43. "Some Reasons, Briefly Hinted At," Trask Library.

44. *WJE* 12:84.

45. *The Works of Jonathan Edwards, 11, Typological Writings*, ed. Wallace E. Anderson and Mason I. Lowance (New Haven: Yale Univ. Press, 1993), 53.

46. "Some Reasons, Briefly Hinted At," Trask Library.

47. *Works, 12*, 257.

Forgiveness and the Party of Humanity in Jonathan Edwards's World

Mark Valeri

Union Theological Seminary of Virginia

In September 1740, Jonathan Edwards preached in the village of Longmeadow, Massachusetts, in response to one of the more publicized events in the history of New England. His cousin Eunice had come to see her family, especially her brother, pastor Stephen Williams, after some thirty-six years living among Catholic, French-allied Indians near Montreal. Captured in the infamous raid on the town of Deerfield, she spoke no English and had a Mohawk husband and children. She already was a celebrity of sorts: the subject of a best-selling account by her father and of much speculation about her conversion to Catholicism. As became clear, she also had no intention of staying in New England. Her much-awaited return, and refusal to resettle in Massachusetts, caused anguish, even shock.[1]

Edwards was among the first to hear her during her visits to Longmeadow, and he preached a three-part sermon series on the occasion. His subject was "keeping God's commands under trials." The word trial, as he used it, had two meanings: trial as a pain to be endured, trial as a discovery of one's guilt or innocence. The first two sermons addressed the temptations to betray God under physical pressure. Here his cousin Eunice came into view. Yet Edwards spent the last sermon addressing New Englanders who did not suffer Indian captivity, the family members and neighbors of Eunice Williams. They too, Edwards averred, were under trial as to whether they would keep God's commands. In their case, the command at issue was this: "Christ has forbidden us to revenge ourselves for injuries." Indeed, Christ had commanded them to "forgive" their enemies.

Edwards admonished English neighbor to forgive offending neighbor, to be sure; but his words hardly could have been heard apart from common sentiments to avenge Mohawk atrocities, the capture and conversion to Catholicism of Eunice, and her alienation from her English family. If "you have a fair opportunity in your hands to avenge yourself," to "humble" your enemy "upon his unworthy treatment of you," and "to forego the opportunity seems" merely to encourage "your enemy," then "let the consideration of what you have heard" of Christ's command stay your hand. "If you take vengeance into your own hands, God will leave it with you to manage it for yourself as you can, and may probably unexpectedly strengthen your adversary against you, and turn on his side." If Edwards's auditors heard him as I have suggested, then they must have been astonished. He claimed that God might turn out to be a patron of Eunice Williams's captors.[2]

This remarkable sermon raises the issue of Edwards's conception of forgiveness as a Christian practice. He followed the standard lexicon of Christian virtues when he urged forgiveness here and in other writings; but the way in which he explained its implications marked a transition figure between older, puritan teaching and a new evangelical ethos of the eighteenth century. Like his puritan predecessors, Edwards sometimes presented forgiveness as a means of solidarity in the local community. In this setting, it denoted a specific behavior—remitting economic debts, charitable speech about one's offenders, refraining from civil litigation—defined by the pastor and regulated through corporate supervision such as sacramental discipline.[3] Yet Edwards also pointed toward the union of individuals into a widespread moral network that reached far beyond the puritan tribe. He parsed forgiveness as an interior disposition—similar to sympathy, mercy, or compassion—that could at least be conceived of as building toward a moral community that confounded customary boundaries.

Although these definitions merit fuller exposition (not to mention some setting in social context), this paper addresses instead one of the intellectual concerns in the background of Edwards's Longmeadow sermon. His advice was part of a larger program to defend evangelical Calvinism against charges that it was irrational and morally dubious. Edwards linked the right practice and conception of forgiveness to a legitimization of revivalist piety in current moral-philosophical idioms. If his auditors would display forgiveness—would exhibit a temper to forego revenge and imagine their Indian adversaries from a divine perspective—then they would show the world that evangelical doctrine produced humane dispositions. Hostilities between English settlers and their French and Indian enemies was not merely a stage for God to enact his control over nations. It also was a stage for believers to display the social virtues of godliness.[4]

Edwards's anxiety about the moral reputation of the evangelical movement rose, in part, from what he perceived to be increased social faction in Northampton. In a January 1740 sermon—four years after a revival had swept through the town—he accused many of his people of being "content to put on a religious face in the meeting house or at private religious meetings" while continuing to "enjoy their covetousness and their pride, and their malice and envy, and their revenge." The trouble, he intimated, was the public reputation of the revivals. Critics of evangelical Protestantism, at home and abroad, demeaned it as emotion without moral substance. They claimed, according to Edwards, that evangelical fervor mimicked the base sensuality and superstitions of Catholicism, or, worse, Islam. To disprove such claims and promote revival, his people should "excel other people in a just and righteous, humble, meek, peaceable, quiet loving conversation one among another." They should be "far from all revenge and ill will, all living in love, studying to promote one another's good; and "apt to forbear with one another, apt to forgive one another." Edwards repeated this last admonition: his people should be "forgiving one another, retaining no grudge against any."[5]

Edwards had more in mind here than the public reputation of the revivals. Strife between creditors and debtors, political contests between customary oligarchies and newcomers, family quarrels, and everyday ill-will between neighbors hurt the town. As pastor, Edwards had plenty of motive to assert his authority over local affairs. Yet on this occasion, as in many others, Edwards stressed the importance of forgiveness as a sign to the world outside of the Connecticut River Valley that piety promoted the common good. If the people of Northampton showed forgiveness, they would "make" doubters "believe that there is indeed something in our profession. It will have a greater tendency to convince the world about us . . . and it will stop the mouths of them that ben't convinced."[6]

The unconvinced, in a provincial scope, were the liberal Protestant clergy of Boston; but Edwards also took great note of scoffers from London and Glasgow, the so-called party of humanity, the party of deists and skeptics, of the Third Earl of Shaftesbury and David Hume.[7] He did so in his private notebooks and international correspondence, and also in his regular preaching. Take, for example, his early 1730s sermon on Matthew 5:44, Jesus' admonition to love enemies. As in other notes and sermons, Edwards here argued that "Christian morality greatly excels the morality of the Heathen Philosophers."[8] In a technical sense, he referred to the superiority of New Testament teaching to that of the ancients. As he glossed this contrast, however, he employed the vocabulary of contemporary British writers associated with what we might call, for shorthand purposes, the Enlightenment. They argued that orthodox Christianity contradicted common sentiment, the law of nature, and reason. It was therefore inhumane. Yet, according to Edwards, their own ideas lacked compassion. "The light of nature," he maintained, "seems to suggest" that "iniquity ought to be Revenged." Because skeptics "have no knowledge of a superiour Invisible being to whom it belongs to the care" of such matters as "justice," they must conclude that it is a human duty to avenge, rather than forgive, moral offense. Christians, however, and especially Calvinists, trusted in providential power over human affairs. As private individuals they had no need to avenge wrongs, seeing that God was both capable and willing to exact vengeance. Also, being Calvinists, they could not predict the ultimate spiritual state of anyone. So, freed from the obligation to procure justice for themselves, believers could embrace the moral mandate to solidarity between all human beings.[9]

Edwards's contrast here, between a spirit of revenge that sought justice on human terms, and that of forgiveness, which relied on divine justice, can be neatly compared to the most widely read contemporary British essays on the topic. Edwards had made notes of these essays, written by the Anglican Joseph Butler and printed in Butler's *Fifteen Sermons Preached at the Rolls Chapel* (London, 1726). Butler's text was the very one used by Edwards from Matthew 5, which Butler took to concern the relationship between resentment and forgiveness. Resentment, according to Butler, was a "natural feeling" of indignation in response to injury. When it led to passions for revenge, resentment no longer served to protect the injured; it became self-defeating. It was irrational in such terms. Forgiveness was the overcoming of bad resentment in the sense of checking its expression. It was the benevolent counterweight to resentment. Originating in the emotion of benevolence, it expressed itself as a refusal to take revenge despite contrary feelings.[10]

Edwards clearly reworked such contemporary ethical analyses in his sermon on Matthew 5 as well as in his address on the return of Eunice Williams. He added to Butler a Calvinist incentive to forgive: confidence in divine justice. Butler argued that revenge was irrational. Edwards contended that it was unfaithful. It discounted the rule of God over history—the central theme to his 1738 sermon series on *The History of the Work of Redemption*.

In making this argument, Edwards did not address the political implications of forgiveness: the affairs of the British empire and the moral dynamics of war.[11] He did nonetheless take the concept beyond the local corporatism of old New England. He suggested how it might extend to a community bound together by human nature in the broadest of meanings. In the dynamic conclusion to his sermon on Matthew 5, he argued that Christian or not, all people shared the same human nature, the same moral corruption, the same potential for conversion, and the same prospects for being forgiven:

"We ought to pity and love our Enemies as companions in injury," and "notwithstanding their injuries to us love them as our fellow Creature and partaker with us of the same human nature." "We ought to have a universal benevolence to mankind," and so, "when we see them unjustly hurting us, and injuring and abusing us, we are to consider that there is just the same corruption of nature in our hearts, the same spirit of evil, of malice, which we see in them." "We" especially "ought not to hate them, for we don't know but that God has a design of mercy towards them. We ought not to hate them, for we don't know but that God has from all Eternity put his love upon them" and that "Christ shed his precious blood for them and bestowed his own Image upon them."[12]

Edwards maintained on other grounds that a specifically evangelical morality exceeded the quotient of benevolence recommended by the English and Scottish Enlightenment. Traditional doctrines such as the Atonement, he mused in his private philosophical notebooks from 1744–1752, implied a more complete version of human solidarity, and a more powerful practice of forgiveness, than those implied in rationalist ethics. He once again compared Christian teaching on forgiveness to that of moralists who defined ethics in terms of natural law. They so followed the rule of reward and punishment that they mounted only a half-hearted, highly circumscribed recommendation for forgiveness. "Natural theology," Edwards wrote, "afforded no hope of forgiveness after sinning" because "the law of nature promises" no "pardon for sin." So, contemporary ethicists such as Francis Hutcheson and other "Deists can never show, on their principles" of natural law, any release from past debts."[13]

Edwards did not put it in such terms, but he implied that the urbane detractors of revival dispensed with an ethic of forgiveness for an ethic of contractual obligation and individual right. To speculate, he might have had in mind here the congruence between the Moral Sense ethics of Shaftesbury, Hutcheson, and Hume and an increasingly harsh commercial order. These moralists emphasized benevolence, compassion, honor, and the like, which supposedly bound individuals into networks of social solidarity. Yet such sentiments, as Adam Smith would later make explicit in 1759, concerned merit and demerit, praise or retribution; they tracked the ledger of social debts. They obliged individuals to the inflexible principles of equity and justice embedded in the natural moral law. For Shaftesbury, Hutcheson, Hume, and Smith, natural morality left little room for the seemingly irrational dynamics of sacrificial atonement, faith, and pardon. This explains why forgiveness did not enter into their moral vocabulary. They never explained the concept or urged its practice in their moral treatises.[14]

Edwards turned the Moral Sense stress on benevolence—the affective sympathy of one human being with all other humans—against critics of revival by arguing that benevolence necessitated forgiveness, and that forgiveness implied the truth of divine redemption: the logic of Christ's sacrificial death and offer of justification by faith. The very doctrines derided by rationalists provided a more secure basis for benevolence than the so-called natural law. Evangelical belief could, as it turned out, reach beyond puritan provincialism to establish the bases for an expansive moral community. Edwards later would make this a central assertion of his treatise on *The Nature of True Virtue*.

Edwards well knew that purely theological assertions would not convince skeptics unless evangelical converts turned the doctrine to practice. He culminated his 1746 *Treatise on Religious Affections* with the claim that believers had affections of "forgiveness of those that have injured them, and a general benevolence to mankind," and so—here is the public act that follows—fulfilled "rules of meekness and forgiveness, rules of mercy and charity." Made visible, benevolence "is an evidence to others of their sincerity in their profession, to which all other manifestations are not worthy to be compared." Edwards did not doubt that the awakened experienced gracious affections; but he pleaded mightily with the people of Northampton, as he had with Eunice Williams' family in Longmeadow, to enact these affections as the external, social verification of their internal, regenerate, states.[15]

If, as I have suggested, Edwards's concern to legitimate the revivals prodded him to a more expansive version of forgiveness than that held by his puritan predecessors, then we might reconsider the social import of the evangelical movement for which he was a spokesman. In one sense, he took the moral axioms of puritanism and, through the language of affections, extended them beyond parochial boundaries. He contemplated a moral community of nearly universal scope. In another sense, however, we might at least question his insistence that only evangelical Calvinism provided a full motive for forgiveness. Did this not distance forgiveness from public life, relegating it to the society of believers?

Edwards, of course, would have protested this implicit critique. Better at least the possibility of a genuine forgiveness rooted in regenerate affections, he might have replied, than a complete concession to the inhumane laws of nature and the new social order.

NOTES

1. See John Demos, *TheUnredeemed Captive: A Family Story From Early America* (New York: Vintage Books, 1995); and Richard I. Melvoin, *New England Outpost: War and Society in Colonial Deerfield* (New York: Norton, 1989). The account by Eunice's father was John Williams, *The Redeemed Captive Returning to Zion* (Boston, 1707).

2. JE, Sermon on Ps. 119:56, Sept. 1740.

3. One can see this throughout JE's preaching, but especially in his sacramental sermons, when he urged communicants to examine themselves for evidences of for-

giveness toward neighbor (e.g., *WJE* 17:268–69). The localism and social specificity of puritan teaching, dominated by pastoral concerns, may be sampled in Samuel Willard, *A Compleat Body of Divinity* (Boston, 1726), 912; Cotton Mather, *Bonifacius* [1710], ed. David Levin (Cambridge, Mass.: Harvard University Press, 1966), 62; Peter Thacher, *Christ's Forgiveness Of True Christians, is a Preceptive Pattern of Christian Fraternal Forgiveness*, which was printed with the equally illustrative work by John Danforth, *Holy Striving Against Sinful Strife* (Boston, 1712). For the social function of these admonitions, see David D. Hall, *Worlds of Wonder, Days of Judgment: Popular Religious Belief in Early New England* (New York: Knopf, 1989); Hall, "Narrating Puritanism," in *New Directions in American Religious History*, ed. Harry S. Stout and D. G. Hart (New York: Oxford University Press, 1997), 51–83; and Jane Kamensky, *Governing the Tongue: The Politics of Speech in Early New England* (New York: Oxford University Press, 1997).

4. In 1740 England technically was not at war with France and her Indian allies in Canada. This period of relative peace partly explains Edwards's turn to the theme of forgiveness in this period.

5. JE, "Mercy and Not Sacrifice," in *WJE* 22:128, 133–34.

6. JE, "Mercy and Not Sacrifice," in *WJE* 22:130–131, 134. JE's appeal for New Englanders to convince Old World skeptics evokes the famous passage from John Winthrop's "Model of Christian Charitie" speech: "the eyes of all the world" are on New England.

7. The phrase "party of humanity" comes from *The Enlightenment: A Comprehensive Anthology*, ed. Peter Gay (New York: Simon & Schuster, 1973), 679. Ample evidence is provided in the "Miscellanies" and in the secondary literature of JE's engagement with Shaftesbury, Hume, Hutchinson, et. al.: see, e.g., Norman Fiering, *Jonathan Edwards's Moral Thought*; Gerald McDermott, *Jonathan Edwards Confronts the Gods*.

8. JE, Sermon on Matt. 5:44, n.d. (early 1730s).

9. JE, Sermon on Matt. 5:44, n.d. (early 1730s).

10. Butler, *Fifteen Sermons*, quoted in Paul A. Newberry, "Joseph Butler on Forgiveness: A Presupposed Theory of Emotion," *Journal of the History of Ideas* 62 (2001): 233–244, 236. I have used Joseph Butler, *Fifteen Sermons . . . to Which Are Added, Six Sermons* (London, 1836), esp. 85–89.

11. When Anglo-French hostilities heated up again during the late 1740s, JE supported the British war effort. See, for JE and the colonial wars, Marsden, *Jonathan Edwards*, 306–19.

12. JE, Sermon on Matt. 5:44. For further discussion of this issue, with particular reference to JE's *Treatise on Original Sin*, see Rachel Wheeler's essay, printed below.

13. "Miscellanies," no. 1023 (references to ancient moralists), in *WJE* 20:356; and nos. 1206, 1226, 1230 (which employ modern terminology in the same line of argument), in *WJE* 23:126, 157, 161.

14. I take this from a survey of the chief works: Hume's *Principles*; Shaftesbury's *Manners*; Hutcheson's *Essay*; and Smith's *Theory of Moral Sentiments*, all published from the 1720s through the 1750s. The American Samuel Johnson followed suit in his widely-used *Ethices Elementa*. Johnson eschewed the idea of pardon or release from

past debts. Unlike the Scots, he did mention forgiveness; but only in terms of the duty of the guilty party: "if" they had "done any Wrong," it was their "duty," for the sake of "good Neighbourhood and the public Tranquility" to "repair the Injury and make Restitution and ask Forgiveness." Aristocles [Samuel Johnson], *Ethices Elementa: or, the First Principles of Moral Philosophy* (Boston, 1746), 57. JE's anti-commercial sentiments have been documented in several places; see, e.g., Mark Valeri, "The Economic Thought of Jonathan Edwards," *Church History* 60 (1991): 37–54.

15. *WJE* 2:417, 419.

Lessons from Stockbridge: Jonathan Edwards and the Stockbridge Indians

Rachel Wheeler

Indian University-Purdue University at Indianapolis

Almost ten years ago, when I was in search of a dissertation topic, Harry Stout remarked to me, almost casually, "Well, no one's really looked at Edwards and the Stockbridge Indians." It seemed perfect—a way to combine my interest in cultural encounter and American intellectual/religious history. Frustrated by Edwards scholarship that gave short shrift to the mission and by ethnohistorical scholarship that had a largely mercenary interest in missionaries as sources for information on Indians, I hoped to write a history of religious encounter at a mission site. Of course, I have since discovered why there has been so little crossover interest in the Stockbridge mission: there is seemingly little in the Stockbridge sources that promises to shed light either on Edwards's theological projects or on the Stockbridge Indians' experiences as members of Edwards's congregation. In this respect, the Stockbridge mission is a microcosm of larger issues in the study of early American history. Despite longstanding calls for an integrated narrative of Indian and white history, one that delineates the influence of cultural encounter on whites as well as Indians, such a project has been slow to materialize.[1] A close look at the Stockbridge sources and what they can and cannot tell us about the mutual influences of Edwards and the Stockbridge Indians is thus suggestive of the prospects for the larger project of creating a new narrative able to hold together white and Indian, social and intellectual history. Here then, I survey the Stockbridge sources, exploring possible vectors of influence between Edwards's mission experience and his theological reflections. Then, I turn to the even sparser evidence of Edwards's influence on the formation of Mahican Christianity.[2]

THE STOCKBRIDGE INFLUENCE ON EDWARDS

The largest category of sources from Edwards's Stockbridge years is also the best known: the theological and philosophical treatises, including, most famously, *Freedom of the Will, The Nature of True Virtue,* and *Original Sin.* Of these three, *Original Sin* contains the most explicit references to American Indians, although these are few and far between. And on the surface, these references appear to be little more than restatements of general English assumptions about the inferiority of native culture. Pointing to the "multitudes of nations" of North and South America, Edwards asked, "What appearance was there when the Europeans first came hither, of their being recovered, or recovering, in any degree from the grossest ignorance, delusions, and most stupid paganism?" On the other hand, Edwards found Indians to be "mere babes as to proficiency in wickedness, in comparison of multitudes that the Christian world throngs with."[3] Yet even such seemingly positive mentions are intended less to laud native peoples than to shame Europeans for their state of irreligion despite prolonged access to gospel revelation. The two other major Stockbridge treatises, *Freedom of the Will* and *The Nature of True Virtue,* contain scarcely any mention at all of Indians.

One obvious explanation for the absence is that Edwards's mission experience left no discernable trace on his theological endeavors. We can at least safely conclude there was no *conscious* influence. In part, this absence reflects the realities of colonial power—Edwards could hold to his Christianity without any conscious challenge from his mission experience, while Mahicans could not pretend to be unaffected by European presence. Viewed this way, a different set of questions emerges: what were the structures that rendered English culture so seemingly immune to encroachment? Are those structures at work in Edwards's texts? And do these texts work in any way to shore up the cultural power that they reflect or do they challenge that power?

I have argued elsewhere that *Original Sin* both reflects and challenges the colonial setting in which it was written.[4] This reading surfaces when *Original Sin* is considered in light of Edwards's sermons to the Stockbridge Indians. Edwards preached over two hundred original sermons to his Stockbridge audience. Despite their number, these sermons seem to promise few rewards. They are mostly in outline form, thus making them considerably shorter than the manuscripts of sermons to his Northampton congregation, and they seem to be theologically rudimentary. They are indeed simpler than his sermons to the English, as Stockbridge schoolmaster, Gideon Hawley, observed when he remarked that Edwards was a "plain and practical preacher" who refrained from displaying "any metaphysical knowledge in the pulpit."[5] In aggregate, these sermons yield evidence of Edwards's efforts to tailor their form and content to suit what he perceived to be the needs of his audience. Thus, Edwards relied heavily on images and parables, believing these had the power to reach straight to the heart of the listener.

While the form of Edwards's Stockbridge sermons was noticeably different from his sermons to his English congregations, the Calvinist doctrine was essentially unchanged; Edwards elaborated the sinfulness of human nature, God's justice in punishing sinners, and the absolute necessity of divine grace for salvation. Only when we compare the Indian sermons with his sermons to his English congregation at Stockbridge does the distinctiveness of the Indian sermons emerge more clearly. The doctrine preached for English and Indian was identical, but Edwards often provided encouragement to his Indian audience where he chided the English.

For example, in one sermon, Edwards encouraged his Indian congregants to take tender care of their souls, to "forsake wickedness and seek after Holiness" and not to "act the part of Enemies of Enemies [sic] to your soul," but rather to "be friends to our own souls."[6] In another sermon, Edwards consoled his audience that although in this world "good men have Enemies" who "hurt 'em and afflict 'em," in heaven they "shall be set on high out of the reach of all their Enemies" where nothing can hurt them and "all Tears shall be wiped away from their Eyes."[7] "God is willing," promised Edwards, that all "whose hearts are joined to Christ should have Christ and his blood to wash 'em from sin." If repentance is earnest, Edwards preached, "there is forgiveness offered to all nations," for Christ "did not die only for one nation" but made clear "his design of making other nations his People," even those that "had been Heathens."[8] Christ offers himself "readily and freely" to suffer for sinners, "let 'em be who they will of what nation soever they are."[9] In a baptismal sermon Edwards preached, " 'tis the will of Christ that all nations shall be taught." Christ recognized "no difference" among the nations; Christ had "died for some of all /all need / all alike."[10]

By contrast, in his sermons to the English at Stockbridge Edwards often strove to shame and frighten his listeners into leading a godly life. Interestingly, Edwards composed very few original sermons for the English in Stockbridge—only about twenty.[11] The rest were repreached from old Northampton sermons. The tone of the new sermons is generally cautionary, as a few examples will suggest. In a sermon preached in October 1751, Edwards cautioned his English audience to "be sensible of your own Blindness" and not think "you can open your own eyes."[12] Sometime that same year, Edwards sought to humble the wealthy and the proud, reminding them "Those that obtain the [highest] degree of worldly wealth and honour and enjoy the most pleasure in their carnal enjoyments can retain them but for a moment all suddenly vanishes away like a vapor that is dissipated by the winds."[13] On another occasion, Edwards chastised those who remained indifferent to gospel preaching: "how selfish are they who have not so much as any reliable signs of their being at good terms with God and yet take no thorough care to get any.[14] And when Edwards turned to his sermons previously preached for his Northampton congregation, he seems to have chosen those which chided rather than those that comforted. In one lecture to the English children at Stockbridge, originally preached at Northampton in 1740, Edwards railed, "I had rather go into Sodom and preach to the men of Sodom than preach to you and should have a great deal more hopes of success."[15]

So what does this difference in tone mean? To be fair, Edwards did indeed deploy warnings of the terrors of hell to his Indian congregation, yet the tone of the sermons suggests that Edwards did not find Indian sins to be a personal affront or representative of a willful disregard of his gospel preaching in the same way he responded to English recalcitrance.[16] But still, without some evidence that this distinctive preaching crept into his theological treatises, we cannot conclude that Edwards was markedly shaped by his mission work, but only that he did what all New England ministers were taught to do—tailor his message to his audience.[17]

Had it not been for his mission experience, I believe Edwards might not have emphasized in *Original Sin* the equality in human depravity to the extent that he did. In this treatise, while the American Indians, together with other examples of "pagan" peoples, serve as examples of the absolute necessity of divine revelation in acquiring knowledge of "true religion," the conclusion Edwards wanted his readers to absorb was that all of humanity would be in a similar state were it not for the grace of God. Europeans were not inherently more virtuous than Indians. Any superiority evident in European society could be explained by the advantages of having long had access to true religion through the written revelation of the gospel. At the end of the treatise, Edwards underscored the ethical implications of the doctrine of original sin. Far from resulting in "an ill opinion of our fellow-creatures" thereby promoting "ill-nature and mutual hatred," as his opponents argued, the affirmation of the doctrine of original sin should induce humility. By contrast, to disown "that sin and guilt, which truly belongs to us," in Edwards's view, leads only to a "foolish *self-exaltation* and *pride*." Acceptance of the doctrine would have the salutary effect of teaching "us to think no worse of others, than of ourselves," and convincing people that "we are *all*, as we are by nature, *companions* in a miserable helpless condition." This, in turn, "tends to promote a mutual *compassion*." If the doctrine of original sin is abandoned in favor of faith in human reason then sin is simply a matter of choice. This in turn leads to the belief that "the generality of mankind are very wicked, having made themselves so by their own free choice, without any necessity:

which is a way of becoming wicked, that renders men truly *worthy of resentment.*"[18] In a strange way then, *Original Sin* emerges as a call to human fellowship rooted in a conviction of equality.

But before we (or at least I) get too carried away thinking Edwards was the champion of the downtrodden, it is important to remember that it was a related doctrine of universal applicability that underwrote New World colonization and mission efforts. If humans are naturally sinful, then all need Christ as savior, and it is therefore incumbent upon those in possession of the written revelation to bring it to those without. It was the universalism (not in the theological sense) of Christianity that both sponsored colonialism and promised equality. If this analysis of the relationship between Edwards's treatise on *Original Sin* and his pastoral work with the Stockbridge Indians is correct, then it suggests that the dual themes of American egalitarianism and exceptionalism are not easily dismissed as simply paradoxical, but are in fact symbiotic, in much the same way that Edmund Morgan has argued that slavery and freedom were mutually implicated.[19]

EDWARDS'S INFLUENCE ON THE STOCKBRIDGE INDIANS

Edwards's influence on his Stockbridge Indian congregants is even harder to trace than the influence of his mission experience on his theology. There are few sources in the mission records that shed even the most diffuse light on Indian experiences. Edwards wrote much of the political infighting among the overseers of the mission, but absolutely nothing about his perceptions of the Indians' encounter with Christianity. The difficulty of accessing native perceptions of colonial encounters would seem to be a universal feature of colonial manuscripts. But when the Stockbridge records are compared with the Moravian records from their mission to the Mahicans just forty miles from Stockbridge, it becomes apparent that there was something quite unique about English mission sources. All sources left by missionaries are problematic as sources for native experiences, but they are problematic in different ways. The Moravians recorded extensive details about the lives of mission residents—making it possible to reconstruct detailed family trees and gain some understanding of the meaning of communion to native communicants, for example—while the English missionaries, Edwards included, scarcely ever mention a name at all. I am not entirely sure what to make of this, but I suspect that the answer lies where culture, power, and perceptions of the self intersect. In Edwards's New England, "Christ" and "Culture" (to use Niebuhr's terms[20]) were so closely linked that entrance into the corporate body was of primary significance, not the distinctiveness of individual experience. Thus, English missionaries tended to measure success by the number of individuals who entered the corporate identity through a profession of belief. By contrast, the Moravians, as outsiders in colonial society, dreamed less of creating Christian nations than of transforming individuals through participation in ritual, and so Moravian sources provide vastly richer sources on Indian individuals' experiences of Christian ritual.[21]

So what hope is there of gaining insight into the Indian encounter with Christianity under Edwards's ministry? Unfortunately very little, at least not in any direct way. But like the treatises and sermons, with some massaging, the Edwards sources do, I think, yield up some clues. By my count, individual Stockbridge Indian names appear in Edwards's vast writings exactly thirteen times.[22] Eight of these appear in Edwards's "diary and memorandum book," where he recorded marrying four Indian couples.[23] Two letters contain reference to Edwards's interpreter, John Wauwampequunnaunt. And another is not actually by Edwards—it is a piece of handwriting practiced by Ebenezer Maunnauseet (eleven times over he penned: "he who lives upon hope may dy of Disappointment"), later drafted into service by Edwards for his sermon notes.[24]

The two remaining names, Cornelius and Mary Munneweaunummuck, appear in Edwards's hand at the bottom of a long profession of faith. In almost all respects, this profession of faith (along with several other similar professions, all unsigned) is entirely unexceptional. It begins, "And I do now appear before God and his People solemnly to give up my self to God to whom my Parents gave me upon my Baptism having so far as I know my own Heart chosen Him for my Portion and set my Heart on Him as my greatest and sweetest Good," and ends, "I profess universal forgiveness and good will to mankind and promise to be subject to the Government of this Church during my abode here."[25] Because it is so formulaic and written in Edwards's hand besides, we would perhaps be justified in dismissing the profession as having little to tell us. But, given that Edwards was willing to lose his job for his insistence on a profession of faith, we can safely assume Edwards did not treat these professions as merely *pro forma* recitations. He must have been persuaded that Cornelius and Mary's testimony, though scripted, was an apt representation of their inner lives. While this does not tell us anything at all about what it meant to Cornelius and Mary, it does suggest that there had been significant exchange between the candidates and Edwards on the subject of Christian belief and practice.

Other Stockbridge sources—letters, petitions, deeds—allow for a fairly thorough depiction of the secular affairs of the mission, but those two professions of faith are the sum total of information regarding Indian religious experiences at Stockbridge under Edwards's tenure.[26] We can get a bit closer however, by employing the "upstreaming" strategy long used by ethnohistorians.[27] Commonly, upstreaming is used in the attempt to recover traditional or pre-contact cultural practices, not to speculate about Christian practice among the first generation of self-identified Christian Indians. The life and writings of Hendrick Aupaumut, chief of the Stockbridge Indians in the late eighteenth and early nineteenth century, allow for a glimpse into native Christianity at Stockbridge. Aupaumut was born in Stockbridge in 1757, and, presumably, baptized by Edwards. Throughout his life, Aupaumut was identified as Christian and Mahican, yet he has received scholarly attention primarily for his role as "cultural broker," having served as intermediary between the newly formed United States and the hostile Ohio and Great Lakes Indians.[28]

Two obscure letters provide tantalizing evidence of Edwards's influence on the Mahican engagement with Christianity. The first is a letter sent by Aupaumut to Edwards's son Timothy, in which he requested, "I should be thankful if you would lend me a Book. The Author is your Father—Concerning Affections or if you han't such—wish to have the other mention[ed]—the Will."[29] We have no way of knowing whether Aupaumut read Edwards's treatises or what he made of them at the time, but the letter does suggest genuine engagement with Christianity—not the superficial and/or subversive practice sometimes attributed to Christian Indians.

A 1795 speech delivered by an unidentified tribal speaker, most likely Aupaumut, suggests that the theology of Edwards and the New Divinity movement had had some influence. The Stockbridges thanked the Quaker missionaries who had recently arrived to undertake work among the neighboring Brotherton Indians: "Brothers we thank the great spirit above that he has put it into your hearts to come this long journey to make us this friendly visit. We have swallowed all your words and good council with pleasure and delight, we are convinced they are the sentements of your hearts. Brothers, we heartily thank you for the many tokens of your disinterested love and friendship towards us poor Indians."[30]

One further clue, from near the end of Aupaumut's long life, suggests that he found in Christianity support for a vision of a common humanity, although it was one he had come to believe would only be realized in another world. In 1818, a missionary arrived in New Stockbridge, New York, on a fundraising tour to raise money for the conversion of the Jews in the holy land. After taking up a collection (of $5.87) Aupaumut wrote a letter to be delivered by the missionary, addressed to "the head men of the remnant of the Children of Abraham, Isaac and Jacob." Aupaumut first established a common humanity with the Jews by citing the Bible's teaching that "all nations in the world descend from one man and woman, and that Jesus came to die for all, so we can call you brothers and address you as such." In concluding his letter, Aupaumut imagined a time when the

Jews and "all the faithfull Gentiles will be received into heaven," where there would be "no distinction between the different Tribes, wheather white, red or black."[31] Edwards's audience for *Original Sin* may have disregarded its message of equality in depravity, but it appears that the Stockbridge Indians kept alive an egalitarian Christian tradition.

In closing, at the risk of claiming too much from an admittedly thin evidentiary base, I would suggest three possible lessons from Stockbridge. First, colonial texts, even those seemingly unrelated to the colonial project, should be interrogated for how they interact with colonial structures of power. In other words, does *Original Sin* or *Freedom of the Will* look any different when we remember that it was written in Stockbridge? Second, a commitment to human equality is often inextricably linked to forces of colonialism. And third, scholars of native Christianity have often asked the wrong question. We should ask not whether Indians understood Christian theology, but rather we should ask *how* did they understand Christian theology, and thus how did they indigenize Christianity?

NOTES

1. See "The Indian Impact on English Colonial Culture," in Axtell, *The European and The Indian: Essays in Ethnohistory of Colonial America* (New York: Oxford University Press, 1982), 272–316. Nancy Shoemaker's recent book is an excellent contribution to this project. Her decision to organize her book topically rather than chronologically allows her to demonstrate how various concepts (land, race, gender, etc.) evolved in white and Indian communities out of their interactions with each other. Shoemaker, *A Strange Likeness: Becoming Red and White in Eighteenth Century North America.* (New York: Oxford University Press, 2004).

2. For the most part, I will not here be explicitly considering the substantial body of JE's Stockbridge letters, which have recently been made readily available in *WJE* 16. These letters are, however, invaluable in understanding the local politics of the mission.

3. *WJE* 3:124, 151, 160, 183.

4. The argument that follows is a shorter version of one I present in "'Friends to Your Souls': Jonathan Edwards's Indian Pastorate and the Doctrine of Original Sin," *Church History* 72 (Dec. 2003): 736–65.

5. Gideon Hawley, "A Letter from Rev. Gideon Hawley of Marshpee, Containing an Account of His Services among the Indians of Massachusetts and New-York, and a Narrative of His Journey to Onohoghgwage," in Massachusetts Historical Society, *Collections* ser. 1, vol. 4 (Boston: Massachusetts Historical Society, 1794), 51. JE believed Indians were generally not capable of understanding metaphysical discourse, as he wrote in *Original Sin*: "from what I know and have heard of the American Indians . . . there are not many good philosophers among them." *WJE* 3:160.

6. Punctuation added for clarity. JE, Sermon on Prov. 19:8, June 1756, box 13, f. 985.

7. JE, Sermon on Heb. 9:27, Jan. 1751, box 14, f. 1127.

8. JE, Sermon on Luke 24:47, Oct. 1751, box 14, f. 1078.

9. JE, Sermon on Rev. 3:20, Feb. 1751, box 14, f. 1141.

10. Undated ms. fragment from baptismal sermon, on back of letter from Gideon Hawley to JE, Dec. 28, 1756.

11. This number was reached using the Beinecke Library's guide and includes all sermons dated after August 1751 that are not marked with "St. Ind." This yields about 25 sermons, which is reduced even farther when the manuscripts are consulted. At least five of these are actually Indian sermons or are misdated and actually predate JE's tenure at Stockbridge.

12. JE, Sermon on Ps. 119:18, Oct. 1751, box 13, f. 972.

13. JE, Sermon on Prov. 3:16, 1751, box 3, f. 199 (previously preached in 1750 at Middletown, Windsor, and Salem Village).

14. JE, Sermon on II Kgs. 20:1–3, Aug. 1753, box 2, f. 286.

15. JE, Sermon on Matt. 13:3–4, 1740, repreached May 1756, box 6, f. 463.

16. JE was certainly not soft on Indian sins, and warned his Stockbridge congregation: "if you go on in drunkenness and other wickedness, the gospel will be in vain. You will be the devil's people and will go to hell notwithstanding, and you will have a worse place in hell than those that never heard the gospel preached." JE, Sermon on Acts 16:9, Aug. 1751, box 14, f. 1093. On another occasion, Edwards counseled: "Take heed that you don't refuse to hearken to the gospel. You [who] have heard the gospel, it will be worse with you than other Indians." JE, Sermon on Matt. 10:14–15, Mar. 1755, box 13, f. 1027. See also JE, Sermon on Luke 13:7, June 1751, box 14, f. 1067.

17. See especially Harry S. Stout, *The New England Soul* (New York: Oxford University Press, 1986), and J. William T. Youngs, *God's Messengers: Religious Leadership in Colonial New England, 1700–1750* (Baltimore, Md.: Johns Hopkins University Press, 1976).

18. Emphasis in the original. *WJE* 3:424.

19. Edmund Morgan, *American Slavery, American Freedom: The Ordeal of Colonial Virginia* (New York: W. W. Norton, 1975).

20. H. Richard Niebuhr, *Christ and Culture* (San Francisco: Harper Collins, 1956).

21. For a sample of the types of sources kept by the Moravians, see Rachel Wheeler, "Women and Christian Practice in a Mahican Village," *Religion and American Culture* 13 (Winter 2003):

22. I am not counting the various letters regarding the Mohawk presence at Stockbridge, which include mention of several Mohawk leaders.

23. JE, Diary and Memorandum Book, 1733–1757, box 21, f. 1267.

24. It is tempting to think the sermon JE outlined on that leaf of paper in some way responded to Ebenezer's abandonment of hope; Edwards counseled his listeners that Christ "Lights the way / of our salvation / food for our souls / means of the greatest / Comfort / God bestows his blessing." JE, Sermon on Ps. 27:4, Oct. 1756, box 13, f. 960.

25. Indian Professions of Faith, n.d., box 21, folder 1245.

26. Actually, a few additional details can be gleaned from the Moravian records, which include several accounts of Mahican-Moravian visitors to Stockbridge.

27. See, for example, Axtell, *The European and the Indian.*

28. Alan Taylor, "Captain Hendrick Aupaumut: The Dilemmas of an Intercultural Broker," *Ethnohistory* 43 (Summer 1996): 431–457.

29. Aupaumut was referring to *A Treatise Concerning Religious Affections* (1746) and *Freedom of the Will* (1754). "Hendrick A." to "Hon'ble Timothy Edwards, Esq. Stockbridge or Wunnuqhqtoqhoke," 1775, Stockbridge Library, Stockbridge, Mass. The date on this letter was added later, and a more likely date is the early 1790s. I thank Lion Miles for pointing this out. Lion Miles, personal communication, Aug. 31, 2004.

30. Sergeant diary, entry dated May 18, 1795, Harvard Grants for Work among the Indians. Journals of John Sergeant, 1790–1909, Harvard University Archives.

31. This letter is signed by Aupaumut, listed as sachem, and five counselors. Aupaumut excerpt quoted in John Sergeant, diary entry dated April 8, 1819, Society in Scotland for Propagating Christian Knowledge, Rauner Special Collections, Dartmouth College, Hanover, New Hampshire. Aupaumut was among the tribal elite and we cannot infer from his experience that this was the shared experience of the tribe. On missions and tribal factionalism, see Daniel Richter, "Iroquois Versus Iroquois: Jesuit Missions and Christianity in Village Politics, 1642–86," *Ethnohistory*, 32 (1985): 1–16.

African American Engagements with Edwards in the Era of the Slave Trade

John Saillant

English and History, Western Michigan University

Between 1680 and 1760 several churchmen standing at least partly in the Calvinist theological tradition expressed views against the slave trade, colonial slavery, or masters' abuse of slaves. Although the number of commentators is small, they inaugurated a tradition of thought and judgment that came to include a vigorous Calvinist-inspired abolitionism—one in which black people themselves were authors—that flourished from the 1770s to the 1810s. Little of the commentary before 1760 was explicitly antislavery by modern standards, but was important in the history of abolitionism and it has been little understood. The leading characteristics of this tradition were an acceptance of slavery as a social institution appropriate to a fallen world and, yet, a definition of just slavery that in effect undermined the legitimacy of virtually all colonial American slavery, both mainland and West Indian. Churchmen like Morgan Godwyn, Jacobus Elisa Johannes Capitein, and Jonathan Edwards never declared slavery immoral or unlawful, but they left New World slaveholders little ground on which to stand in defense of their practices.

Morgan Godwyn (1640–c. 1695), a minister of the Church of England, served in Barbados and Virginia from about 1666 to about 1680.[1] Godwyn insisted that slavery was an acceptable form of social subordination and that Christianity would render slaves docile and tractable. Such ideas would reappear in the proslavery states in antebellum America. However, Godwyn was the most daring and persistent opponent of slaveholders in the seventeenth-century Anglo-American world.[2] He criticized the current forms of slaveholding so thoroughly that virtually nothing would have been left of the institution had his recommendations for better treatment of slaves been followed.

Godwyn's views on doctrine are unknown, but his family was noted for its anti-Catholicism and his father was graduated from Trinity College, Dublin, a Puritan institution. The younger Godwyn, however, took his degree in 1665 from Christ Church, Oxford, a college not known in the mid-seventeenth century for its Puritanism.[3] In migrating to Virginia, he entered a colony marked by conflicts between slaveholders and Anglican ministers, some of the latter with Puritan sympathies. He praised the religion of the New England colonies and perhaps he assented to the predestinarian parts of the Thirty-Nine Articles of the Church of England, but we cannot denominate him a Puritan. He seems to have disagreed energetically with local tobacco growers over their treatment of slaves, particularly the cruel punishments, sale of children away from parents, and unwillingness of masters to allow ministers to bring Christianity to the unfree. Some of the clearest commentary on the abuse of slaves as well as on the racist opinions of English settlers appears in writings that Godwyn began publishing in 1685. Mistreatment of blacks in England itself also caught his attention. He hoped for an amelioration of the conditions of slaves' lives and an improvement of Christian faith and practice in the Church of England. Like abolitionists of a century later, he believed that the leaders of Parliament and of the Church of England possessed the political or moral authority to counter the slave traders and slaveholders.[4]

Similarly, the reputable Puritan Samuel Sewall, a judge not a minister, granted in 1700 that at one time God may have decreed the enslavement of some tribes or societies, though he doubted that any scripture declared that Africans were to be cursed with slavery. But his objections to slavery, as did Godwyn's, undermined New World slavery. Slaves can hardly be moral beings, he noted, and masters themselves were tempted to sin by the presence of slaves. Americans had no way of ascertaining, he continued, whether African captives were taken in just wars—those in favor of the Atlantic slave trade were claiming that those taken by victors in a just war were legitimately sold—and indeed had reason to suspect the pursuit of unjust wars that ensnared the purchasers of slaves in a web of immorality. Finally, Christians could not recognize the distinction between brother and stranger that had made certain people or groups liable to enslavement according to the Old Testament. "*Ethiopians,* as black as they are, seeing they are the Sons and Daughters of the First *Adam,* and Brethren and Sisters of the Last Adam, and the Offspring of God," Sewall concluded, "ought to be treated with a Respect agreeable."[5]

Godwyn and Sewall represent a transition in Anglo-American thought that reached its conclusion less than a century after they flourished. In the last quarter of the eighteenth century, enemies of the slave trade and slavery granted that enslavement had seemed legitimate both to Jews of the pre-

Christian era and to Christians themselves. Yet this legitimacy, abolitionists argued, was contingent upon both good and fair treatment of slaves and, in the Christian era, proper interpretation of the New Testament. Both the Atlantic slave system and a Reformed reading of Scripture suggested that the slave trade and New World slavery were immoral. At the beginning of this transition from a provisional acceptance of slavery and an abolitionist insistence on its illegitimacy, thinkers like Godwyn and Sewall eviscerated defenses of slave-trading and slaveholding by pointing out the great distance between the legitimate and the current forms of enslavement.

Jacobus Elisa Johannes Capitein (1717–1747), born in West Africa, was taken as a young boy by slave-traders of the Dutch West India Company to Holland, where he was educated in languages and theology.[6] Of course, Capitein relied on Calvin as well as referring to English Puritans. Capitein's book, *Political-Theological Dissertation Examining the Question: Is Slavery Compatible with Christian Freedom,* has typically been understood as a defense of slave holders, but it actually pursued a strategy similar to that of Godwyn's *Advocate.*[7] Capitien argued that slavery resulted from humankind's "degeneracy" and that it was not inconsistent with the Christian faith of both master and slave, since the Atonement freed the soul, not the body.[8] He also pointed out that manumitting slaves who professed Christianity created an incentive for them to sin by fabricating religious convictions. "For all people, and consequently also slaves," he declared, "can easily feign Christ's name." However, Capitein also asseverated that slave and master alike were free under natural law, that Christian kindness may lead owners to free slaves, and that Holland had ended slavery by law. Kindness, indeed, was obligatory, though under "divine law" liberation was only optional.[9] Capitein concluded:

> Slavery in no way contradicts Christian freedom—slavery, which indeed has been repealed here in the Netherlands out of some sense of benevolence or clemency or for political expediency, not because of divine law. From this it follows naturally that slavery does not impede the spread of the Gospel in those Christian colonies where it prevails right up to the present day. For this reason, a kingdom most amicable and pleasing to God can and should be built for both masters and slaves, educated in the better religious practices. This is what Paul recommends to Philemon (v. 16). And in this way slaves will certainly in the end be as prepared as possible for the will of their masters, as we read in Ephesians 6:5–8: *Slaves, be obedient to those who are your earthly masters, with fear and trembling, in singleness of heart, as to Christ.* On these lines, another passage will grow deep roots in the minds of those masters who have not cast off the character of a Christian gentleman (v. 9): *Masters, do the same to them, and forebear threatening, knowing that he who is both their master and yours is in heaven, and that there is no partiality with him.*[10]

Capitein never traveled to the New World, but he surely remembered the ships of the Dutch West India Company on which he sailed with many slaves. He would have known that the standard he drew from Philemon was irrelevant to slave-traders. Thus, Capitein's proslavery thesis so separated legitimate enslavement from the realities of the Atlantic world that its slave system —purchase, transport, sale, and labor alike—was inevitably stripped of any justification.

The end of Capitein's life—he died a missionary in West Africa—brings us to the height of Edwards's theological career. The attractions and uses of Edwardsean religion for the first black abolitionists were many. Some parts of Edwardsean religion brought African Americans across the threshold into New England Christianity, while others allowed blacks to understand their own situation as part of Christian history as well as to argue for the abolition of the slave trade and slavery. The earliest black abolitionists believed that there was no antislavery and pro-black argument sustainable outside the Calvinist tradition. The initial attractions of Edwardsean religion deserve mention here, but the more substantial black approaches to Edwards and the New Divinity are the subject of most of the remainder of this essay.

First, several of the first generation of Anglophone black authors learned to read and write in American Calvinist households, which thus endowed their young servants or slaves with a species of property (in an older sense of a skill) that could never in the long run be squared with enslavement. Second, although Edwards himself was a slave owner, a number of those who affiliated themselves to his theology, along with others with a more general connection to Calvinism (heirs, like Ezra Stiles, of the "old Calvinists") became leaders in eighteenth-century abolitionism.[11] Third, the War of Independence drew from the New Divinity men not only a vigorous endorsement of the republican cause, which many blacks understood as a slaves' cause, but also a statement about the effect of unfreedom on human life. It produced, the New Divinity men argued, melancholy and despair—not the worst states according to the Reformed tradition, but heavy weights upon one's life. This argument about melancholy and despair certainly hit home for American slaves, and perhaps the fact that Edwards himself had wrestled with periods of anxiety and depression led him to a theology with which the enslaved could readily feel affinity. Fourth—and here is a general point about eighteenth-century Calvinism—blacks in various parts of the Atlantic world were attracted to Calvinist preaching. There were significant populations of black Huntingdonians in Nova Scotia and Sierra Leone. Some black city-dwellers favored the preaching of moderate Calvinists like Ezra Stiles and Timothy Dwight, both of New Haven, as well as that of extremists like Samuel Hopkins of Newport and William Romaine of London, a leading Huntingdonian. The famed Wesleyan evangelical, Thomas Coke, bemoaned the successes of "the Calvinists" who were evangelizing the slaves of the West Indies and thus competing with his own Wesleyan brethren, who sometimes suffered "a Calvinistic missionary on each side . . . if not more than two." And although the documentation is scanty, an examination of Richard Allen's surviving writings suggests that at least early in his career even he was preaching doctrines friendly to the Calvinist tradition, although in retrospect we tend to associate him with the Wesleyan Methodists.[12]

The elements of Edwardsean religion meant either in and of themselves, or with some extension, that the slave trade and slavery were wrong and that a Christian society must be fair, free, and open for blacks and whites alike. The first generation of African American Christianity bloomed under the light of Edwards beginning about 1770, grew during the War of Independence and the trans-Atlantic agitation against the slave trade and slavery, then declined around 1820 as blacks began committing themselves to free-will religion. The second generation saw the establishment of new churches and denominations as well as a renewed battle against slavery, but it lost the Calvinist-inspired vision of its predecessors.

The early expressions of Godwyn, Sewall, and Capitein notwithstanding, Edwards provided the linchpin of abolitionism as it developed in the second half of the eighteenth century—his notion of disinterested benevolence. Edwards himself owned several slaves at various points in his adult life, but the Edwardsean understanding of virtue was elemental in early abolitionism, both black and white. Second-generation and third-generation Edwardseans like Samuel Hopkins, Levi Hart, Sarah Osborne, Job Swift, and Lemuel Haynes developed this abolitionism, even if in some cases only erratically. And prominent among black critics of the slave system were Ottobah Quobna Cugoano, Olaudah Equiano, John Marrant, and Phillis Wheatley, who were apostles of Calvinists like George Whitefield, William Romaine, and Selina Hastings, the Countess of Huntingdon. Benevolence figured more prominently in the writings of blacks who were closer to Edwards, but it was still prominent in those of blacks whose influences were more strongly Huntingdonian. If one is obliged to love others disinterestedly as creatures of God, then one is obliged to free the enslaved. Enslavement involved not only suffering, which might, after all, be ameliorated, as some of slavery's defenders argued, but also melancholy and despair deriving from the very state of unfreedom. Indeed, this sense that slavery itself was universally wrong—something purportedly understood only by those who read the New Testament accurately—was essential to the first abolitionism, distinguishing it from the more common and less radical positions.[13] Moreover, one of the advances black abolitionists made in the Edwardsean tradition was that slaves desire to be free not for themselves, not for selfish purposes, but rather to achieve mental and civic states in which they could worship God properly. The enslaved could never be virtuous, they argued. And slaveholders could never have the reformed hearts demanded of them in the Edwardsean tradition.

The Edwardsean notion of divine providence struck a chord deep in the heart of nearly every early black Christian writer—and blacks came to be among the most vigorous proponents of an Edwardsean providentialism. One of the crucial texts of early black America is an apparently sympathetic autograph thirty-five-page commentary by Prince Hall on Edwards's *History of the Work of Redemption.* Unfortunately its content is now obscure, but it is possible that this text—virtually the Holy Grail of early African American writing—may come available to scholars some day. Early in the twentieth century it was examined by several scholars who were interested in Hall's social activity but not his religion. But we find providentialism everywhere in early black writing: God provided both evil and good, suffering and salvation, as part of a divine benevolent design. The injunction to the believer was to approach the divine mind, to seek to understand God's reason for evil and suffering. Probably nothing more than this allowed black people to comprehend their experience and order their lives. It provided a vision of one suffering at first in ignorance, then achieving a self-determination arising from one's understanding of God's benevolent actions within one's life. In this, Edwardsean theology shaped blacks' self-understanding and provided them biblical models, including, above all, Joseph.[14]

Moreover, the Edwardsean understanding of the will allowed early black abolitionists to envision the end of slavery and the nature of a postslavery society. The reformed will was to guide individuals to do good, not for natural purposes or as an incidental result of other deeds, but out of a benevolent intent. Simply put, the early black abolitionists argued that essential to the end of slavery was the benevolent urge to be good to black people, in effect, to free slaves and to welcome blacks into American or English society as full members. Although the question of the will might seem too subtle for many modern observers, it was this more than anything else that separated eighteenth-century abolitionism from nineteenth-century abolitionism. Antebellum abolitionists, black and white alike, anticipated a degree of separation between blacks and whites that their predecessors never envisioned. William Lloyd Garrison himself abjured the goal of benevolent social relations as an impediment to the termination of slavery.[15]

Each one of these themes—virtue, providence, will—has been pursued in scholarship on early black authors and their abolitionist arguments. This essay emphasizes another feature of Edwardsean theology that appealed to blacks—typology. With good reason, black people became typologists. There was a typological argument to be made against slavery that matched Edwards's typologizing and that also answered the proslavery argument that the Old Testament authorizes slavery, albeit a benign variety. Eugene D. Genovese, for instance, has recently argued that nineteenth-century Southern Christian ministers, Calvinist and Arminian alike, defended slavery in good faith based on an accurate reading of the Old Testament.[16] Defense, yes, but good faith, no—simply because the Southern argument abandoned not just Edwards but typological understanding. And this abandonment occurred not with a commitment to the higher criticism that was in the nineteenth century to undermine typologizing, but almost certainly because of a willed desire to efface an antislavery Bible. The typological argument against slavery, which was developed at length by black abolitionists like Quobna Ottobah Cugoano and Lemuel Haynes, was that the Old Testament had a spiritual meaning that was misapprehended by the Jews, then became available for a true understanding by Christians, even if they at large came to understand the truth only over time, most notably because of the Reformation. The Old Testament commentary on slavery was meant by God to be symbolic or figurative, referring to human impulses, including sinful ones, that should be controlled and subjugated to a virtuous life or to a God-fearing community. The laws governing slavery were spiritual, not social. Those laws never authorized the enslavement of persons, whether for good or bad treatment, and those who appealed to the Old Testament in support of slavery were improperly allowing the old dispensation to pollute the new.[17]

It should come as no surprise in our time that the typological argument involved a swipe against Islam as well as against Judaism. Muslim slave-traders were active in the second half of the eighteenth-century, and they were the coastal middlemen responsible for the flow from Senegambia of slaves into the West Indies and North America. Not only did black abolitionists know this—indeed the diatribe against Islam is deep in their work—but also they accepted the eighteenth-century fallacy that Islam was an offshoot of Judaism with little relation to Christianity. Current translations of the Qur'an may have encouraged that view, but, in any event, it gave black abolitionists leverage against the slave trade and slavery, which could be seen as features of the Muslim world (and behind that, the Jewish world) imported into Christian America. That was in the eighteenth century potentially a very powerful critique of the slave trade and slavery.

Moreover, whatever else early black abolitionists believed of the Bible, they believed it to be a book of types and antitypes. Joseph, the model for many black writers, was a type of Jesus, but also a type of the black abolitionist. The Qur'anic Joseph, of course, differed from the Old Testament Joseph on a detail that was crucial for the black abolitionists: in the Qur'an

Joseph understood the divine will from the moment he was thrown into the pit, while in the Old Testament Joseph understood the divine will only much later in the story when he became the savior of his brethren. The latter accorded with the black abolitionists' self-understanding—as when Olaudah Equiano moved from a slave-trading and slaveholding society, into the Middle Passage, then into the overseeing and the trading of slaves himself, and, finally, into abolitionism. Unlike the Qur'anic Joseph, Equiano never understood the divine will while he was in the dark pit of the slave ship.

That blacks understood the Bible as a book of types and antitypes explains much about early black texts and early black abolitionism. When John Marrant —now famously—described the talking book, the example he gave of its activity was Isaiah 53 and Matthew 26, which were thought to be typologically related in the figures of the suffering servant and Jesus.[18] Indeed, we might recast the "talking book thesis" by noting that the texts themselves support, in addition to the idea that the book talked to white people, a notion that the book talks to *itself*—it is a book of types and antitypes—and that white people had merely learned to overhear the conversation. The Bible may have been a sign of power held by whites but not blacks, but it was also a book situating black people in history and divining their essential future. A commitment to typology also helps to explain the heavy reliance by nearly all early black writers on the Book of the Prophet Isaiah—Allen, Cugoano, Equiano, Haynes, and Marrant all relied on him—as well Phillis Wheatley's use of Virgil. Isaiah was an important book for typologists, while Virgil had credence among the orthodox for seeming to have noted the birth of a child who could have been a type of Christ or could even have been Jesus himself.

Moreover, black people experienced themselves as types and antitypes in ways foreign to their white contemporaries. If we gather these various threads together—Edwards's God, the slave trade, slavery, abolition, freedom, Islam, Christianity, Africa, America—we can understand that black people in the second half of the eighteenth century saw themselves as moving in a generation or two, sometimes, as with Equiano, even in *one lifetime*, from Old Testament to New Testament, from type to antitype. As abolitionists, they were living and breathing antitypes. Edwards's typology represented that long tradition of interpretation to them, but Edwards himself could never have claimed such experience. His was always the world defined by the New Testament. Black abolitionists had traveled from the world of the Old Testament (Africa, Islam, the slave trade, slavery, all of which were then mentally linked in ways that today we may find unrealistic and even offensive) to the world of the New Testament (America, abolition, freedom, a hoped-for equality). The structure of the book of types and antitypes was the very form of their lives.

A number of scholars have noted accurately that Edwards expanded typology by finding types not just in Scripture but in nature as well as in other religious traditions. In the second half of the eighteenth century, blacks made a parallel move. Islam, for instance, although condemned as the religion of West African slave traders, was seen as prefiguring important elements of the lives of free blacks in America and England: a sense of honor, sagacity in trade, and, above all, a commitment to literacy directed to religious purposes. Early black authors were fascinated with characters who passed from ignorance to understanding of God's will. Joseph was one such man, as were Nicodemus and Zaccheus, who were thought by some to have become followers of Christ. The transitions that such figures seemed to have made reflected the trajectory of the lives of the first black Christians of America and England. All scholars examining this generation would today accept that it lived in a world of signs. The signs included the types in which Edwards believed. James Albert Ukasaw Gronniosaw described them as "wonderful impressions."[19] If one type was the despairing slave longing for freedom, the antitype was the committed abolitionist. If another type was Islam (as, apparently, for Wheatley) or a polytheistic faith (as for Gronniosaw), then the antitype was Christianity. The miracles that many early black writers reported as having occurred in their lives were also part of the type–antitype relationship. But the antitypes were themselves signs of things to come, which were for blacks, the free as well as the enslaved, truer forms of faith, freedom, and equality.

NOTES

1. "Godwin, Morgan," in *The Dictionary of National Biography*, ed. Sir Leslie Stephen and Sir Sidney Lee (London: Oxford University Press, 1917), 8:62; Betty Wood, "Godwyn, Morgan," in *Oxford Dictionary of National Biography*, ed. H. C. G. Matthew and Brian Harrison (Oxford: Oxford University Press, 2004), 22:630–631.

2. Alden T. Vaughan, "Slaveholders' 'Hellish Principles': A Seventeenth-Century Critique, in Vaughan, *Roots of American Racism: Essays on the Colonial Experience* (New York: Oxford University Press, 1995), 55–81.

3. M. M. Knappen, *Tudor Puritanism: A Chapter in the History of Idealism* (Chicago: University of Chicago Press, 1939), 472–475.

4. Morgan Godwyn, *The Negro's and Indians Advocate, Suing for Their Admission into the Church; Or a Persuasive to the Instructing and Baptizing of the Negro's and Indians in Our Plantations* (London, 1680).

5. Samuel Sewall, *The Selling of Joseph, A Memorial*, in *Am I Not a Man and a Brother: The Antislavery Crusade of Revolutionary America, 1688–1788*, ed. Roger Burns (New York: Chelsea House Publishers, 1977), 10–14, quotation p. 13.

6. Grant Parker, "The Agony of Asar: An Introduction to the Life and Work of Capitein," in *The Agony of Asar: A Thesis on Slavery by the Former Slave, Jacobus Elisa Johannes Capitein, 1717–1747*, ed. Grant Parker (Princeton, N. J.: Markus Wiener Publishers, 2001), 7–11.

7. Typical of the judgement on Capitein is Leyla Keough, "Capitein, Jacobus Elisa," in *Africana: The Encyclopedia of the African and African American Experience* (New York: Basic *Civitas* Books, 1999), 371–372.

8. Jacobus Elisa Johannes Capitein, *Political-Theological Dissertation Examining the Question: Is Slavery Compatible with Christian Freedom*, in *The Agony of Asar,* 81–132, quotation p. 99.

9. Capitein, *Political-Theological Dissertation,* 97, 104, 115, 117–121, 127, 131, quotations pp. 97, 114–115, 131.

10. Capitein, *Political-Theological Dissertation,* 131–132.

11. For JE's comments on the slave trade and slavery, see Kenneth P. Minkema, "Jonathan Edwards's Defense of Slavery," *The Massachusetts Historical Review* 4 (2002): 23–59. On Ezra Stiles's interaction with black New Englanders and his opposition to the slave trade, see John Saillant, *Black Puritan, Black Republican: The Life and Thought of Lemuel Haynes, 1753–1833* (New York: Oxford University Press, 2003), 89, 129–134.

12. For Thomas Coke on preaching to West Indian slaves, see John Vickers, *Thomas Coke: Apostle of Methodism* (Nashville: Abingdon, 1969), 149–172, 300–301, quotations pp. 301–302. For information on blacks' interactions with Calvinist ministers and church members, see Joanna Brooks, *American Lazarus: Religion and the Rise of African-American and Native American Literatures* (New York: Oxford University Press, 2003), 87–113, 171–173; *"Face Zion Forward": First Writers of the Black Atlantic, 1785–1798,* ed. Joanna Brooks and John Saillant (Boston: Northeastern University Press, 2002); Charles E. Hambrick-Stowe, "The Spiritual Pilgrimage of Sarah Osborne (1714–1796)," *Church History* 61 (1992): 408–421; Charles Hambrick-Stowe, "All Things Were New and Astonishing: Edwardsian Piety, the New Divinity, and Race," in *Jonathan Edwards at Home and Abroad: Historical Memories, Cultural Movements, Global Horizons,* ed. David W. Kling and Douglas A. Sweeney (Columbia, South Carolina: University of South Carolina Press, 2003), 121–136; John Saillant, "Antiguan Methodism and Antislavery Activity: Anne and Elizabeth Hart in the Eighteenth-Century Black Atlantic," *Church History* 69 (2000): 86–115.

13. For JE on a new, Reformed understanding that slavery counters God's will, see Minkema, "Jonathan Edwards's Defense of Slavery," 38.

14. Phillip Richards, "The 'Joseph Story' as Slave Narrative: On Genesis and Exodus as Prototypes for Early Black Anglophone Writing," in *African Americans and the Bible: Sacred Texts and Social Textures,* ed. Vincent L. Wimbush (New York: Continuum, 2000), 221–235.

15. For differences between Garrison and earlier abolitionists, see Saillant, *Black Puritan,* 186–187.

16. Eugene D. Genovese, *Consuming Fire: The Fall of the Confederacy in the Mind of the White Christian South* (Athens: University of Georgia Press, 1998).

17. For an example of antislavery typologizing, see Saillant, *Black Puritan*, 33–34.

18. John Marrant, *A Narrative of the Lord's Wonderful Dealings with John Marrant a Black, (Now Going to Preach the Gospel in Nova-Scotia) Born in New York, in North-America*, in *"Face Zion Forward,"* 47–75.

19. James Albert Ukasaw Gronniosaw, *A Narrative of the Most Remarkable Particulars in the Life of James Albert Ukasaw Gronniosaw, an African Prince, as Related by Himself*, in *Unchained Voices: An Anthology of Black Authors in the English-Speaking World of the Eighteenth Century*, ed. Vincent Carretta (Lexington: University Press of Kentucky, 1996), 32–58, quotation p. 34.

Jonathan Edwards in the Twenty-First Century

George M. Marsden

University of Notre Dame

What can we learn from Jonathan Edwards today? When I was writing a biography of Edwards, I tried to keep that prescriptive question in the background and to focus on understanding him first in his own eighteenth-century context. Now I want to make explicit what was mostly implicit in the biography and ask what is most significant that we might appropriate about Edwards in the twentieth-first century.

I recognize, of course, that the answer to this inquiry will depend substantially upon who the "we" is that we are talking about. Those who have close theological affinities to Edwards will find much more to appropriate than will those who find his theology essentially wrong-headed or even offensive. Almost everyone who looks at Edwards seriously finds some things to learn from or admire and some things that they reject or deplore, but the lists of what is on the positive or negative sides vary immensely. So, acknowledging that I cannot speak for everyone, let me say what I find as especially useful for our own time.

AMERICAN PERSPECTIVES

Beginning with a topic of the broadest interest, understanding Edwards helps us better to understand the American experience. One of the great puzzles about the United States is that it is simultaneously so secular and so religious. Twentieth-century histories that celebrated progress and modernization did not explain that paradox well. If we rather recognize that Edwards and the movements he represented left a lasting legacy in America, we balance more conventional histories that quickly leave behind the religion of the colonists in order to get to the American Revolution and the political-economic forces that began to shape a modern world. Edwards's cultural significance is found particularly in his close association with the emergence of revivals in America, one of the most influential of modern instruments for promoting religious vitality. Although Edwards did not invent revivals nor perfect them in what became their most characteristic American forms, he is still worth studying because he was one of the major fountainheads from which this immensely influential movement flowed.

It is especially important for understanding nineteenth-century America that the most powerful intellect of the colonial era was also its leading apologist for the awakenings. Edwards and the Edwardsean tradition helped assure that revivalism in America was not only a populist movement that would be marginal to the mainstream high culture. Rather, for more than a century it was a cause dear to the hearts of many leading educators and clergy,[1] hence inspiring young men and women from all levels of American culture to carry on the evangelical cause, whether on the mission field, in social work and reform, or in more ordinary vocations.

In twentieth-century progressive America, by contrast, to the extent that Edwards was remembered it was almost always by way of *Sinners in the Hands of an Angry God* or, in other words, as an example of what Americans had progressed from. At mid-century Perry Miller attempted to counter that approach by rehabilitating Edwards on the grounds that Edwards and Edwardseans represent one of the most formidable of American indigenous intellectual traditions. Miller succeeded among academics in inspiring something of an Edwards industry among academics. Yet at the same time, Edwards faded from the American collective memory in the late twentieth century. Although he still makes brief appearances in American literature courses, he is seldom seriously considered in popular history or texts. The priority of New England, despite the region's demonstrably vast influence on the shared public culture, has become unfashionable, and in a canon already with too many white males, the controversial Edwards is easy to ignore. The overall result—whether from early twentieth-century progressivism or late twentieth century multiculturalism—is an historical distortion that impoverishes the collective heritage.

Going beyond the question of the usefulness of a recovery of Edwards for *understanding* American culture, a case can also be made that more positive attention to Edwards would be beneficial as part of America's collective historical memory. The usual American self-image is so upbeat, emphasizing our abilities to overcome our problems and inviting belief in our invincibility, that we could do with a touch of warning and realism in our histories. America needs more popular histories written in a minor key. Even though Edwards's specific political views are hopelessly out of date, he did emphasize, as did his Puritan forebears, that God's covenants with nations were *conditional*. Nations have heavy moral responsibilities, not just promises of success and blessing. Further, and more important as a general principle, Edwards ceaselessly warned against trusting just in human abilities to solve humanity's problems. Humans are first of all very limited creatures who tend to think they are far more in control of their destinies than they really are.

THEOLOGICAL PERSPECTIVES

Such perspectives on human pretension bring us to the heart of the matter that concerns not just what Edwards might mean for America and American history, but what specifically from his theological legacy might be appropriated by people in the twenty-first century.

In order to answer that larger question, it is helpful first to be reminded of the context in which Edwards was working. In my view it is especially important to view him as someone who was deeply loyal to the Puritan and wider Reformed or Calvinistic traditions of the seventeenth century and who was also informed by the Newtonian revolution and profoundly challenged by the British Enlightenment of his own era. One of the things that makes Edwards so interesting is that the Puritan side of him looks back to the Christendom of the Middle Ages and the Reformation, while the Newtonian and Enlightenment issues he was addressing look forward to the modern era. Facing the juxtaposition of these two vastly different outlooks so directly, he was acutely alert to some of the most significant implications of modernity. Just because the Puritan-Reformation-Medieval side of his outlook is so different from most of our assumptions, he sometimes startles us with insights from another era that are wonderfully applicable to our own.

The first and the most important principle that should challenges us—even if it is not at all unique—is that Edwards always begins with God. Most of us today begin with the human condition. Secularists, of course, have nowhere else to begin. Even many of today's Christians and other theists, however, are in the habit of starting with their own understanding of human needs, moral principles, or desirable ideals and tailoring God to them. Edwards recognized this growing tendency in the enlightened and liberal Christian thought of his own time and so insisted all the more adamantly on God and God's revelation as the starting point for all questions.

Closely related is that he started with a dynamic loving God of personal relationships. That view grew out of his trinitarian theological tradition which led him to see the most essential dynamic of reality as the intra-trinitarian love of God. God's creation of the universe is an expression of that overflowing love and a need to share that love with other personal and responsible beings. To borrow and modify a current metaphor, Edwards viewed the origin of the universe as a sort of "big bang" of God's creative love in which God's personal creative force *continues* directly to shape an ever-expanding reality. The creation of the universe is not just something that happened long ago. Rather it is an ongoing intimate process. The creation is the very language of God. "The heavens declare the glory of God," as Psalm 19 says. So all creation bears a relationship to God that is analogous to the relationship of our language to us. It is not identical to God but is still an intimate communication of God's being. Since the universe is new every moment, at each instant it is an expression of God's love and would not exist if God withdrew his creative power. For those of us, such as myself, who have been reared in Presbyterian or Reformed traditions that emphasized "the sovereignty of God" but sometimes treated that as an abstract legal principle, the loving dynamics that Edwards adds can be exhilarating.

Edwards himself may have been reacting to some tendency toward abstraction in his own scholastic Reformed heritage, but he was more explicitly countering the Deist views that were emerging in British thought. Deists distanced God from creation by presenting him as the perfect creator who built the great machinery of the universe and then allowed it to run according to natural laws without interference. Edwards went in the opposite direction. He insisted on God's intimate relationship to every atom of the universe. Well-versed in Newtonian physics, Edwards saw God as continually working through the laws by which the Creator guided the ever-changing physical relationships in the universe. Edwards's universe was, like Newton's, a universe of relationships. A change in one part changed the relationships of the whole. Yet Edwards's universe, while having room for scientific laws of physical relationships, was ultimately a universe of persons and of personal relationships.

In contrast to Edwards's view, quasi-Deism has prevailed in the modern world, once again even among many Christian believers. Our tendency is to think of the physical world as an independent entity run by the laws known by natural science.[2] Technology vastly increases the influence of that seemingly self-contained world by shaping much of our lives, determining how we earn livings, how we spend our money, how we value other people, how we communicate, how we are entertained, and often how we worship. Religious believers typically *supplement* that largely autonomous world with beliefs in a higher spiritual reality and some moral principles that may somewhat qualify the way they relate to the technological society and the natural world. They may also believe in occasional divine interventions, especially with respect to unusual spiritual experiences or concerning matters of personal health.

Edwards's starting point in the Triune God's ongoing love provides a basis for attempting to cultivate some alternative sensibilities. For Edwards the most essential dimension of all reality is the spiritual and personal that pervades everything. These are not beliefs that are added on to what we believe about the material world but rather dimensions that define it and everything else. All creation is an expression of the redemptive love of God in Christ. Hence when we view nature, we do not see it properly unless we see it in its primary relationship, its relationship to God. Since that relationship is personal, our most basic response to nature ought to be affective. Edwards saw the material world as "Images of Divine Things." In his notebook of that title he recorded some of his many reflections on how the beauties of Christ's love were revealed in everything around us. Since nature is corrupted by sin, its revelations are also of Christ's *redemptive* love. The beauties of the universe are the harmonies of right relationships that we sometimes get glimpses of in the beauty of trees and flowers. Edwards often uses musical analogies to speak of that beauty. If we view nature in its right relationships, then we sense the beauty of its harmonies in relationship to the whole. If we allow our sin to limit our sensibilities, for instance in being preoccupied with our selfish physical pleasures, or if we reject the love at the center of things, then we fail to participate in and perceive the larger harmony. It reminds me of some first reactions to Bach among some of my contemporaries in the town where I grew up. They just heard meaningless, boring sounds.

Some of Edwards's most profound and frequently reiterated reflections are on the foolishness of allowing our affections to be controlled by the transitory material desires. Such affections, even if we discipline and temper them, foster preoccupation with self. The only way to begin to break such deeply engrained tendencies is to be granted a glimpse of the beauty of God's ineffable love revealed in Christ. If we ever truly see that overwhelming beauty, if we are given the immense gift of eyes to see, then our deepest affections will be drawn to it. We cannot help loving beauty when we perceive it.

Edwards's view of God's love as overwhelming beauty is also a useful way of explaining the paradox of God's grace and our choice. When we perceive something immensely beautiful we can not help but be drawn to it. Yet certainly it is our own will that is acting according to our deepest desires. Edwards points out that being able to act according to our deepest desires is the highest coherent meaning of free choice.

In this life, our sense of God's beauty is never perfected and our wills remain fickle, but only with that life-changing revolution in our affections can we begin to view the universe with God at the center, rather than ourselves. Only then can we begin to sense how our preoccupations with mundane desires alone are expressions of self-centered self-delusion. In a universe where God's love is the light, we recognize that our unredeemed hearts are like black holes that absorb but do not reflect that light. The revolution that a glimpse of the beauty of Christ's love begins to effect is one in which we revalue all those mundane desires as good only if used for God's loving purposes.

This radical change in perspective changes the way we view history and hence society. Edwards hoped that the great culminating work of his career would be a comprehensive "body of divinity in an entire new method, being thrown into the form of an history." The theme of this historical theology would be the redemptive work of Christ. First, he would develop a Christocentric biblical theology. All of Scripture was to be interpreted as pointing to Christ. Although we today might work out the details of how to do that rather differently, the essential principle fits with some of our most fruitful Christocentric biblical-theological traditions. Edwards, however, extended the centrality of Christ's redemption to be the key to all of history. Today, every school of biblical interpretation would dissent from Edwards's specific conclusions. He hoped to break the code of biblical prophecies and coordinate them with specific historical events, especially those of his own time. Nonetheless, I think we might learn from the broader principle involved.

Our culture is preoccupied with understanding history and contemporary societies as a product of material, social, economic, and cultural forces. Such approaches can tell us a great deal and some of us spend our careers examining them. Nonetheless, it is important to be reminded, if one is a religious believer, that such accounts are sadly misleading. As Richard Lovelace suggests, it as though we are analyzing a great contest or game in which only half the participants are visible.[3] I find it helpful to add that we—and here I mean by "we" those whose religious beliefs have a Judeo-Christian lineage—are like the characters in *The Lord of the Rings*. We need to recognize that we are in a cosmic contest in which we have a role to play. Yet, while we may be confident of the final outcome, we have little idea what challenges we may face at the next turn in the road. We can do our best at reading our maps and trusting in the larger principles that are revealed to us. Still, we remain largely in the dark about the specific meanings of our historical experience, even if we need to be reminded that ultimately they fit into a larger pattern that in this life has only been partially revealed.

EDWARDS AND ENLIGHTENED MODERNITY

Edwards's God-filled view of the universe also provides the basis for a critique of some of the most fundamental principles our Enlightenment modernity that still are taken for granted in much of our world. Especially important (in addition to the quasi-Deism already mentioned) is the widespread modern belief that human happiness must be the controlling concern in any adequate religious view or philosophy. Theologians since the eighteenth century have tended to work from the premise that the universe must be designed for our happiness. They then proceed to identify principles that seem to contribute to human happiness and to characterize God according to those principles. Most secular philosophers do much the same thing, only recognizing better than the theologians that God is not a necessary term in the equation. Why not, they ask, just say that the good is whatever promotes human happiness and leave out the distracting claims about God?

Edwards, by contrast, insists on the premise that the Triune God as revealed in Jesus Christ defines whatever is good. God is essentially a loving being and the communication of that love is the very reason for creation. Why God permits evil is a mystery ultimately beyond our comprehending. Whatever the reason, it must be a sub-dimension of God's loving design, since God defines what is good. Edwards himself, eager as he was to answer the enlightened critics, did not always leave the matter there. He attempted to show, at the least, that Reformed versions of the biblical accounts presented no more serious problems than did their Enlightenment alternatives. Sometimes he went further than that in trying to justify God's ways. Nevertheless, he rested ultimately on the conclusion that, as he put it at the conclusion of his treatise on *Original Sin*, [God] . . . is able to make his own truths prevail; however mysterious they may seem to the poor, partial, narrow and extremely imperfect views of mortals, while looking through a cloudy and delusory medium."[4]

Leaving aside the question of the merits of Edwards's precise way of addressing the problem of evil, many theists today might benefit from the general stance of holding to a robust theology of a personal loving and just God, yet recognizing our limits—á la Job—in understanding God's larger purposes. Today in the Western world the prevailing conception of God is that he exists to protect our happiness and to prevent calamities. In Christian churches, at least, there is so much emphasis, especially in prayers, on the good that God can do for us and our friends that it is easy to lead to disillusion. A common attitude, especially among those who have left religious communities, is that "I could not believe in a God who would allow such and so to happen." Such attitudes reflect the widespread tendency, even of believers, to start with our own standards of justice and morality, or even just with our partisan interests, and then attempt to construct a God of our own design.

Edwards also provides a basis for criticizing the assumptions, inherited from the Enlightenment, that humans can both construct and follow a humanistically based moral system that will bring moral progress. Even today, when it is fashionable to critique "the Enlightenment project," so-called postmodernist philosophers are likely to speak as if there are self-evident moral principles and that with sufficient enlightenment people will come to see that they should follow them.[5] For instance, they would think it self-evident that all persons should be treated equally regardless of their race, gender, or sexual orientation. Or advocates of abortion on demand will talk about "a woman's right to control her body" as a universally valid moral principle. In the modern and post-modern outlooks, the assumption is that nature is normative for understanding the self and that self-understanding is essential to morality. Edwards, in *The Nature of True Virtue* argues against the possibility of humans following some sort of rationally derived or intuitively based moral system. Basically he points out in Augustinian fashion that humans in their natural condition are essentially selfish. Elaborating on the perennial ethical "problem of the stranger," he shows that even in the best cases people by nature set their highest affections on something too small. Although they might be greatly admired for sacrificial love to family, self-sacrificing service to community, or heroic loyalty to nation, their love for their own kind comes at the expense of love to everyone else. Only the common love of their Creator-Redeemer could unite them. Only if they receive the grace to participate in God's love, can they begin to have their affections turned to what is truly good in the interest of the whole. Then they would do whatever they could to bring all nations to love the same God. As Robert Jenson remarks concerning this problem of how to "universalize solidarity" (as the Marxists put it): "The joint worship of God can do it; and no other plausible suggestion is yet on the table."[6]

Edwards, as a person whose political views were shaped entirely before the era of the American Revolution, may have underestimated some of the short-term benefits of the new enlightened morality which have done much to bring principles of equal treatment under the law within some modern states. Although he did, in *The Nature of True Virtue*, grant that such limited virtues might be good in so far as they go, he also implicitly pointed out the limits of political solutions. To cite Robert Jenson again, one such limit that is especially apparent today is that democracies are notably blind to the problem of the stranger.[7] While it might be possible to establish at least some relative equality before the law within democracies, there is no way a modern state could extend that equality to all outsiders. Edwards himself did not propose a viable political solution,[8] yet he did recognize the problem of relying on politics alone.

HUMAN DEPRAVITY

In contrast to most western people in the twenty-first century, Edwards saw all people as naturally sinful and corrupt. We must hasten to add, of course, that also he believed each human being was a creature made in God's image and therefore of infinite worth. Today, most westerners need to balance their commendable rhetoric about human worth with this more realistic view of universal human depravity. For one thing, it simply fits the evidence better. As is often said, human depravity is the traditional Christian doctrine that has received the greatest empirical verification in the twentieth century. More practically, it provides a leveling principle in analyzing social and personal problems that is more realistic than is such leveling based on optimistic views. Social and psychological analysts today tend to place the blame for human evil on forces other than the community or person for whom they are speaking. Others are to blame: the capitalists, the poor, the government, foreigners, one's parents, social or economic forces and so forth. While such analyses often have some validity, most of us would benefit from keeping in mind that there are serious flaws in human nature itself, even our own. Calvinists such as Edwards, although making strong distinctions between those who have grace and those who lack it, at least do not exempt themselves from the faults common to humanity and from the continuing deceitfulness of the human heart.

Although Edwards was thoroughly hierarchicalist in his social views, his emphases on universal human depravity and on the arbitrariness of God's grace had leveling implications that might be well appropriated today. In God's eyes the world's hierarchies are turned upside-down. The truly spiritual person, whether a child, a woman, a slave, or an Indian is superior to the "gentlemen" of the ruling classes. Even though Edwards was closely allied with a few powerful magistrates whom he regarded as truly spiritual, he was especially suspicious of white gentlemen as a class. Often they were his chief antagonists. In fact the white gentlemen of his day were increasingly becoming champions of liberty and equality—that is, liberty and equality for white gentlemen, including sexual liberty. One of Edwards's problems in Northampton grew from the fact that he was trying to preserve older Puritan principles regarding sexual morality at a time when New England's white males were beginning to assert their sexual privileges. For instance, he ran afoul of some influential Northamptonites over two cases in which he insisted that a young man should marry the woman by whom he had fathered a child.[9] Most of his spiritual models were women, including some who were the closest to him: his sister Jerusha, his wife Sarah, and his daughter Jerusha. The white male he most revered was David Brainerd, one who gave up usual earthly power in order to serve others. In Edwards's first sermon to the Mohawks in 1751, he enunciated the leveling principle in a view of human nature as fallen. "It was once with our forefathers as 'tis with you," he assured them. "They formerly were in great darkness." All people, whether wealthy Europeans or Indians in the forest needed the same light. "We are no better than you in no respect," he explained, "only as God has made us to differ and has been pleased to give us more light. And now we are willing to give it to you."[10]

We, of course, do not need Edwards to learn about the importance of treating all persons equally regardless of race or gender, and some who are politically correct today will object both to his assumption of European cultural superiority[11] and to his evangelical insistence that God's light, revealed particularly in Christ, is the only way to bring the world together. Nonetheless, even from a secular perspective it is worth noting that a realistic view of human nature can promote egalitarian sentiments as well as can the more naïve view that people are naturally good.

EDWARDS FOR EVANGELICALS

Some of the same lessons that could be learned from Edwards by today's heirs of the Enlightenment might also be applied to today's evangelicals. First, to the extent that history serves to shape a group's self-understanding, American evangelicals would benefit from wider recognition of a progenitor who had high respect for intellect. Not that such recognition should entail that most evangelicals should become Edwardseans or agree with all his theology. Rather it would be only to counter the anti-intellectualism such as that which Mark Noll so sympathetically deplored in *The Scandal of the Evangelical Mind*.[12] Ironically, today's American evangelicals seem to be more followers of Benjamin Franklin than of Edwards. They admire practicality, friendliness, moralism, easy formulas, and quantifiable results. While these Franklinesque traits are not all bad, they sometimes contribute to evangelical superficiality. Purveyors of the spiritual equivalent of junk food have long capitalized on evangelicalism's market-driven economy. Awareness and respect for the Edwardsean part of their heritage would be a healthy balance.

That leads to the more substantial point that modern evangelical Christianity, especially of the American varieties that are so widely influential throughout the world, is itself partly a product of the Enlightenment. Mark Noll in *America's God* and Nathan Hatch in *The Democratization of American Christianity* have documented how in both theology and popular religion Americans accommodated Christianity to the ideals of the new republic.[13] That adjustment to the culture is a key to American evangelicalism's remarkable vitality and resilience. Yet it comes at a price that Edwards was one of the first to point out. Many of the later American developments have been accentuations of traits already apparent in New England's first Great Awakening. Often modern evangelicalism's emphasis on conversion and testimony gets turned into celebration of one's own experience. Such human-centeredness appears also in the emphasis on what God does to promote one's welfare or to bring prosperity and success. Sometimes it is notably individualistic. Salvation becomes largely a matter of one's self in relation to God and one's relationship to one's immediate congregation of fellow worshippers. Even if one concedes that authentic Christianity often prevails among groups with such tendencies, since Scripture and some basic Christian theology are so pervasive in their discourse, Edwards would be correct to note the dangers involved.

Edwards was, of course, first of all a *defender* of the innovative and often intense manifestations of the Great Awakening, but in his great treatise on *Religious Affections* he also provided his definitive critique of the perennial tendency of religion to get turned to serving the self. In order to guard against that danger he proposed several sorts of tests of authenticity. First, as a way of ensuring the experience was truly God-centered, he insisted that it be informed and bounded by God's revelation in Scripture, rather than by our own spiritual "impulses." Second, he looked for evidence of sustained balance in Christian life that would reflect traits resembling the "fruits of the spirit" of Galatians 6—"Love, joy, peace, . . ." and the like. Finally, he believed the best tests to be in "Christian practice."[14] Since true religion involves one's affections, which guide the will, the best test of faith was whether people lived according to God's revealed will. Did they love what God loved? Although Edwards makes practice the test of faith, as many today would agree, he insists on keeping it within his God-centered framework.

BEAUTY

Going beyond that critique of some us-centered evangelical practices, it seems to me, in conclusion, that we must return to Edwards's emphasis on beauty as the point that best encapsulates what evangelical Christians and many others can learn from him today. Our tendency is to separate beauty from practicality. We think of beauty as what we see on vacations. Or it has to do with lonely mystics, esoteric artists, and ancient forms of aesthetic worship. "Beauty" is seldom a word that comes to mind when we think of evangelical or Reformed culture, which is one reason why so many intellectual evangelicals are drawn to High Anglicanism or Eastern Orthodoxy.

Edwards, by contrast, recognizes blazing beauty at the center of the universe and sees it both as of infinite eternal significance and as the basis for the most practical Christian fervor. Because of its intra-Trinitarian origins, beauty for Edwards is essentially personal. It is the beauty of love. One of his favorite themes is of the church as the bride of Christ. Any true encounter with such personified beauty is transforming. It draws our highest love to it. It captures our most fundamental affections. Our will, driven by our affections or loves, is transformed to love what God loves. Hence beauty is the source of fervent action based on love to God and all God's creatures.

In modern society, which is so often driven by functionalism and efficient managerial technique, even in much of its religious life, beauty is a rare category except as it is trivialized or as a sort of personal refuge from the machinery of modernity. It is especially scarcely a source of our practical motivations. Much as the Benjamin Franklins of the world have contributed to our comforts and health, if such is the epitome of our heritage, we are ultimately left with deadening instrumentalism. Superior physical or cultural power is ultimately our only recourse. Edwards points us to an overwhelming beauty that is not just a temporary escape but which is the basis for a way of life that is both practical and exhilarating.

NOTES

1. Avihu Zakai, *Jonathan Edwards's Philosophy of History: The Re-enchantment of the World in the Age of Enlightenment* (Princeton: Princeton University Press, 2003), helpfully points out JE's influence in putting God's work in awakenings at the center of history.

2. Zakai, *Edwards's Philosophy of History*, 85–127, provides a recent overview of JE's concern to reject mechanistic philosophies.

3. Richard Lovelace, *Dynamics of Spiritual Life: An Evangelical Theology of Renewal* (Downers Grove, Ill.: Intervarsity Press, 1979), 256.

4. *WJE* 3:435–37. *Original Sin* was the least influential of JE's major theological works. In the nineteenth century even some of his admirers, such as the conservative Reformed theologians at Princeton Theological Seminary, were critical of his metaphysical theories regarding the divinely constituted identity of humankind. See Joseph Conforti, *Jonathan Edwards, Religious Tradition, and American Culture* (Chapel Hill: University of North Carolina Press, 1995), 122–23.

5. For instance, Richard Rorty, "The Moral Purposes of the University: An Exchange," *The Hedgehog Review* 2:3 (Fall 2000): 106–107, affirms as, in effect, self-evident tests for a "constructive" religious community that it "has gay clergy and solemnizes gay marriages" or that it "preaches the social gospel."

6. Robert Jenson, *America's Theologian: A Recommendation of Jonathan* Edwards (New York: Oxford University Press, 1988), 171.

7. Jenson, *America's Theologian,* 171.

8. In fact, JE's own politics were thoroughly committed to the "Protestant interest" which he thought God had, for the time being, placed particularly in the hands of the British nation. Working within such a Constantinian framework, he saw religious justification for wars against Catholic nations.

9. See Ava Chamberlain, "Jonathan Edwards and the Politics of Sex in Eighteenth-Century Northampton," printed above.

10. "To the Mohawks at the Treaty, August 16, 1751," in *The Sermons of Jonathan Edwards: A Reader,* 108.

11. JE was not, however, a racist and did not see limits to the cultural potentials of others. "It may be hoped," he assured his Northampton congregation concerning the fast-approaching millennium, "that then many of the Negroes and Indians will be divines, and that excellent books will be published in Africa, in Ethiopia, in Turkey—and not only very learned men, but others that are more ordinary men, shall then be very knowing in religion." *WJE* 9:472, 480. On his views of Indians, see Gerald McDermott, "Jonathan Edwards and American Indians: The Devil Sucks Their Blood," *New England Quarterly* 72:4 (Dec. 1999): 539–57.

12. Mark A. Noll, *The Scandal of the Evangelical Mind* (Grand Rapids: Eerdmans, 1994).

13. Mark A. Noll, *America's God: From Jonathan Edwards to Abraham Lincoln* (New York: Oxford University Press, 2002); Nathan O. Hatch, *The Democratization of American Christianity* (New Haven: Yale University Press, 1989).

14. *WJE* 1:383.

Index

Aaron, 59
Abihu, 59
abolitionism, xii, 141–49
Abraham, 56, 59
Absalom, 61
"Account of Abigail Hutchinson" (Edwards), 95
Acts, Book of, 139n16
Adam, 79
Adams, Abigail, 84n60
Adams, John, 69, 70, 83–84n60
aesthetics, 93–94. *See also* beauty
"African American Engagements with Edwards in the Era of the Slave Trade" (Saillant), xii, 141–51
African Americans: as abolitionists, xii, 144–49; and Calvinism, 144–45; Edwards's view of, 164n11; and slavery, xii, 141–49
Age of Reason (Paine), 42
Aldridge, Alfred Owen, 30, 81n8
Allen, Ethan, 42, 43
Allen, Richard, 145, 148
Amalek, 57
Amalekites, 57
American Indians: Edwards on capabilities of, 21, 138n5, 164n11; Edwards's sermons to, 132–33, 134, 161; Eunice Williams's life with, 21, 123–24, 126; massacres of, by American colonists, 67; Moravian missionaries to, 135–36; sin of, 133–34, 139n16; Stockbridge Indians and Edwards, xii, 18, 131–38, 161
The American Jeremiad (Bercovitch), 91
American literature, xi, 86–96
American Renaissance (Matthiessen), 90
American Revolution, 65
American Tract Society, 87, 95
"American Writers Series," 89–90
America's God (Noll), 161
America's Theologian (Jenson), viii
Amos, 21
"The Anachronism of Jonathan Edwards" (Niebuhr), 20
anger of God, 59, 75
animal sacrifices, 59
Anselm, Saint, 84n74
Antichrist, 61–62
Antiochus Epiphanes, 61
Aristotle, 2, 9
Arminianism, 99, 102
"Articles of Belief and Acts of Religion" (Franklin), 66
Astronomical Principles of Natural and Revealed Religion (Whiston), 44

astronomy, 44–46
atonement, 74–75, 84n74, 127, 143
Augustine, Saint, 31–32, 159
Aupaumut, Hendrick, 137–38, 140n31

bad book affair, 111, 117
Bahmins, 79
Baptist Missionary Society, 104
Baptists, 102–4, 108
"Bartleby the Scrivener" (Melville), 95
beauty, xii, 3, 12, 29, 73, 74, 84n72, 93–94, 156, 162–63
Bedford, Arthur, 26
Beecher, Henry Ward, 93
Bellamy, Joseph, 86–87
Bercovitch, Sacvan, 91
Beveridge, Albert, 21–22
Bible: Bolingbroke on, 69; critical interpretation of, 38–49; Edwards's exegesis of, x, 25–32, 49n1, 54–55; Edwards's study of, 25–26, 33n5; Franklin on, 76; Jefferson Bible, 71; Jefferson on, 69, 76, 85n81; Mosaic authorship of Pentateuch, x, 41–43, 51–52n16; as revelation, 27–29, 76; and science, 43–47; on slavery, 142, 143, 147; types and antitypes in, xii, 16, 31, 59, 91, 120, 146–49; violence in, x, 54–63
blacks. *See* African Americans
"Blank Bible" (Edwards), x, 34n10, 55
Blithedale Romance (Hawthorne), 95
Block, James E., 37n23
Bolingbroke, Viscount, 50n11, 69, 70, 82n28
"Book of Controversies" (Edwards), 85nn85–86
Brainerd, David, 160–61
Breitenbach, William, viii
"Bringing the Ark to Zion a Second Time" (Edwards), 23n17
Brodhead, Richard, 96
Brooks, Cleanth, 91
Brown, Robert E., x, 31, 38–53
Buell, Lawrence, 94

Burnet, Thomas, 44
Butler, Joseph, 126
Byrd, William, 94

Calvin, John, 70
Calvinism: and Bible, 27; and Franklin, 65–66, 68, 82n27; Holmes on, 88; Jefferson on, 70; Mumford on, 89; and slaves, 144–45; Twain on, 89
Capitein, Jacobus Elisa Johannes, 141, 143–44
Carey, William, 104
"Catalogue" (Edwards), 52n22
Catholicism, 16, 61–62, 123–24, 125
Chalmers, Thomas, xi, 106–8
Chamberlain, Ava, xi, 111–22
Champion, J. A. I., 40, 42, 50n9
Christ. *See* Jesus Christ
Christian practice, 11, 19. *See also* forgiveness; sacraments; virtue
Christianity. *See* religion
Chronicles, Book of, 52n16
Chubb, Thomas, 84n74
Clark, Harry Hayden, 90
Clemens, Samuel, 89, 94, 98
Coke, Thomas, 145
Collins, Anthony, 65–66, 68
comets, 44, 45–46
communion controversy (1748–1750), 111, 118–19
Complete History of Connecticut (Trumbull), 92
Concerning the End for Which God Created the World (Edwards), 34n9, 84n67
Conforti, Joseph, viii, 94
Constitutional Convention, 67, 81n8
conversion, 60, 64n25
"Conversion of President Edwards" (Edwards), 95
Cook, Captain, 104
Coolidge, John, 30–31
Cooper, Anthony Ashley. *See* Shaftesbury, Third Earl of
Cooper, James F., 117

Index

Crane, R. S., 90
creation by God, 4–12, 155
critical interpretation of Bible, 38–49
crucifixion of Jesus, 59–60
Cugoano, Ottobah Quobna, 145, 147, 148
Cummins, Maria, 95

Dana, James, 98
Daniel, Book of, 61
Danks, Samuel, 111, 117
David, 57, 61
Dayton, Cornelia Hughes, 115–16
"The Deacon's Masterpiece; or the Wonderful 'One-Hoss Shay'" (Holmes), 88
Deerfield, Mass., 123
deism: and atonement, 84n74; diversity within, 82n23; Edwards on, 16, 28, 51n12, 73–74, 76–79, 125, 155; and Franklin, x–xi, 65–68, 73, 79–80; and Jefferson, x–xi, 68–73, 79–8; and natural law, 127; writers influenced by, 82n28
The Democratization of American Christianity (Hatch), 161
Deuteronomy, Book of, 58, 117, 120n1
Dewey, John, 40
Dillinger, John, vii
"Discourse on the Trinity" (Edwards), 13n9–10
dispositions, 2–4
Dissenters, 103–4, 105, 108
A Dissertation on Liberty and Necessity, Pleasure and Pain (Franklin), 66
The Distinguishing Marks of a Work of the Spirit of God (Edwards), 28, 34n9
"A Divine and Supernatural Light" (Edwards), 34n10, 84n79
"Divine Love Alone Lasts Eternally" (Edwards), 34n7
"Does History Matter to God?: Jonathan Edwards's Dynamic Re-conception of God's Relation to the World" (Lee), ix, 1–13

Douglas, Ann, 95
Druids, 79
Duyckinck, Evert, 88
Dwight, Sereno Edwards, 33n5, 39, 92
Dwight, Timothy, 144

Early American Literature, 86, 92
Edwards, Jerusha (daughter), 160
Edwards, Jerusha (sister), 160
Edwards, Jonathan: and aesthetics, 93–94; in American literary canon, xi, 86–96; and bad book affair, 111, 117; biblical exegesis by, x, 25–32, 49n1, 54–55; bibliographies of scholarship on, vi, 29–30; bicentennial of, vi–vii; biographers of, v, xii, 15, 90, 92; and communion controversy (1748–1750), 111, 118–19; and critical interpretation of Bible, 38–49; disappointment of, in Northampton congregation, 17–20, 125; and disciplinary action for sex-related offenses, 111–20; dismissal of, from Northampton pastorate, 111, 119; eighteenth-century reputation of, 86–87; grand narratives by, ix–x, 14–22; legacy of, v–ix, xii, 32, 152–63; in New York City, 54; pastoral narratives by, ix–x, 17–22; politics of, 65, 164n8; prose style of, 93, 95; on religion, 72–80; salary of, 111; and science, 43–47, 77, 154, 155; slaves owned by, 145; and Stockbridge Indians, 18, 131–38, 161; study of Bible by, 25–26, 33n5; tercentenary of, v–vi; twentieth-century scholarship on, vi–ix; Yale Edition of collected works of, v–vi, 26, 93. *See also* sermons by Edwards; and specific works
Edwards, Sarah Pierpont, vi, 160
Edwards, Timothy, 137
"Edwards as American Theologian: Grand Narratives and Pastoral Narratives" (Pauw), ix–x, 14–24

Edwards in Our Time, viii
Elements of Criticism (Kames), 101
Elliott, Emory, 94
Emerson, Ralph Waldo, 86, 91, 95
The End for Which God Created the World (Edwards), 8, 9, 12n7, 13n24, 13nn13–21, 34n9, 84n67
end in creation, 4–7
Enlightenment, 32, 125–27, 154, 157–59
Enoch, 79
An Enquiry Concerning Political Justice (Godwin), 105, 106
An enquiry into the obligations of Christians, to use means for the conversion of the heathens (Carey), 104
Ephesians, Epistle to, 61, 143
Epictetus, 70
Epicurean philosophy, 70
Epicurus, 70
equality, 81n1, 133, 134, 137–38, 159
Equiano, Olaudah, 145, 148
Erskine, John, 102, 103
eschatology, 11–12, 31, 43–47
Essays on the Principles of Morality and Natural Religion (Kames), 101–2
Esther, Book of, 57
eternity, 9–12. *See also* heaven; hell
Eternity of Hell Torments Considered (Whiston), 44, 45
Ethices Elementa (Johnson), 129–30n14
evangelicalism, ix, xii, 32, 124–25, 161–62
Evans, Caleb, 103
evil, 16, 18, 58, 146, 160–61. *See also* Satan; sin
Exodus, Book of, 34–35n10, 57, 117
"Experience" (Emerson), 95
Exposition on the Epistle to the Ephesians (Goodwin), 61
Ezra, 42, 52n16

Faithful Narrative (Edwards), 64n25, 94, 95

Fall of Man, 44, 56
"False Light and True" (Edwards), 34n10
Faulkner, William, 94
Faust, Clarence, 89–90
Feuerbach, Ludwig Andreas, 72
Fifteen Sermons Preached at the Rolls Chapel (Butler), 126
"The Final Judgement" (Edwards), 84n67
Finney, Charles Grandison, 92, 98
flood in Bible, 18, 44, 56
forgiveness, xi, 21, 84n74, 123–28, 128–29n3, 129–30n14
"Forgiveness and the Party of Humanity in Jonathan Edwards's World" (Valeri), xi, 123–30
fornication cases, xi, 111–20, 160
Foxcroft, Thomas, 86–87
Franklin, Benjamin: in American literary canon, 88, 89, 90, 91, 92, 94; at Constitutional Convention, 67, 81n8; and evangelicals, 161; influence of, 163; politics of, 65; on religion, x–xi, 65–68, 72–73, 76, 79–80, 81n8, 82n27; tercentenary of, v
"Franklin, Jefferson and Edwards on Religion and the Religions" (McDermott), x–xi, 65–85
free will. *See* will
Freedom of the Will (Edwards), xi, 87–88, 93, 98–108, 132, 140n29
Fuller, Andrew, xi, 102–4, 107–8

Galatians, Epistle to, 162
Garrison, William Lloyd, 146
Gay, Peter, 30, 31, 32
gender roles, 118. *See also* women
Genesis, Book of, 56, 62, 63n9
Genovese, Eugene D., 147
Gill, John, 104
Gladstone, William, 106
glory of God, 5–6
God: anger of, 59, 75; and beauty, 3, 12, 73, 74, 93–94, 162–63; creation

by, 4–12, 155; Deists' view of, 66, 69, 74, 79–80, 155; forgiveness by, 84n74; Franklin on, 66–68, 81n8; glory of, 5–6; grand narratives of, ix–x, 14–22; happiness of, 7–9; Jefferson on, 68–69, 83n60; love of, 62, 154–59; as moral governor, 76; pastoral narratives of, ix–x, 17–22; providence of, 67, 146; relationship between world and, ix, 1–12; revelation of, 27–29, 30, 76, 79, 80; Son of, 4, 12; as starting point for all questions, 154–57; and temporality, 7–10; and Trinity, 3–4, 15, 19, 77; twenty-first century view of, 158
Godbeer, Richard, 112
"God's Care in Times of Public Commotions" (Edwards), 22n2
Godwin, William, xi, 105–8
Godwyn, Morgan, 141–42, 143
The Golden Day (Mumford), 89
Goldsmith, Oliver, 101
Goodwin, Thomas, 61
grace, 17, 20
grand narratives, ix–x, 14–22
Graves, Hannah, 117
Great Awakening, 86, 92, 162
Great Awakening, Second, 87, 92
Griswold, Rufus, 88
Gronniosaw, James Albert Ukasaw, 149
Gura, Philip F., xi, 86–97

habits, 2
Hall, David D., 19, 119
Hall, Prince, 146
Hall, Robert, Sr., 103
Haman, 57
Hampshire County Ministerial Association, 117, 119
happiness, 5–9, 158
Haroutunian, Joseph, viii
Hart, Levi, 145
Hastings, Selina, 145
Hatch, Nathan, 161

Hawley, Elisha, xi, 111–20, 121nn7–8, 121n14, 122nn25–26
Hawley, Gideon, 132
Hawley, Joseph, 113
Hawley, Joseph III, 113, 116, 118–19, 121nn7–8, 122n25
Hawley, Rebekah, 113–16
Hawthorne, Nathaniel, 93, 94, 95
Haynes, Lemuel, 145, 147, 148
heaven, 12, 45, 62
Hebrews, Epistle to, 34n8, 34–35n10, 139n7
"Heeding the Word, and Losing It" (Edwards), 33n2, 34n8
hell, 43–46, 52n21, 53n28, 62
Henry, Matthew, 56, 58
Herbert of Cherbury, Lord, 66
Hermes Trismegistus, 79
Herod, 58
hierarchy, 80–81n1
historiography, 47–48, 50n9
An History of the Corruptions of Christianity (Priestley), 71, 83n48
History of the Work of Redemption (Edwards), ix–x, 14–16, 20, 50n9, 126, 146
Holmes, Oliver Wendell, 40, 88, 92, 98
Holy Spirit, 4, 11
Home, Henry (Lord Kames), 100–102, 107–8
Hopkins, Samuel, 33n5, 49n1, 70, 92, 111, 144, 145
human nature: Franklin on, 67–68; and human depravity, 160–61; Jefferson on, 69; of Jesus Christ, 12, 60; and love, 159; and prejudice, 75; and reason, 68–69, 73, 75–77, 79–80
Humble Attempt to Promote Visible Union of God's People in Extraordinary Prayer for the Revival of Religion (Edwards), 87, 103
An Humble Inquiry (Edwards), 23n22, 118, 119, 120
Hume, David, 82n28, 101, 125, 127
Huntingdon, Countess of, 145

Hutcheson, Francis, 94, 127
Hutchinson, Abigail, 64n25

illegitimacy, 112, 114–15
"Images of Divine Things" (Edwards), 34n8, 156
immanence of God. *See* grand narratives; pastoral narratives
"The Importance and Advantage of a Thorough Knowledge of Divine Truth" (Edwards), 33n2, 34n7, 34n10
In the American Grain (Williams), 89
Indians. *See* American Indians
The Inquiry into the Freedom of the Will (Edwards), 87–88, 98–108, 132, 140n29
Isaac, 56, 59
Isaiah, Book of, 46, 148
Islam, 16, 67, 125, 147–49

James, William, 40
Japheth, 79
Jefferson, Thomas: in American literary canon, 89; on Bible, 69, 76, 85n81; and Jefferson Bible, 71; on Jesus Christ, 69, 70–72, 85n81; politics of, 65; on religion, x–xi, 68–73, 76, 79–80, 83–84n60, 85n81
Jefferson Bible, 71
Jenson, Robert, viii, 13n22, 159
Jericho, battle of, 57
Jerusalem, Roman siege of, 58, 61
Jesus Christ: birth of, 58; conflicts between Jews and, 58; crucifixion of, 59–60; on forgiveness of enemies, 123–26; freedom of, 100; human nature of, 12, 60; Jefferson on, 69, 70–72, 85n81; love of, 156; as Mediator, 12, 74; miracles of, 53n30, 60; Priestley on, 71; redemptive work of, 59–60, 74, 75, 100, 127, 157; resurrection of, 48–49; and saints, 62; as Son of God, 4, 12
Jews. *See* Judaism
Job, Book of, 57–58, 158

John, Gospel of, 27, 53n30, 60, 63n9
Johnson, Samuel, 129–30n14
Johnson, Thomas H., 89–90
Jonah, 52n21
Jonathan Edwards (Miller), 90–91
Jonathan Edwards: Representative Selections (Faust and Johnson), 89–90
"Jonathan Edwards and the Cultures of Biblical Violence" (Stein), x, 54–64
"Jonathan Edwards and the Politics of Sex in Eighteenth-Century Northampton" (Chamberlain), xi, 111–22
"Jonathan Edwards in the Twenty-First Century" (Marsden), xii, 152–64
"Jonathan Edwards's *Freedom of the Will* Abroad" (Noll), xi, 98–110
Joseph, 16, 146, 147–48, 149
Josephus, 58
Joshua, 57
Journals and Miscellaneous Notebooks (Emerson), 86
Judaism, 58–59, 69, 79, 83n48, 137–38, 147

Kames, Lord, xi, 100–102, 107–8
Kelley, Shawn, 40
Kimnach, Wilson, 73
King, Eleazar, 117, 118, 119
King, Martin Luther, Jr., 22
The Kingdom of God in America (Niebuhr), viii
Kings, Second Book of, 139n14
Kippis, Rev. Andrew, 105
Knapp, Samuel Lorenzo, 87–88, 93
Kuklick, Bruce, 26

The Lamplighter (Cummins), 95
Lawrence, D. H., 89
Lectures on American Literature (Knapp), 87–88
Lee, Sang Hyun, ix, 1–13
legal system, 114–16, 118
Lesser, M. X., 29–30

Index

"Lessons from Stockbridge: Jonathan Edwards and the Stockbridge Indians" (Wheeler), xii, 131–40
"Letter from China" (Franklin), 67
Levine, Joseph, 41
Levitical priesthood, 59
Leviticus, Book of, 58, 59
The Life of David Brainerd (Edwards), xi, 95
"Life Through Christ Alone" (Edwards), 34n7
light, 28–29
"Light in a Dark World, a Dark Heart" (Edwards), 34nn9–10
Lincoln, Abraham, 22
Lincoln, Bruce, 39, 49n2, 50n4
Locke, John, 3, 26, 73, 93, 94
"'Longing for More and More of It'?: The Strange Career of Jonathan Edwards's Exegetical Exertions" (Sweeney), x, 25–37
Longmeadow, Mass., 123–24
Lord's Supper, 111, 118–20
"Lost and Found: Recovering Edwards for American Literature" (Gura), xi, 86–97
love: of Christ, 156; of God, 62, 154–59; of humans, 159
Lovelace, Richard, 157
Lucretius, 83n60
Luke, Gospel of, 27, 34nn7–8, 34n10, 64n20, 139n8, 139n16
Lyman, Mercy, 113

Mahicans. *See* American Indians
Main Currents in American Thought (Parrington), 89
manliness, 118
"Man's Natural Blindness in Things of Religion" (Edwards), 84n69, 84n77
Marrant, John, 145, 148
marriage: pregnancies of brides, 112–13; as sacrament, 120. *See also* sexual morality
Marsden, George M., v, xii, 15, 152–64
Martha, 27
Mary, 29, 58
Mary of Bethany, 27
Mather, Cotton, 89, 93
Mather, Increase, 90
Matthew, Gospel of, 23n30, 33n2, 34n7, 53n30, 58, 60, 64n31, 120n3, 125, 126, 129nn8–9, 129n12, 139n15, 139n16, 148
Matthiessen, F. O., 90, 95
Maunnauseet, Ebenezer, 136
Maurice, Matthias, 103
McDermott, Gerald R., x–xi, 65–85
Mead, Sidney, 19
Melville, Herman, 37n23, 91, 95
Menand, Louis, 40
"Mercy and Not Sacrifice" (Edwards), 23n23, 129nn5–6
The Metaphysical Club (Menand), 40
Miles, Lion, 140n29
Miller, Charles A., 83n60
Miller, Hugh, 106
Miller, Perry, v–vi, vii, 26, 30, 90–91, 92, 96, 153
"The Mind" (Edwards), 93
ministers, 15
Minister's Wooing (Stowe), 95
Minkema, Kenneth, ix, 19
miracles of Christ, 53n30, 60
"Miscellaneous Observations on the Holy Scriptures" (Edwards), 34n10, 55
"Miscellanies" (Edwards), 12n1, 12n3, 12–13nn6–14, 13n23, 22n3, 23n5, 23n7, 23n16, 23n26, 28, 34n7, 45, 51n12, 51n15, 52–53n21–23, 53n25–28, 55, 61, 84nn67–68, 84n71, 84nn73–75, 85nn82–84, 85nn87–89, 129n13
"Modern Question," 103
Modernism, 89
modernity, 157–59
Mohawks. *See* American Indians
Moral Sense ethics, 127
morality, xi, 67, 69–70, 76, 77, 78, 80, 159

Moravians, 135–36
Morgan, Edmund, 135
Morison, Samuel Eliot, vii
Moses, 34–35n10, 41–43, 51–52nn15–16, 57
Muhammad, 67
Mumford, Lewis, 89
Munneweaunummuck, Cornelius, 136
Munneweaunummuck, Mary, 136
Murdock, Kenneth, vii, 90
musical analogies for beauty, 156
Muslims. *See* Islam
mystery, 77–78
myth, 39, 49n2, 50n4

Nadab, 59
Narrative of the Communion Controversy (Edwards), 118
Native Americans. *See* American Indians
"Natural Philosophy" (Edwards), 2, 53n24
natural theology, 127–28
nature, 15, 27, 28–29, 73, 156
The Nature of True Virtue (Edwards), 105, 128, 132, 159
New Divinity movement, viii, xii, 137
New Testament. *See* Bible; Jesus Christ
New Theory of the Earth (Whiston), 44
Newton, Isaac, 26, 44, 48, 154, 155
Nicodemus, 149
Niebuhr, H. Richard, viii, 20, 26, 31, 135
Noah, 18, 79
Noll, Mark, viii, xi, 98–110, 161
Northampton, Mass.: bad book affair in, 111, 117; communion controversy (1748–1750) in, 111, 118–19; disciplinary committee of Edwards's church in, 117; dismissal of Edwards from pastorate in, 111, 119; Edwards's disappointment in congregation of, 17–20, 125; Edwards's pastoral ministry in, 18–20; Edwards's salary in, 111;
revivals in, xi, 16, 17, 19, 124–25; sexual morality in, xi, 111–20, 160
Norton, Mary Beth, 113
"Notes on Scripture" (Edwards), x, 18, 23n18, 42, 51n13, 52n21, 55
"Notes on the Apocalypse" (Edwards), x, 52n21, 55, 61, 63n5
"Nothing on Earth Can Represent the Glories of Heaven" (Edwards), 84n67
Numbers, Book of, 57

occasionalism, ix, 2
"Of Atoms" (Edwards), 2, 12n4
Old Testament. *See* Bible
Original Sin (Edwards), xii, 21, 84n79, 132–35, 138n5, 158, 163n4
Orpheus, 79
Osborne, Sarah, 145
Owen, John, 104

Paine, Thomas, 42, 43
Parker, Theodore, 93
Parrington, Vernon Louis, 89
pastoral narratives, ix–x, 17–22
Pauw, Amy Plantinga, ix–x, 14–24
"Perpetuity and Change of the Sabbath" (Edwards), 84n67
"Personal Narrative" (Edwards), xi, 34n7, 34n10, 92, 95
Peter, First Epistle to, 33n2
Philemon, Epistle to, 143
Philosophical Transactions (Royal Society), 77
Pierce, Charles S., 40
Pierpont, Benjamin, 55
piety, 125
Plato, 79
Plotinus, 7, 10
Poe, Edgar Allan, 88
Political-Theological Dissertation Examining the Question: Is Slavery Compatible with Christian Freedom (Capitein), 143–44
politics, 65, 164n8

Poole, Matthew, 26
Pope, 61–62
pragmatism, 40
predestination, 104, 107
pregnancies of brides, 112–13
prejudice, 75
premarital sex, xi, 111–20, 160
Presbyterians, 106–7
Prideaux, Humphrey, 26
Priestley, Joseph, 71, 82n28, 83n48
Princeton Theological Seminary, 163n4
prisca theologia, 79, 80
problem of the stranger, 159
"Profitable Hearers of the Word" (Edwards), 34nn7–8, 34n10, 37n22
Prohibition Era, vii
Prose Writers of America (Griswold), 88
Proverbs, Book of, 58, 139n13
providentialism, 146
Psalms, Book of, ix, 15, 34n10, 57, 128n2, 139n12, 139n24, 155
"The Pure in Heart Blessed" (Edwards), 34n10
Puritanism: and Edwards, 88, 128, 154; and gender roles, 118; and sexuality, 112; twentieth-century scholarship on, vii, 30–31, 89
Pythagoras, 79

Quakers, 137

race. *See* African Americans; American Indians
Racializing Jesus (Kelley), 40
Rahab, 57
Ramsey, Paul, 12
Rawlyk, George, 22
reason: and deism, x–xi, 68–69, 73, 75–77, 79–80; and historical authenticity of the Bible, 40–42; revelation versus, x–xi, 28, 30, 76, 79, 80. *See also* deism
Reason the Only Oracle of Man (Allen), 42

redemption, 14–22, 59–60, 74, 75, 100, 104, 127, 157
Reformation, 147, 154
religion: Edwards on, 72–80; Franklin on, x–xi, 65–68, 72–73, 76, 79–80, 81n8, 82n27; Jefferson on, x–xi, 68–73, 76, 79–80, 83–84n60, 85n81; mystery in, 77–78; Priestley on, 71, 83n48; tests of authenticity of, 162; violence and Christianity, 16. *See also* evangelicalism; Islam; Judaism
Religious Affections (Edwards), xi, 19, 78, 87, 93, 95, 119, 128, 140n29, 162
religious freedom, 72
repentance, 75
resurrection, 48–49
revelation, 27–29, 30, 76, 79, 80
Revelation, Book of, 61, 64n31, 64n33, 69, 139n9
revivals, xi, 15–16, 17, 19, 86, 87, 124–25, 153
Romaine, William, 144, 145
Roman Catholicism. *See* Catholicism
Romans, 58, 61
Root, Esther, 114, 120n4, 121n18
Root, Hezekiah, 121n14
Root, Martha, xi, 112–18, 120, 120n4, 121nn7–8, 121n18
Rorty, Richard, 163n5
"Rough Notes" (Edwards), 51n15
Royal Society, 77
Ryland, John, Jr., 103

sacraments, 119–20, 128–29n3. *See also* Lord's Supper
"The Sacred and the Profane Connected: Edwards, the Bible, and Intellectual Culture" (Brown), x, 38–53
Saillant, John, xii, 141–51
saints, 12, 16, 46, 62
St. John, Henry. *See* Bolingbroke, Viscount
Samuel, Second Book of, 61
Sarah, 56

Satan, 16, 58, 60. *See also* evil
satisfaction theory of atonement, 74–75, 84n74
The Scandal of the Evangelical Mind (Noll), 161
Schafer, Thomas A., 51n13
The School of Hawthorne (Brodhead), 96
science, 43–47, 77, 154, 155
Scottish Presbyterians, 106–7
Scripture. *See* Bible
Second Great Awakening, 87, 92
Seneca, 70
sermons by Edwards: on Christian practice, 19; on Christ's miracles, 53n30; on forgiveness, 123–26; on God's ordering of public commotions, 14; at Longmeadow, 123–24; in Northampton, 19; on reason versus revelation, 28; "Sinners in the Hands of an Angry God," 53n23, 92, 153; to Stockbridge colonists, 48–49, 133–34; to Stockbridge Indians, 132–33, 134, 161
Sewall, Samuel, 142, 143
sexual morality, xi, 111–20, 160
Shaftesbury, Third Earl of, 65–66, 82n28, 125, 127
Shem, 79
Shields, David, 92
Shoemaker, Nancy, 138n1
sin: of American Indians, 133–34, 139n16; Fuller on, 104; and human depravity, 160–61; original sin, 67, 134–35; and reason, 76; suicide as, 113. *See also* evil
Sinners in the Hands of an Angry God (Edwards), 53n23, 92, 153
slavery and slave trade, xii, 141–49
Smith, Adam, 127
Socrates, 71
Sodom and Gomorrah, 56
Some Thoughts Concerning the Revival (Edwards), 16, 23n9, 67

Spinoza, Baruch, 42
"A Spiritual Understanding of Divine Things Denied to the Unregenerate" (Edwards), 34n10
Stein, Stephen J., x, 31, 51n13, 54–64
Stiles, Ezra, 87, 144
Stockbridge, Mass., colonists, 48–49
Stockbridge, Mass., Indians, xii, 18, 131–38, 161
Stoddard, John, 114
Stoddard, Solomon, 113
Stoic philosophy, 70
Stout, Harry S., 31, 131
Stowe, Harriet Beecher, 89, 95
stranger problem, 159
Studies in Classic American Literature (Lawrence), 89
"Stupid as Stones" (Edwards), 34n7
"Subjects of Enquiry" (Edwards), 51n15
"Subjects to Be Handled in the Treatise on the Mind" (Edwards), 2
suffering, 146
suicide, 113
Sweeney, Douglas A., x, 25–37, 94, 95
Swift, Job, 145
Sybils, 79

Taylor, Edward, 91
Taylor, Nathaniel William, 94
telescope, 77
temporality, 7–12
theological legacy of Edwards, 154–57
Theorizing Myth (Lincoln), 39
Thomas, Isaiah, 87
Titus, Epistle to, 120n3
"Treatise on Grace" (Edwards), 34n10
A Treatise on Religious Affections (Edward), xi, 19, 78, 87, 93, 95, 119, 128, 140n29, 162
Trinity, 3–4, 15, 19, 77. *See also* God
Trumbull, Benjamin, 92
Tully, 70
Twain, Mark, 89, 94, 98
Tyler, Moses Coit, 88–89
"Types Notebook," 22n2

typology, xii, 16, 31, 59, 91, 120, 146–49

Ulrich, Laurel Thatcher, 115
Unitarianism, 72
United States: evangelicals in, 161–62; imperialism of, 21–22; legacy of Edwards for, 152–53; self-image of, 153–54
upstreaming strategy, 137

Valeri, Mark, xi, 21, 123–30
violence: in Bible, x, 54–63; of Christianity, 16; of Prohibition Era, vii
Virgil, 148
virtue, 67–68, 78, 106, 108, 162
Voltaire, 50n11, 69, 82n28

Wainwright, William J., 75–76
Wait, Thomas, 111, 117
Walters, Kerry S., 66, 82n27
Warner, Susan, 95
Warren, Robert Penn, 91
Wauwampequunnaunt, John, 136
"The Way of Holiness" (Edwards), 34n7
Westphal, Merold, 23n14
Wheatley, Phillis, 145, 148, 149
Wheeler, Rachel, xii, 21, 131–40
Whiston, William, 44–45, 46, 52n22
Whitefield, George, 82n27, 145

Whitman, Walt, 95
widows, 113
will: and abolitionism, 146; Chalmers on, 106–8; freedom of, 98–108; Fuller on, 102–4, 107–8; and God's love as beauty, 156; Godwin on, 105–8; Kames on, 101–2, 107–8
William and Mary Quarterly, 92
Williams, Eunice, 21, 123–24, 126
Williams, Roger, 89
Williams, Rowan, 24n34
Williams, Stephen, 123
Williams, William Carlos, 89
Winslow, Ola, 30
Winthrop, John, 129n6
women: Edwards on new image of, 118; and fornication cases, xi, 111–20, 160; pregnancies of brides, 112–13; as spiritual models for Edwards, 160; as widows, 113
The Works of Jonathan Edwards (Yale Edition), v–vi, 26, 93
world: dispositional ontology and reality of, 1–3; relationship between God and, ix, 1–12

Yale Edition of Edwards's collected works, v–vi, 26, 93

Zaccheus, 149
Zoroaster, 79